THE JOHN HARVARD LIBRARY

Bernard Bailyn
Editor-in-Chief

The John Harvard Library

THE
COOPERATIVE
COMMONWEALTH

By

LAURENCE GRONLUND

Edited by Stow Persons

THE BELKNAP PRESS OF
HARVARD UNIVERSITY PRESS
Cambridge, Massachusetts
1965

CONTENTS

THE

COOPERATIVE
COMMONWEALTH

INTRODUCTION

THE three decades following the American Civil War were not auspicious ones for social criticism and protest. The war had brought an end to the public-spirited idealism which had marked the years between 1830 and 1860. This idealism had expressed itself in a number of reform movements variously designed to educate the young, emancipate women, free the slave, rehabilitate the criminal, preserve the peace, or purify the faith. The intensification of the slavery controversy after 1850 inevitably engulfed these diverse forces of reform in the common struggle, and with the achievement of emancipation and reunion the spirit of reform seemed to consume itself and expire.

The reformers of the prewar era had labored in an exhilarating atmosphere of personal freedom, and with the enthusiasm of men and women who had seen the promised land. Their object was to guide their less fortunate fellows to a realization of the happiness they themselves already knew. Content with the essential features of their society they focused their reforming energies on the specific institutions and practices which momentarily denied full self-realization. The wide range and variety of these causes gave the movement as a whole a decidedly miscellaneous character. Protection of personal health by a scientifically regulated diet and rational clothing was in its way just as important as the eradication of ignorance or the extension of the true faith. Although there had been a certain amount of interchange of personnel among the various reform movements, resulting in the development of the reformer as the distinctly recognizable type which Emerson celebrated, for the most part reforms were strictly limited in their objectives to designated institutional abuses. Insofar as reform rested on a social theory at all it was simply the emerging democratic theory of pluralism. Men were presumed to be free to manipulate their institutions at will. Whether the transformation of one institution would effect others was not a matter for concern.

Only a few of the more speculative among the communitarian socialists had perceived that a practical interest in reform should be reinforced by an appropriate sociological theory. John Humphrey Noyes, the founder of the Oneida Community, had developed a general theory of reform from his religious perfectionism, and had attempted unsuccessfully to persuade William Lloyd Garrison that the abolitionist could not consistently stop short with a program designed merely to end slavery. An even more comprehensive social theory underlay the communitarianism of the Fourierists. As disseminated in America by Albert Brisbane and Parke Godwin, Fourierism rested on a conception of universal history as the progressive emancipation of the human emotions or passions. History was said to consist of a succession of epochs each of which revealed the freeing of the passions through institutional modifications. As a general theory of reform based on historical dynamics Fourierism set the stage for Marxism.

The social changes resulting from rapid industrialization in the years after Appomattox made impossible an immediate reconstitution of the old army of reformers. The middle class to which the reformers had confidently appealed was now in no mood to listen. A new "chromo-civilization," of which E. L. Godkin was to complain, based on mass production and glorifying materialistic accomplishments, would have to establish itself and work out its implications before the critical spirit could again achieve a hearing. Furthermore, a new intellectual foundation for social criticism more appropriate to the needs of the industrial age than was the old romantic individualism would have to be laid. For these reasons, the voices of the old reformers, many of whom lived on into the Gilded Age and continued to talk about religious or intellectual emancipation, seemed strangely muffled and ineffectual.

In the simpler, rural environment of ante-bellum days the organization of communitarian settlements appeared to many reflective minds to be an appropriate mode of attack upon the shortcomings of Protestant, capitalistic individualism. Communitarianism had been a kind of strategic flanking movement, offering a practical working model of a better order, that appealed not only to rural zealots, but even to hard-headed city journalists. Now the copper wires and steel rails of communication and transportation drew the country tightly together in a mesh of economic activities, and the self-sufficient and isolated communitarian settlement seemed irrelevant.

Simultaneously, the strengthening of the national state and development of a nationwide industrial economy, both direct results of the war, at once rendered communitarianism obsolete and prepared the way for a theory of political socialism. America was now ripe for the invasion of Marxist ideas. The role of Laurence Gronlund was to popularize the Marxist brand of social criticism aimed specifically at the evils of industrial capitalism. Marxism was itself a form of naturalistic determinism with which educated Americans were already familiar in less controversial guises. The Social Darwinism of Herbert Spencer and his disciples, and the historical positivism of Comte and Buckle were versions of naturalism well known in this country. Both shared with Marxism a conception of social structure in which technology and economy were assigned a primary role as the sources of social change. Innovations in technology and economy were presumed to trigger changes in the nonmaterial culture, thus transforming the entire structure of the society. These theories presupposed the sensitive responsiveness of ideas and institutions in an industrialized and nationalized state. The apparent relevance of the Marxist critique was undoubtedly enhanced by the assumptions which it shared with these other less controversial social doctrines. As a political movement Marxism was to be of negligible importance in the United States, but as a style of thinking the somewhat diluted version represented by Gronlund was to have a far-reaching and pervasive influence.

German immigrants of the 1850's had been the first to introduce Marxism to the United States, but for many years their influence was narrowly confined to German-speaking circles. It would be difficult to say whether their Marxism functioned primarily as an expression of their aspirations for the working class or as a means of sustaining their ethnic and cultural identity in an alien world.

These immigrants, led by such men as Wilhelm Weitling, Friedrich Sorge, and Joseph Wedemeyer, were oriented toward Europe and absorbed in the bitter factional struggles among Marxists, Lassalleans, and anarchists, which they did their best to perpetuate in America. When the Marxists were threatened with the loss of control of their organization the headquarters of the Marxist International Workingmen's Association was transferred in 1872 from London to New York, where it expired four years later. In 1877 several small groups united to form the Socialistic Labor Party, a heterogeneous collection of anarchists, trade-unionists, and political actionists. In 1883, the year before the publication of the *Cooperative Commonwealth*, the party numbered a mere 1500.[1]

Laurence Gronlund (1846–1899) was born in Denmark and studied law at the University of Copenhagen, where he received the master's degree in 1865. Two years later he emigrated to the United States and continued the study of law in Milwaukee while supporting himself by schoolteaching. He was admitted to the bar in Chicago in 1869. In view of the highly disparaging remarks on legal theory and practice which he inserted in the *Cooperative Commonwealth* one must conclude that Gronlund's brief legal career was far from a happy one. As his socialist convictions ripened he grew understandably estranged from a profession so largely concerned with the adjudication of conflicting property interests. He came to regard litigation as a form of warfare in which the lawyer ignored justice and morality in order to secure the verdict for his client.

Little is known of the circumstances surrounding Gronlund's conversion to socialism save for a reported remark that he had been converted by reading Pascal's *Pensées* — hardly a relevant preparation for the acerbities of the Socialistic Labor Party. In any event, his interest in the cause of socialism became impassioned, and by 1878 he had abandoned the law for the more congenial if less remunerative work of journalism and political lecturing. He became a familiar figure in the radical circles of New York City, where in 1883 he was reported to be earning ten dollars a week and saving three of them to defray the costs of publishing his magnum opus,

[1] Howard H. Quint, *The Forging of American Socialism: Origins of the Modern Movement* (Columbia, S.C., 1953), p. 23.

the *Cooperative Commonwealth,* which appeared in the following year.[2]

The spirit of the indigenous American communitarian socialism of the ante-bellum era had been generous and humane. The sense of social justice which it had shared with socialists of all kinds had not been stained by the bitterness which was to become all too common a feature of the so-called "scientific" socialism of the industrial age following the war. Its vision had been fastened upon the human relationships of the ideal community where love was presumed to reign supreme. The Marxists contemptuously dubbed this tradition "utopian." It was true that a radical disjunction between vision and reality had always confronted the utopians, and their sporadic ventures into community founding, which seemed the obvious way to actualize their visions of the good society, had been notoriously ineffectual.

To bridge the gulf between present and future and demonstrate how to realize the ideal became the historic mission of Marx and Engels. They offered a theory of social dynamics which explained how the laws of economic development would lead to an inevitable crisis of capitalism out of which a socialist society would emerge. To guide and hasten this process a disciplined and militant socialist organization of workers would be essential. Marxist theory underscored the distinction between means and ends; and the Marxist attack on the utopians forced a choice between sound (that is, Marxist) means and visionary ends. Thus Marx and Engels divided socialist history into its earlier utopian and modern scientific phases.[3]

The last two decades of the nineteenth century were a transitional period in the history of socialist thought. In spite of the attempts of Marxists to purge socialism of its utopian elements the movement continued to be permeated with a utopian flavor. Christian Socialists, Bellamyite Nationalists and assorted communitarians mingled their appeals to the spirit of love and brotherhood with

[2] Charles Albro Barker, *Henry George* (New York, 1955), p. 437. For a brief summary of what is known of Gronlund's personal career see the *Dictionary of American Biography* article by W. Ellison Chalmers.

[3] Daniel Bell, in D. D. Egbert and S. Persons, eds., *Socialism and American Life* (2 vols. Princeton, 1952), I, p. 229.

the rancorous tones of the proponents of the class struggle. The *Cooperative Commonwealth* was a product of this fluid situation, blending the elements to form its own distinctive amalgam.

Gronlund's professed object in writing the book was to demonstrate that society was moving inevitably toward socialism, and that each individual was consciously or unconsciously contributing his mite toward the ultimate consummation. In view of its inevitability it was idle to ask whether socialism would be a good or bad thing; fortunately, it would of course prove to be an immense good. Social and economic conditions in the more highly developed countries, notably the United States and Great Britain, were ripe for the great transformation.

Inevitability and uncertainty went hand in hand in Gronlund's socialist analysis. It would not do, he said, to court a fatalistic complacence, for while the revolution was itself inevitable its outcome was highly uncertain. Without the guidance of an informed and dedicated leadership society could easily revert to barbarism; and he pointed ominously to the abundant evidences of corruption and decadence in the Gilded Age which suggested an analogy with Augustan Rome. In that precedent, the feudal stage of social evolution with its serf labor which eventually succeeded ancient slavery was able to emerge only after centuries of the Dark Age — a prime example of a mismanaged revolution. To avert a comparable fate it was essential to recruit a dedicated band of socialists who would be able to lead society safely through the possibly chaotic conditions of the revolution to the good society of the future.[4] These potential leaders were to be found among the intelligent and public-spirited readers of all classes to whom Gronlund addressed his book. This was not to be an intramural book for socialists in which the author would sharpen the fine points of orthodoxy. Although it would touch all the bases of Marxist analysis it would be concerned primarily to persuade nonsocialist readers that the capitalist system must collapse and that a socialist order satisfying all social and humanitarian ideals should replace it.

Throughout the book Gronlund made a strenuous effort to avoid

---

[4] Gronlund was at first optimistic enough to believe that ten thousand dedicated socialists in a population of seventy-five million would be able to accomplish this task. Their function would of course be simply that of leadership; the revolution would make itself. See p. 238. Six years later, in his revised edition, Gronlund mentioned no figures. Revised edition, p. 294.

the sectarian issues which then divided the international socialist movement into warring camps. He refused to commit himself on the thorny question of whether socialists should put primary emphasis on political or economic action. He was careful to speak respectfully of both Marx and Ferdinand Lassalle as cofounders of scientific socialism. Nevertheless, despite his intentions he was forced toward the side of political action by the heterogeneous nature of the audience to whom he appealed. Because the American readers were presumed to be found in all classes, rich and poor, professionals and laborers, their common denominator was reflective intelligence rather than class interest; Gronlund could not appeal to them as to a dispossessed proletariat. Thus beyond bestowing his blessing on working class organizations he had little to say about economic action. Yet inasmuch as it became apparent that his conception of the socialist program was primarily political, Gronlund's way was again blocked, now by the conventional notion of Marxists as to the superficial character of political action.

The first chapter of the *Cooperative Commonwealth* is the only portion of the book devoted to Marxist economic analysis. In some twenty pages Gronlund reviewed in nontechnical language the labor theory of value, the iron law of wages, the theory of the increasing misery of the laboring class and the impending crisis of capitalism. Some two thirds of the book described the cooperative commonwealth which was to emerge out of the revolution. Gronlund was careful to point out that scientific socialists were not utopian architects with blueprints of the good society in their pockets. Instead, he explained, they limited their predictions to such general features as were presumed to be logical developments from present institutions or practices, much as a paleontologist with his knowledge of skeletal structure reconstructed the whole animal from a few fossil fragments. In spite of professing such restrictions, however, Gronlund allowed himself a generous latitude in projecting the features of the coming society, often furnishing considerable detail. As in all literary utopias, these features, which need not be reviewed here, are of interest so far as they provide insight into the author's feeling for the strengths and weaknesses of his own society.

An implicit nationalism ran through all of Gronlund's thinking, and the cooperative commonwealth which he envisioned was a sovereign national state—the United States of America shorn of its archaic dual federalism. The coming revolution was to be the product of American conditions, while the social values to be realized in the cooperative commonwealth were the values indigenous to the American democratic ideology. The internationalist aspect of Marxism with its solidarity of working men without a country was conspicuously absent from Gronlund's thinking. At the same time he failed to foresee the problems of foreign policy among socialist republics, his attention being riveted upon "socialism in one country." In 1884 Gronlund believed that the first attempts to establish socialism would occur in Germany or France because of their advanced economies; six years later he was convinced by its rapid economic development that socialism would come first in the United States.

The ambiguities in Gronlund's treatment of the class struggle in the *Cooperative Commonwealth* invited misunderstanding. It has sometimes been said that by suppressing the doctrine he deviated from Marxist orthodoxy.[5] In the introduction to the book he promised an analysis of social evolutionary transformation free from any "vindictive feelings against *persons,* who are from circumstances what they are." This statement should not be taken to imply a repudiation of class struggle. To feel "nonvindictive" about individuals was one thing, while to exonerate the social class of which they might be members was quite another; and Gronlund had no intention of excusing the class which monopolized the benefits of the existing order. Excoriation of the capitalist class is a leitmotif which runs throughout the book. Gronlund followed Marx faithfully in distinguishing the successive historical epochs of slavery, feudalism, and capitalism, each of which was characterized by its distinctive mode of production and form of economic exploitation. To be coldly analytical about the inevitability of the social process and at the same time morally indignant at the injustices perpetrated by the plutocrats was simply to be a Marxist, and by this test Gronlund was fully qualified.

Nevertheless, in later years it is true that class struggle was the issue on which Gronlund was to become an apostate from Marxism.

---

[5] Quint, *American Socialism,* p. 28. In other respects Quint's excellent account of Gronlund acknowledges his Marxist orthodoxy. Chester Destler, *American Radicalism, 1865–1901. Essays and Documents* (New London, Conn., 1946), p. 199n.

After witnessing the revival of middle class reform activity in the 1880's and 1890's it was to become increasingly apparent to him that American experience was not conforming to Marxist expectations. The most promising signs of change were the awakened social consciences of religious and professional leaders whose activities pointed toward remedial legislation supported by an informed public opinion. Gronlund's earlier decision to appeal to the middle class was confirmed by the course of events, and much of the apparatus of Marxist analysis was finally abandoned. But all of this was in the future, and in 1884 Gronlund still professed formal allegiance to the basic Marxist doctrines.

The conciliatory tone which establishes the dominant mood of the book was integral to Gronlund's grand strategy in appealing to thoughtful Americans of all classes. It was not his principal object to arouse the emotions of hatred or anger called forth by such documents as the *Communist Manifesto*. If his Marxist orthodoxy was in any way suspect it was because he saw little practical hope of achieving the good society in America by the unaided efforts of the laboring proletariat, whatever the formal doctrines of his creed might dictate. And so he addressed himself to the types which had long been the principal reservoir of humanitarian idealism and public spirit. His task was to detach these readers from their historic allegiance to capitalistic individualism. Sensing the challenge of big business to the social status and self-esteem of the lower middle and professional classes Gronlund dared to hope that by analysis, persuasion, and appeals to hopes and anxieties he might induce those classes to commit themselves to the coming revolution.

In order to disseminate Marxist ideas most effectively it was necessary for Gronlund to locate them in an intellectual context familiar to the types of readers whom he hoped to influence. In doing this he demonstrated the effectiveness of his Americanization. The context of Gronlund's ideas was primarily British in origin, and in establishing it he was greatly aided by the fact that Marx himself had relied heavily upon the British political economists. Besides Ricardo, with his labor theory of value, Gronlund showed himself familiar with Malthus, Bentham, and John Stuart Mill, and could thus demonstrate how socialism would be the fitting culmination of a course of economic development already illumined in part by a galaxy of minds long venerated by educated Americans. To these older authorities Gronlund also added the familiar contemporary names of Carlyle, Ruskin, and Frederic Harrison. But much the most striking of Gronlund's accomplishments was the finding of a place in this sequence of thinkers for Herbert Spencer, the patron saint of the Social Darwinists. To bring the authority of Spencer's name to the elucidation of socialism in the Gilded Age seemed a master stroke and Gronlund made the most of it.

In his synthetic philosophy Spencer had found a prominent place for the analogy of the social organism. Society was presumed to be like a plant or animal, its various functions being analogous to the specialized parts of a living organism. It was to say the least anomalous for a champion of extreme *laissez-faire* to indulge himself in such a conceit, and Gronlund was quick to see that the idea was far more useful to the socialist than to the extreme individualist. The mutually interdependent functions of the cooperative commonwealth could very appropriately be exemplified by the coordinated parts of the organism, in which each cell played its indispensable role. Spencer moreover provided an excellent illustration of Gronlund's contention that socialism was growing naturally out of the existing capitalist society. Behold the best of the philosophical apologists for capitalism laying the intellectual foundations of socialism with his theory of the social organism! Spencer was in short an unconscious socialist.

The conciliatory and analytical tone which generally prevailed in Gronlund's discussion could yield on occasion to what appears to be calculated anger. When he discussed the anarchy of class warfare intensified by the constricting spasms of capitalism in its death struggles his bitterness overflowed. "Monopolists," "Jews," "gamblers," "parasites," "fleecers," "robbers," and "vampires" were mercilessly flayed for causing the evils men were suffering under capitalism. Somewhat apologetically, perhaps, Gronlund explained that in all of the great revolutionary movements in history the release of passion had been necessary in order to accomplish the transition to the new order. No one could tell whether violence would accompany the downfall of capitalism; that would be determined largely by the behavior of the capitalists. But that men must be nerved by passion to overthrow the system there could be no doubt.

Like so many Americans at the end of the nineteenth century Gronlund assumed that the current trend toward monopoly would continue unchecked until virtually complete monopoly would prevail not only in manufacturing, but in transportation, banking, merchandising, and land owning as well. A few millionaires would gobble up the capital of the entire middle class. To check or avert the course of monopolization was presumed to be impossible; the laws of economic development decreed it with utter finality. For Gronlund the true utopian was the antimonopolist. Gronlund put as much emphasis on the threat to the small merchant and employer as on the increasing misery of the workers. Even the independent farmer was declared to be threatened by the rapidly spreading bonanza farms owned by large corporations.

As the ultimate collapse of capitalism approached, signaled by the quickening tempo of depression, unemployment, and business failure, the clamor from all sides for remedial measures could be expected to become increasingly insistent. Many such measures were already being strenuously advocated in Gronlund's day. Besides the efforts to check monopolies a vigorous movement was underway to secure an eight-hour law limiting the working day. Labor was beginning its drive for unionization and a voice in determining wages and working conditions. Producers' and consumers' cooperatives designed to offset the tolls exacted by middle-men were being organized with increasing frequency and success. What position would socialists take on these so-called immediate demands? They were clearly a popular response to the tightening tentacles of capitalist control, and the socialists could expect to increase their following by adding such measures to their political program. The difficulty was that these measures were remedial rather than revolutionary. To the extent that they might be successful they would strengthen the capitalist system and postpone the day of final reckoning. Many socialists including Gronlund consequently turned their backs on immediate demands. Gronlund insisted that neither political regulation nor economic pressure could be effective in a society in which the ultimate power was held by capitalists. He conceded rather grudgingly, however, that such measures had had some success in England, where workers were partially reconciled to their wage slavery, thus deferring the coming revolution. By insisting upon revolutionary purity and refusing to temporize with immediate demands the socialists sacrificed much potential labor and farm support.

Gronlund had little to say about the circumstances under which the transition from capitalism to socialism was to occur beyond noting the need for a trained and dedicated band of socialists who would take charge. Nothing was said of a dictatorship by the proletariat. The reader gets the impression that for the United States at least Gronlund envisioned some kind of middle-class revolution managed by the kind of people to whom he addressed his book. He preferred to hurry on to paint as attractive a picture as possible of the socialist society of the future.

The organic analogy suggested the essential features of the cooperative commonwealth. Gronlund insisted that society — or the State, as he preferred to call it — is, together with the land it occupies, quite literally a living organism. Once freed from the incubus of class rule it would have no other function than to provide for its own welfare. It would take full charge of all productive and distributive machinery, assigning to each individual his duties and providing him with nourishment in accordance with his functions. Just as the cell exists for the body so each individual would realize his highest potentialities in service to the whole society. Interdependence would replace the archaic doctrine of individual rights, and society would be unified by the sentiment of solidarity. The individual citizen would for the first time realize freedom in restraint, that is, leisure, self-determination, and the ability and means to do the right thing.

Gronlund distinguished between communism (communitarianism) in which all property is held in common, and socialism in which only the means of production and distribution are brought under collective control. Under socialism, where productive employment would be provided for all citizens, demand for goods and services would be high, and everyone would acquire such personal property as might be desired. The workers in each industry would have full control, and would receive the full value of their labor. Labor checks to be exchanged for goods and services would replace money as wages. Necessary public revenue would be derived from a sales tax and a home tax. Profit, interest, and rent would all disappear. It would be the crowning glory of the cooperative commonwealth that the whole proceeds of labor would be distributed among those who did the labor.

According to Marxist theory, government is always the instrument of control by the ruling class. Logically, therefore, in the cooperative commonwealth where all would labor there would be no ruling class and no government. If government did not wholly wither away it would at least shrivel up to mere administration. Anticipating John Dewey[6] by nearly half a century Gronlund rejected the conventional distinction between public and private. Every function of social value is a public function, and every citizen is a public official responsible to the whole community for the conscientious performance of his duties.

In each industry the workers organized democratically would be in control, choosing their officials and holding them to strict accountability. These industry officials would in turn choose coordinators for the several industrial sectors, thus forming a hierarchical structure of administration which would be at once political, economic, and social. Gronlund believed that compared with the importance of economic and industrial relations government and administration were trivial matters. Such occasional issues of public policy as might require popular approval would be submitted to referendum.

As a social organism the cooperative commonwealth would have a central regulative system analogous to the brain and nervous system of higher animals. It is difficult to reconcile this analogy with the idea of democratic participation in decision making. It is even more difficult to believe that Gronlund's administrative officers would have no power in the usual sense. He solemnly affirmed that their functions would be restricted to superintendence, arbitration, and the gathering of statistics. Thus blithely was the problem of government transcended.

In his attempt to paint as attractive a picture as possible of the cooperative commonwealth Gronlund inevitably addressed himself to several social issues of current interest. Although the emancipation of women was proceeding rapidly, the objective of economic equality between the sexes was far from being realized. To the socialist this was the key to all social problems. Once women were placed on an equal footing with men economically all other prob-

[6] John Dewey, *The Public and Its Problems* (New York, 1927), pp. 33, 71.

lems would quickly find their solution. Gronlund did not propose that women should compete with men, which would be undesirable, but that the sexes should be placed on an equal footing by the assignment of appropriate functions to each. When a woman could earn her own living she would be free to enter the marriage relationship as an equal, and domestic life would be vastly improved. Gronlund shared with Catholics the feeling for the importance of family integrity, although he emphatically rejected the doctrine that church and family should share coordinate authority with the state. Like so many of the utopians, Gronlund found in the ethics of the family relationship his norm for social relations in the larger community. Self-love and regard for others would be reconciled in devotion to the larger good.

Mass education in the United States confronted the socialists with a problem similar to that of the immediate demands. It was one of their dogmas, which Gronlund faithfully repeated, that capitalism was hostile to public education. Nevertheless, the rapid growth of public education systems was a fact that stared him in the face, and Gronlund deftly sought to turn it to account by citing it as an indication of the trend toward socialism, because it was inconceivable that an educated people could tolerate class domination. In any event, the cooperative commonwealth would provide effective universal education for the first time.

Gronlund entertained the startling notion that when knowledge had become common property all would think and feel alike. It was only natural, he believed, for healthy men to share common convictions. Difference of opinion — that is to say, anarchy of opinion — was an enormous evil. Gronlund was shortly to deplore the relatively primitive militaristic flavor of Bellamy's labor battalions, but his own, paradoxically enough, was a far more pervasive and fundamental totalitarianism. It was now apparent that the analogy of the social organism was no idly chosen figure, but that it furnished accurate insight into Gronlund's vision of the cooperative commonwealth as a society composed of individuals so closely integrated in activities and outlook as to resemble the cells of a living organism. Once the individual had achieved a sense of complete identification with the social whole there would no longer be any possible discrepancy between individual and group interests. Human evolution could then be consciously guided by selective processes to rationally determined ends.

Although the *Cooperative Commonwealth* was a Marxist book its position with respect to the fundamental dogma of class conflict had been at least ambiguous, and out of this ambiguity the course of Gronlund's subsequent career began to unfold. As author he had formally adhered to the doctrine of class struggle both in history and theory, yet when he assayed to gather the forces which were to guide the course of the socialist revolution he found the theory of class conflict irrelevant to his purposes. He had identified his revolutionary cadre as a respectable minority of intelligent and public-spirited individuals to be found in all social classes. Class conflict and its resolution had played little or no part in his analysis of the dynamics of the coming revolution.

The rather mystical feeling for solidarity which had made Spencer's idea of the social organism a congenial one to Gronlund also strengthened his latent religious impulses. He noted the awakened sensitivity to social injustice among Protestant clergymen which resulted in the Social Gospel movement, and he was drawn into close personal association with the Rev. W. D. P. Bliss, a founder of the Fabian movement in America. Gronlund contributed to the *American Fabian,* and served as vice-president of the Social Reform Union which Bliss organized in the nineties.[7]

Gronlund's influence extended in other directions as well. Although he disapproved of the primary emphasis placed by Henry George on the nationalization of land on the ground that in the United States at least other issues were more pressing he nevertheless joined with other socialists in supporting George's vigorous campaign for mayor of New York in 1886. Gronlund believed that to press the land question would alienate the farmers, although he conceded that ultimately farms would have to be collectivized. At the moment, however, his position on land reform undoubtedly strengthened his appeal for J. A. Wayland, the agrarian radical, who was converted to socialism by reading Gronlund's book. In the nineties Gronlund hoped to harness Populist discontent to the

[7] Joseph Dorfman, *The Economic Mind in American Civilization* (3 vols. New York, 1946–1949), III, pp. 157–158.

socialist movement, advocating the formation of a Plebeian Party in which farm and labor grievances could be brought together. Whatever the correct position on immediate demands might be there was now at least no hesitation as to the desirability of socialist cooperation with agrarian radicalism.[8]

Undoubtedly Gronlund's most eminent disciple was Eugene Debs. The socialist leader told a presidential investigating commission in 1894 that he was not a socialist because his ideas had come from Gronlund rather than from Marx.[9] Although there may be some doubt as to the accuracy of this account of Debs's conversion there can be no question that it was distinguished testimony to the effectiveness with which Gronlund had sugar-coated the Marxist pill.

Four years after the publication of the *Cooperative Commonwealth* there appeared a far more famous book, Edward Bellamy's utopian romance, *Looking Backward*. Although Gronlund was critical of certain details of Bellamy's version of the cooperative commonwealth he was on the whole an enthusiastic admirer of Bellamy, and threw himself energetically into the Nationalist movement which burgeoned spontaneously in the wake of *Looking Backward*. The extent to which either man was indebted to the other has been a matter of scholarly dispute. According to Howard Quint, the *Cooperative Commonwealth* had made a deep impression on Bellamy, who incorporated much of its socialist message in *Looking Backward*.[10] Arthur E. Morgan, on the other hand, denies that Bellamy was acquainted with Gronlund's book, and holds on the contrary that it was the reading of *Looking Backward* that persuaded Gronlund to abandon the Marxist doctrine of class struggle.[11]

In the history of thought it is often more fruitful to consider the relationship between recorded ideas rather than to attempt to establish the personal dependence of one thinker upon another. If one compares *Looking Backward* with the *Cooperative Commonwealth* what can be said about their relationship? When the ma-

---

[8] Bell, in *Socialism and American Life*, I, p. 259; Quint, *American Socialism*, p. 224.

[9] Ray Ginger, *The Bending Cross. A Biography of Eugene Victor Debs* (New Brunswick, N.J., 1949), p. 156.

[10] Quint, *American Socialism*, pp. 30, 78. Dorfman also shares this view. *Economic Mind*, III, p. 150.

[11] Arthur E. Morgan, *Edward Bellamy* (New York, 1944), p. 388.

chinery of fictional romance is stripped away from Bellamy's book it at once becomes apparent that *Looking Backward* bears a striking resemblance to its predecessor. Both books have been described as utopias, and both are utopias of the same peculiar kind. In them the good society is not detached from the author's world by space or some other fanciful barrier. It is rather the residuary legatee of his world, the devoutly to be desired fulfillment of social tendencies and forces already observable and at work. It is not enough for the writer to point the contrast between the actual and the ideal; he must also show mankind how it is possible, indeed inevitable, to progress from the one to the other. They are both, in short, post-Marxist utopias.

Both books start with stinging indictments of contemporary capitalistic society, and both show how the internal contradictions of that society lead inevitably to the Commonwealth, a word with venerated associations for both writers. Both make much of the tendency toward monopoly under capitalism, which they feel will continue until a single great monopoly has formed, at which point it will be a relatively simple process for the state to take over. In the first edition of the *Cooperative Commonwealth* Gronlund employed "the foreign word, Solidarity," to designate the fraternal sentiment which was to prevail in the cooperative commonwealth. He removed this reference from the revised edition of 1890, perhaps having discovered in the interim that as early as 1874 Bellamy had forecast his social theory in an essay entitled "The Religion of Solidarity." This humanistic theism received an eloquent statement in the sermon preached by the Rev. Mr. Barton which forms the culminating passage in *Looking Backward*. Gronlund and Bellamy shared a powerful capacity for moral indignation at the callous indifference and inhumanity which were the fruits of early industrialism. Both writers drew vivid contrasts between the family ethic of love and self-sacrifice which would be the prevailing ethic of the cooperative commonwealth and the selfish, competitive individualism inculcated by capitalism. They also shared the common nineteenth-century social evolutionism, with its convenient blend of materialism and spirituality. Possessed of a common heritage their thinking moved in closely parallel channels, and there seems to be little advantage in assigning to either a determinative influence on the other.

Encouraged by the reception of his book both in the United States and in England Gronlund prepared a revision which was published in 1890. Events during the intervening six years as well as the ripening of certain ideas present in germinal form in the earlier version all left their marks on the new edition. The awakened interest in social problems among many of the Protestant clergy encouraged Gronlund to believe that revolutionary leadership would be assumed by devoutly religious minds. After the fashion of George Herron and the Christian Socialists he identified the cooperative commonwealth with the Kingdom of Heaven on earth. A passage in the first edition in which he had ascribed the origins of *laissez-faire* to Protestant influences was now suppressed. The predominant emphasis of the first edition upon economic factors was now supplemented by a stronger moral imperative, as reflected in the changing of many references to "capitalists" to read "philistines."

Events occurring in the latter part of the 1880's undoubtedly persuaded Gronlund to reconsider his position on immediate demands. The formation of the American Federation of Labor in 1886, the Interstate Commerce Act of 1887, and the prospects of antitrust legislation all suggested that American political and industrial society was not the utterly helpless captive of capitalist dynamics that he had earlier assumed it to be. It now appeared likely that government might play a far more important role as a moderating influence than he had believed possible. Gronlund now deleted a passage in which he had proclaimed the futility of a federal eight-hour law, or of any governmental attempt to influence working conditions. He removed a passage in which he had rejected as futile a Greenbacker proposal of federal farm loans at low interest rates. Indeed, Gronlund's conception of the role of government in the socialist revolution was now drastically revised. In the earlier edition he had said that socialists could wait with folded arms for the capitalist order to collapse of its own weight, when the reins of power would drop from impotent capitalist hands into theirs. He now predicted that long before that point was reached "the *State* will step in." In this context the word State clearly meant government. How a government which had played a central role in revolutionary transformation could then be expected to wither away Gronlund did not explain.

Heartened by the signs of growing interest in socialism Gronlund now predicted that the cooperative commonwealth would be
established first in the United States: geographical isolation from
the effects of counterrevolutionary forces as well as the temperament of the American people augured favorably. The influence of
Samuel Gompers had yet to turn the AFL away from socialistic
reform toward pure and simple unionism, and so Gronlund could
persuade himself that the spirit of American unionism was socialistic. He now suppressed passages in which he had earlier appealed
to passion; instead, the final pages of the revised edition contained
an eloquent invocation of the religious spirit of solidarity. The revolution was to consist of "identifying ourselves with humanity —
the redeemed form of man."

In the decade remaining to him Gronlund moved steadily away
from Marxism, although he remained a socialist to the last. While
employed briefly as a statistician in the Department of Labor he
attempted in 1891 to organize a secret society called the American
Socialist Fraternity. Academic economists and young men interested
in enlarging the scope of governmental activity were invited to join.
Appealing deliberately to the intelligentsia rather than to the proletariat Gronlund advocated "not the socialism which is in the interest only of the weak and the inefficient, but that which will
create *glad* and *willing* obedience in all — ORDER — and thus is
even more in the interest of the competent." The object of secrecy
was to protect the influence and usefulness of members in high
places.[12] There is no evidence that Gronlund's plans for the Fraternity came to fruition. He gave up his position in the Labor Department for the precarious career of itinerant lecturer and promoter,
living in dire poverty, and finally was forced in 1898 to appeal to
Henry Demarest Lloyd for financial aid.

Gronlund's last book, *The New Economy*, was published in 1898,
a year before his death. The reformist and revisionist tendencies of
the *Cooperative Commonwealth* were here fully developed. Class
conflict and revolutionary violence were now repugnant to him.
Centralization of the American economy in trusts and monopolies
was a trend to be welcomed, since the seizure and operation of
trusts by government would be a relatively painless procedure.
Evolutionary gradualism in which progress toward collectivism

[12] Dorfman, *Economic Mind*, III, pp. 154–155.

would be guided by an educated and public-spirited leadership was enveloped in a mystical feeling for the inevitable working out of the Divine Will in history. Hopeful and active to the end, Gronlund's final project was a plan[13] for the colonization of socialists in a Western state for the purpose of capturing its government and making a state-wide trial of collectivism — a kind of industrial communitarianism on an appropriately American scale.

Stow Persons

[13] Quint, *American Socialism*, pp. 277–278, 317–318.

A NOTE ON THE TEXT

THE text of *The Coöperative Commonwealth* chosen for the John Harvard Library is the original edition of 1884 published by Lee and Shepard of Boston and Charles T. Dillingham of New York. Save for the correction of typographical errors, of which there were a good many, and the occasional expansion of an abbreviation to recognizable form, Gronlund's text is reproduced verbatim with all of its idiosyncrasies of style and usage. In the interest of the widest possible distribution the generous publishers permitted J. W. Lovell of New York and J. A. Wayland of Girard, Kansas, two well-known socialist publishers, to issue their own editions. Selling at a dollar in cloth and fifty cents in paperback the book enjoyed at least a modest success, with several printings in both the United States and England. The publishers have no record of the number of printings. The subtitle of the original edition read, *An Exposition of Modern Socialism*. The adjective "modern" was intended to denote "German" or "Marxist" as distinct from other and presumably spurious forms of the socialist doctrine. For reasons not now apparent the socialist publisher Lovell changed the subtitle of his editions to read, *An Exposition of Collectivism*, thus removing the word Socialism from the title page.

Gronlund prepared a "revised and enlarged" edition which appeared in 1890. In order to improve the book for English readers the author deleted many references to American events and personalities, thus robbing the work of much of its local color and appeal. At least five editions were issued by S. Sonnenschein of London. Of greater interest to the student of socialist thought were the many modifications of the text which reflected the evolution of Gronlund's thinking during the six years following the original publication. Taken together, these modifications show the extent of Gronlund's deviation from Marxism toward his own brand of reformist and mystical socialism. They are discussed by the editor in the Introduction, pp. xxiv–xxv.

THE

COÖPERATIVE
COMMONWEALTH

IN ITS OUTLINES.

AN EXPOSITION OF MODERN SOCIALISM

BY LAURENCE GRONLUND

"My object is not to make people read,
But to make them think."
[MONTESQUIEU — *Spirit of Laws.*

BOSTON
LEE AND SHEPARD PUBLISHERS
NEW YORK CHARLES T. DILLINGHAM
1884
[transcript of the original title page]

TO

THE ONE WHO HAS BEEN MOST INTERESTED

In the progress of my work;

TO MY SYMPATHETIC WIFE

I dedicate this book.

[INTRODUCTION
TO THE REVISED EDITION,
1890]

Any one who, like myself, has been watching the intellectual movement among Americans during the last dozen years, must be impressed with the way in which socialism, or nationalism, as it has been lately called, has spread among them. I may say that I know that the present work, in the shape in which it first appeared in 1884, has contributed its share to that effect; it has sown the seeds of socialism in all parts of our country, and there is sufficient evidence to show that some of them have germinated. I suppose this is due to the feature, which is peculiar to THE CO-OPERATIVE COMMONWEALTH, that it gives, as well as can at present be done, the constructive side of socialism, — that it attempts to present the new social system in outline.

As far back as August, 1880, when I could count all native American socialists on the fingers of one hand, there appeared a remarkable dialogue in the *Nineteenth Century*, entitled "Political Optimism," in which occurred the following paragraph: —

We see that political systems in all progressive societies tend towards socialistic democracy. We see everywhere that it must come to that. We all of us feel this conviction, — or all of us, I suppose, who have reflected on the matter. We feel, too, that nothing we can do can avert, or possibly long delay, the consummation. Then we must believe that the movement is being guided, or is guiding itself to happy issues.

Now, what I try to do in this book is to take you by the arm, lead you to a new point of view, and if you are not near-sighted, nor wear colored spectacles, nor biased by your interest, you will surely come to the above conviction.

The happiest effect of my book is that it has led indirectly, and probably unconsciously, to Mr. Bellamy's "Looking Backward," the novel which without doubt has stealthily inoculated thousands of Americans with socialism, just because it ignored that name and those who had written on the subject. It should, however, in justice to the cause, be stated, that there are three ideas in that novel for which socialism should not be held responsible, as has been done by Prof. Francis A. Walker, in a criticism. These are a love for militarism, equal wages, and appointments by the retired functionaries. They are decidedly unsocialistic notions, belong exclusively to Mr. Bellamy, and will be further noticed in the course of this volume.

Jules Simon has remarked, "The nineteenth century has, so far, been nothing but a riddle." It looks to me as if the last ten years will give the solution of the riddle. I should not be surprised if we soon should witness an enthusiasm rivalling that of the first crusade. Everything is ripe, especially in the United States, for the great change, except leaders. I am convinced they will come out from among the deeply religious minds among us. What is needed is to convince them that this coming change is God's will; that the society to be ushered in is not a pig-sty, filled with well-fed hogs, but is, indeed, the Kingdom of Heaven on earth; in other words, those of the above dialogue, that "the movement is guiding itself to happy issues." This I have tried to do in an essay, which will be published simultaneously with this volume, entitled "Our Destiny."

LAURENCE GRONLUND.

BOSTON, 1890.

A dialogue on "Political Optimism" in the *Nineteenth Century* for August, 1880, contains the following language:

"We see that political systems in all progressive societies tend toward socialistic democracy. We see everywhere that it *must* come to that. We all of us feel this conviction, or all of us, I suppose, who have reflected on the matter. We feel, too, that nothing we can do can avert or possibly long delay the consummation. Then, we *must* believe that the movement is being guided, or is guiding itself to happy issues."

This passage may serve as a key to the following pages.

They have been written that you may see that the social and political phenomena in all progressive countries, and particularly in our own country and Great Britain, are, in a perfectly natural manner, evolving a New Social Order, a Social Democratic Order, which we have called *The Cooperative Commonwealth;* in other words, — to speak pointedly, — that Socialism is no importation, but a *home-growth,* wherever found. They are written to give you good reasons for expecting that this New Social Order will be, indeed, a "happy issue" to the brain-worker as well as to the hand-worker, to woman as well as to man. They are written to give reasons for our convictions that it must come to that, here as elsewhere, within a comparatively short period, or to barbarism.

Barbarism! — Yes. Let not yourself be led astray by the remarkable increase everywhere of wealth on the whole, — possibly the under-current is, nevertheless, carrying us swiftly backwards. Suppose you had told a Roman citizen in the age of Augustus that his proud country *then* had entered on its decline, — as every schoolboy now knows it had, — he would have thought you insane. Now, the many striking parallels between that period and the times in which we are living must have forced themselves on your attention, if you are of a reflective turn of mind, as we assume you are. You will have observed the same destructive forces to which History attributes the fall of pagan Rome busily at work under your very eyes. You see the same mad chase after wealth; you find every-where the same deadening scepticism in regard to high ideals. You observe in all our centres of activity a corruption — I will not say as great as, but — promising in due time to rival that of the Roman Empire. Be careful not to be too scornful if we prophesy that in, say, twenty-five years from now, — if not the Cooperative Common-wealth should then, perchance, be realized — the demagogues of New York City will buy voters by free public feasts and theatricals, that you will hear the cry of *"panem et circenses"* — "give us bread and circuses," if you live then! Indeed, we have already read in the N. Y. Tribune: "Every one of our civil Justices has given a day's 'outing' to the wives and children of his district." Even now in many of the States wealth seems a pre-requisite to the attainment of Senatorial honors and millionaires and sons of millionaires are bid-ding for seats in the lower house of Congress.

But, for reasons hereafter set forth, we do not believe our race will return to barbarism. The Roman Empire was saved from that fate, finally, by being reanimated. Our age as fully needs reanima-tion as the period of the Cæsars. We shall be reanimated: history will once more see Society reconstructed on a new basis.

Says Huxley: "The reconstruction of Society on a scientific basis is not only possible, but the only political object much worth striv-ing for." True, emphatically true! Except so far as it is implied in this sentence that any individual or any nation can go to work and *arbitrarily* reconstruct Society on a scientific or any other basis.

Socialism — *modern* Socialism, *German* Socialism, which is fast becoming *the* Socialism the world over — holds that the impending reconstruction of Society will be brought about by the Logic of Events; teaches that *The Coming Revolution is strictly an Evolu-tion.* Socialists of that school reason from no assumed first principle, like the French who start from "Social equality" or like Herbert Spencer, when in his *Social Statics* he lays it down as an axiom, that "every man has freedom to do all that he wills, provided he infringes not the like freedom of every other man;" but basing themselves on experience — not individual but universal experience — they can and do present clear-cut, definite solutions.

It is this German Socialism which is presented in the following pages, with this important modification that it has been digested by a mind, Anglo-Saxon in its dislike of all extravagancies and in its freedom from any vindictive feeling against *persons*, who are from circumstances what they are. In the first three chapters we present the Socialist critique of the phenomena of the era in which we are living; in the next three chapters we indicate the coming Social order which will, probably, develop itself out of the present system; in the three that follow we outline the political and legal machinery which very likely will be found necessary to the working of that new order; in chapters X, XI and XII, we point out the principal social effects which may be expected to follow from it, and in the last chapter we consider how the revolution — the change — is likely to be accomplished in our country and England.

We believe it is time that a work, containing all the leading tenets of Socialism in a concise, consecutive form should be presented in the English language — in the language of the two countries where the social, and specially the industrial conditions, are ripening quicker than anywhere else. Such a work, in fact, exists nowhere. Whenever any one now wishes to inform himself on the subject he has to wade through innumerable books and pamphlets, mostly German. That such a candid man as John S. Mill, who had a truly Socialist heart, did not become a Socialist we attribute to this fragmentary shape of Socialist thought, and that in a tongue unknown to him; for his "Chapters on Socialism," published after his death, show that he was familiar only with French speculations, of a time when Socialism was yet in its infancy. We can dismiss nearly all that thus far has been written in our language by Socialists on the subject with the remark that it is not exactly adapted to people of judgment and culture. We think that all Americans who simply want to be well-informed ought to make themselves acquainted with this new *philosophy* — and Socialism is nothing less than that — which is believed in by hundreds of thousands of our fellow-men with a fervor equalling the enthusiasm of the early Christians. We think they will make themselves acquainted with it, as soon as it is presented to them in readable English, and applied to American phenomena and American conditions by a writer possessing the American bias for the practical. Such Socialism, whether true or false, whether destined to be successful or unsuccessful, is a matter that concerns *you* personally.

But if the writer of this work did not hope to accomplish something beyond giving some, or even many, Americans more correct notions of the aims of Socialists than those they have, it would never have been written. We have a deeper purpose, far nearer our heart. Most reflective minds, if they do not go the whole length of the one who speaks in the dialogue with which we started, do admit that we are at the brink of an extraordinary change; that a crisis of *some sort* is impending, no matter if it is likely to burst out now or in ten or fifty years from now. We then say that the only thing that can save us and our children from horrors, ten-fold worse than those of the French Revolution, that can save us from the infliction of such a scourge as Napoleon, will be the activity of a minority, acting as the brains of the Revolution. For while there will be a revolution, it need not necessarily be one marked by blood. We hope it will not be such a one: a revolution by violence is to Society what a hurricane is to a ship struggling on the stormy ocean; it is only by herculean efforts that we shall succeed in avoiding the rocks and bring it into the secure haven, and even then we shall be but at the threshold of our task.

But, then, we must first have in our country this minority; a vigorous minority, even if but a small one; a minority of intelligent and energetic American men and women; a minority with sound convictions as to what the crisis means and how it may be made to redound to the welfare of the whole of Society and with the courage of their convictions. Such a minority will be indispensable to render the revolution a blessing, whether it comes peaceably or forcibly. Not that this minority is to *make* the coming Revolution — an individual, a clique, a majority even can as little make a revolution as the fly makes the carriage wheel roll; the Revolution makes itself or "grows itself;" — but this minority is to prepare for it and, when the decisive moment has arrived, act on the masses, as the power acts on the lever. To reach and possibly win this minority — however small — this book has mainly been written.

We shall, for that purpose, address ourselves to the reflective minds of all classes, rich as well as poor, professional as well as working men — and, indeed, many, very many, literary men and women, very many lawyers, very many physicians and teachers are just as much in need of this Coming Revolution as most working men. But we shall assume, reader, that you are not one of those who are personally interested in the maintenance of the present Social Order, or rather *Social Anarchy*, for then it is hopeless to try to win you over. Very likely you will deem it a difficult feat to win you over, to turn you into a Socialist — All we ask of you is with us to view familiar facts of life from a standpoint, very different from the one you have hitherto been occupying, to look at them in other lights and shades, and then await the result. A man is never the same any more after he has once got a new impression. Much that we are going to say cannot but shock your preconceived ideas, but from St. Paul down many have been indignant at first hearing what afterwards became their most cherished convictions. We shall discard all common-places and phrases and throughout be mindful of Samuel Johnson's admonition: "Let us empty our minds of cant, gentlemen!"

CHAPTER I

THE PROFIT SYSTEM

"The working class is the only class which is not a class. It is the nation. It represents, so to speak, the body as a whole, of which the other classes only represent special organs. These organs, no doubt, have great and indispensable functions, but for most purposes of government the State consists of the vast laboring majority. Its welfare depends on what their lives are like." — *Frederic Harrison.*

"They (Political Economists) are men of only one idea — Wealth, how to procure and increase it. Their rules seemed infallibly certain to that supreme end. What did it signify that a great part of mankind was made meanwhile even more wretched than before, provided wealth on the whole increased?" — *Catholic Quarterly Review,* Jan. 1880.

"That the masses of men are robbed of their fair earnings — that they have to work much harder than they ought to work for a very much poorer living than they ought to get, is to my mind clear." — *Henry George.*

We shall commence with an object lesson; it will consist chiefly of figures, and figures are tiresome things; — but the lesson will be a short one. Here are four diagrams, — "cakes" let us call them:

1850.

Wages for 957,000 "hands."	Surplus, 46 per cent.

$ 437,000,000.

1860.

Wages for 1,300,000 "hands."	Surplus, 53 per cent.

$ 805,000,000.

1870.

Wages for 2,000,000 "hands."	Surplus, 53 per cent.

$ 1,310,000,000.

1880.

Wages for 2,739,000 "hands."	Surplus, 48 1-3 per cent.

$ 1,834,000,000.

These "cakes" represent the *net* produce of all manufacturing industries of the United States for the respective years; mark! *not* the gross value of the products on leaving the factories, but only that value which has been given to them in the factories *minus* the wear and tear of machinery. That is to say, we have arrived at the above figures by first adding the value of the raw materials and the depreciation of all machinery, implements and buildings together, and then deducting that sum from the value of the finished products. The value of the raw-materials used, and the gross value we have gathered from the respective U. S. Census Reports, but for the estimate of the wear and tear of machinery &c there are absolutely no data anywhere to be had. We have taken five per cent. of all the capital invested in all manufactures in the respective years as probably a fair estimate of such wear and tear, as but a small part of all capital is invested in machinery and implements, where most of the wear and tear occurs. Supposing that we are somewhat out of the way on one side or the other in this guess, it will not materially affect the conclusions of this chapter.

Observe, first, that these "cakes" grow at an even and a very great rate;

The cake of 1850 has a value of   437 million dollars;
    that of 1860 "   "   "   "   805   "   "
    that of 1870 (reduced to gold) 1310   "   "
    that of 1880 a value of   1834   "   "

Observe, next, that these "cakes" are divided by a vertical line into two very nearly equal portions. That to the left was paid to the workers in the form of wages; that to the right we shall, for the time being, call the "Surplus."

Note, also, — for we do not want to make facts, but simply to declare and explain them — that the portion: wages, increases both absolutely and relatively in proportion to the number of workers:

The average wage in 1850 was 248 dollars;
   "   "   "   " 1860 " 292   "
   "   "   "   " 1870 " 310 (gold.)
   "   "   "   " 1880 " 346   "

The portion: *surplus* grows at a great rate:

In 1850 it amounted to 200 million dollars;
" 1860 it was   426   "   "
" 1870 it was   690   "   (gold.)
" 1880 it rose to   886   "   "

The average "surplus," that is, when divided by the number of establishments, was as follows:

In 1850 it was $1,500.
" 1860 "   "   3,000.
" 1870 it fell to 2,736, because the number of establishments had nearly doubled.

In 1880 it rose to 3,490, the number of establishments being nearly the same as in 1870.

Here ends the lesson. It was all figures; but we should say that to a reflective mind these figures are not dumb, but speaking.

The central point of interest seems to us to be this "surplus." *How does this surplus originate?* For to know what a thing is, we must know the process of its origin. How come these cakes — the net results of our industrial production — to be divided that way? In order to answer these questions we shall have to dissect the system of production which now prevails.

Take a number of moneyed men who agree to invest their superfluities in some industrial enterprise. They come together, form themselves into a joint-stock company and elect officers; such companies, in fact, now own and operate some of our largest establishments, and the tendency is that all industries of any consequence in time will be carried on by them. Suppose then our moneyed men engaged in the cotton, or woolen, or iron and steel industry; either one of these will serve our purpose equally well, as the "surplus" was in 1880 about the same in proportion in all of them. Suppose they engage in the making of cotton cloth. None of these men need have any knowledge whatever of the work to be done, and as a matter of fact the stockholders of existing joint-stock companies have no such knowledge. They need not know anything, indeed, except to add and divide — this is not added impertinently, but simply to emphasize a fact most pertinent to our subject. All that they need do is to hire a manager at a stated salary and place their funds at his disposal.

This manager then rents a factory — a cotton-"mill" — or has one built; goes then into the market and buys spindles, bales of cotton, and other machinery and raw materials. All that now is wanting is Labor; but that is also to be found in the market — plenty of it. The manager buys as much as he wants of it. Note, however, here a difference. The machinery and raw material he has to pay for on, or a short time after, delivery; not quite so with Labor. With that a contract is made to employ it for a week or a month at an agreed price, and then to pay for it *after* having used it.

All these wares — machinery, cotton and Labor — are now taken to the cotton mill, where our men with money may, if they think fit, look on while Labor spins and weaves the cotton into cloth, using up in that process a certain small portion of the machinery and factory. Everybody now knows, that this cloth is not made for the personal use of these moneyed men or their families — and we shall see in another chapter that this fact is a truly distinguishing mark of the era we are living in — but that it is manufactured wholly for other people whom these men never saw or heard of. This cloth is made for the express purpose of being taken into and disposed of in the market of the world. For there, all wares, from guano to gold, from rags to silk, have one quality in common; that of possessing *value*.

Now, please mark that nothing can so effectually kill our cause as the successful impeachment of the answer we shall give to the question: What is value? or the deductions we shall draw from it. Our explanation of what this "surplus" is and what Capital is, hinges on this question, which is, indeed, *"l'idee mere"* — the "mother idea" of Socialism. We shall, therefore, suspend our sketch of the present mode of production, in order first to answer it.

But mark again, our exposition of "value" is none other than that of David Ricardo. Socialists regard Ricardo as the last political economist who made any substantial addition to the science; the one who, in regard to value and wages, advanced it to its highest plane. And it was only after the supporters of the present social order found out, what use could be made of his teachings, that Bastiat and his disciples came to their succor and tried to impugn these teachings. We build on Ricardo as our foundation.

To the question then. By "value" we mean *value in exchange;* we do not mean value in use, or utility, or, what seems to us a more luminous name, and what Locke called it: *worth*. The worth or utility of shoes is their capacity to protect the feet; their value is what they will fetch in the market. Their value is their relation to other wares, in some way or other; is another name for equivalence.

But relation in what way? Not relation of worths. Worth, or utility, is undoubtedly presupposed, but it does not determine the value. That will be seen from the following illustrations:

The reason why a man wants to purchase a pair of shoes, is that he needs them, that they are useful, that they possess "worth" to him. But their usefulness is not at all the reason why he pays $2.00 for them. He does not pay twenty times as much for them as for a ten cent loaf of bread, because they are twenty times as useful to him. Why not? Because the two "worths" or two usefulnesses are just as incomparable as a pound of butter and a peck of apples would be. Again, a loaf of bread is "worth" infinitely more to a man who has not eaten anything for forty-eight hours than to one who just comes from a hearty dinner; yet the former can buy the loaf just as cheaply as the latter. Value, then, is no relation of "worths," of usefulnesses.

Nor has money anything to do with determining values. Wares would have value, the same as they have now, if all money of all kinds were suddenly annihilated. In order to eliminate that disturbing factor: money, we shall suppose an exchange of goods for goods — pure barter.

Assume, then, a shoemaker to exchange one pair of boots for a coat, another similar pair for a table, a third pair for one hundred pounds of bread, a fourth pair for forty bushels of coal, and a fifth pair for a book. All these articles are said to be *equal* in value.

But equality presupposes comparison. We only compare such articles with each other that are similar. In what respect, then, are the above articles similar, except that of being useful, which we saw was no point of comparison?

They are dissimilar in regard to the material, out of which they are made and the purposes for which they are made. They are, on the other hand, similar in this respect that they have been produced by human labor, working on natural products, which, again, have been won by human labor. They have, then, this property in common, that they have sprung from Nature, and contain in them a certain amount of human labor. *Labor is their father and Nature is their mother.*

Nature, however, performs her work gratuitously. It must, then, be human labor which gives these various articles their value.

That is, also, the teaching of Ricardo. He lays it down as a fundamental principle, that the exchange values of wares the supply of which may be indefinitely increased, (as is the case with these articles we enumerated) depend, exclusively, on the quantities of labor, necessarily required to produce them and bring them to market, in all states of society. In another place he says: "In all cases, wares rise in value, because more labor is expended."

These various articles, however, have not only value; they were supposed to have equal value, consequently they must contain an equal amount of human labor. And so it is.

These amounts are first measured by the time devoted to produce these articles. Thus, it is easy enough to say, how much bakering labor is contained in the bread; how much tailoring labor in the coat &c.

These various labors, however, are very different in kind, you will say. Undoubtedly. But the difference consists simply in being more or less complicated. It takes, simply, more time to learn the one than the other. The most complicated kind of work can always be reduced to ordinary unskilled labor, may always be considered as multiplied common labor. Thus digging is easier to learn than type setting. There is contained in every hour's work of the carpenter a part of the time he devoted to learning his trade. This is still more apparent in the literary labor contained in a book. Years may be requisite for the preliminary work, months or even years may have to be devoted to special studies, while the mere writing of the manuscript may take but a few months. One hour of writing may thus be equivalent to twelve, or many more, hours of common labor.

In this connection Ricardo very pertinently remarks "I am not inattentive to the difficulty of comparing one hour's labor in one employment with the same duration of labor in another. But the estimation of different qualities of Labor comes soon to be adjusted in the market with sufficient precision for all practical purposes."

But we are not yet ready to define what Value is. Suppose one man required twice as much time to make a pair of boots as is usually required, and suppose he should then want from the tailor two coats in exchange, instead of one, he probably would get some such answer as this: "I don't care how long time it takes you to make such a pair of boots. I know, that on an average, an average shoemaker can make them in half that time, and therefore your labor is of no more value." Value is not then determined by the time which this or that worker may need.

Again. Suppose tomorrow a machine is invented and generally introduced which will make two pair of boots in the same time that now is required for one pair. Then the Value will be reduced one-half.

We, then, define Value as: *the quantity of common human labor, measured by time, which on an average is requisite, by the implements generally used, to produce a given commodity.*

We should now go on with our illustration and state the deduction which Socialists draw from the definition just given, were it not for some misunderstandings that very likely already have arisen in many a reader's mind.

Thus, one may object: Suppose I find a diamond in the highway. Its value is, certainly, far above the trouble of picking it up. Does not this show that Bastiat's definition of Value: that its measure is "the service done to the buyer, in saving him a certain amount of effort," is the more correct one? We answer: People are not in the habit of finding diamonds in the highways. If they were, diamonds would soon be as cheap as pebbles. Diamonds will come to the finder dear enough, if he were to seek them in Hindostan or Brazil, where they are usually found. Remember that the *average* amount of labor is a part of our definition.

A word more in regard to that theory of "service," which so many reformers in our country have got into their heads without knowing to whom they owe it. Bastiat it was who invented that term in order to get over the apparent mischief Ricardo's theory worked; who expressly selected it because its meaning was equivocal. Its efficacy lies entirely in the shifting uses of an ambiguous term. Bastiat's definition really amounts to saying, that the value of a railroad-ticket from Boston to Worcester is measured by the time, trouble and expense which I may "save" in not walking or driving that distance! Why, our progress depends on exactly the reverse! On this, that values of articles become constantly less and less in proportion to the trouble I should have to undergo in producing them by my own efforts! So that, finally, values and troubles of mine bear no relation at all to each other.

Again, we shall, of course, be charged with having disregarded the law of Demand and Supply. And yet, we distinctly mentioned, that we, so far, only spoke of articles that may be indefinitely increased. Wares, that cannot be thus increased, like rare pictures and wines, and other wares in times of scarcity, have what is called, a "monopoly value," that is, their value is not measured by the labor contained — *crystallized* — in them at all, but by Demand and Supply, exclusively. And even with regard to wares that may be indefinitely increased (the vast majority of all wares) we, with Ricardo, do not deny that "there are accidental and temporary deviations of the actual market from their primary, and natural price."

That which we lay stress upon is, that the labor expended on wares measures, and *is*, their primary and natural value. Labor expended constitutes, so to speak, their *level* value. Demand and Supply have, as to those wares, simply the effect of making their price (that is, their value expressed in money — in gold and silver) vibrate, now a little above, now a little below that level value of theirs; exactly as the wind raises and depresses the waves in respect to the level of the sea.

We claim, then: — First, in the words of Ricardo: "Nature by the aid of machinery adds to utilities (to "Worths") by making society richer; but the assistance which it affords, adds nothing to Values, but always makes the latter fall."

And, on the other hand, that *Human Labor and Scarcity create all Values.* But since it is evident, that Scarcity cannot create anything real, we must conclude that the Values which are due to it, are unreal ones; and that it is human Labor alone that creates all real values. [This of course, does not imply, that there is not much Labor which does not create any Values at all.] So it is not only now, but so it has always been. So it will always be under any industrial system.

We can now return to our sketch. We left the manager having taken the cotton cloth into the world's market for sale. Suppose one hundred hours of common labor (that is, the unskilled labor to which, as we have seen, all skilled labor can be ultimately reduced) necessary, under the prevailing mode of production, to make this cloth, and another hundred hours of common labor requisite to produce the bales of cotton and that part of the machinery which has been used up, then the value of the finished cotton cloth is two hundred hours of common labor. That is, they will exchange with that amount of labor crystallized in any other ware. Suppose they are exchanged (disregarding for the moment the oscillating influence of Demand and Supply) for an amount of gold, embodying two hundred hours of common labor. That gold is then taken to the office of our company.

But, since equal amounts of labor are exchanged, why do these moneyed men engage in this operation? Do they do it for fun?

Not a bit of it. We have now arrived at the Socialist deduction which is drawn from our definition of value, and which made it so important, that it should be thoroughly understood. Our moneyed men first deduct from that heap of gold lying before them their outlay for raw materials and the wear and tear of machinery. The balance — the "cake" in fact — they divide into two, let us say, equal portions. The one portion they give to Labor, and the other — ?

Remember that we stated, that there is plenty of labor in the market. Labor now-a-days is a ware. Being a ware it possesses both Worth and Value. Its *worth* is its ability to produce our "cakes" — Values. Labor creates these. And its (labor's) *Value* is precisely what the value of other wares is: *the amount of common human labor, necessary to "raise" and maintain a laborer,* in the manner customary at a given time and in a given country.

Labor as Ricardo says, "has its natural value — depending on the price of necessaries — and its market price," vibrating above and below the former. The laborer, in other words, must sell his labor for wages, now a little above, now a little below what it costs him to live and bring up his family.

That which we have hitherto called "the surplus," then arises, because the laborer gets only about half of what he produces. And what becomes of it? Fancy these moneyed men reasoning to themselves: "True, this surplus is the product of our Labor, but didn't we agree to pay a stated price for that; and haven't we paid it? True, also, that we have done nothing but going through the effort of hiring our manager and looking on. Never mind! *we call it profit.*" That name they give it and put it into their pockets.

From this point we have no more use for the vague word "Surplus"; we are now entitled to call it by the appropriate name: Fleecings. If there was an English word for the process of abstracting honey from the bees, we should prefer that, for the process of pocketing the proceeds of Labor is also a stealthy one. Let it, however be distinctly understood that in adopting this word "fleecings" we have not the remotest idea of reflecting upon *persons;* we use it, and shall use it repeatedly, to condemn as impressively as possible the system which allows and sometimes compels one class of men virtually to say to another class: "If you will work five hours a day for us gratuitously, we will enable you to work the other five hours for yourselves" — that is, to condemn the *Profit System,* the Wage-System. Observe that we said "one class of men." For, while in our illustration we assumed that the owners of the cotton mill had all the means, needed for their enterprise, we know that in many cases employers have to rent land on which to build their factories and to borrow money to defray their expenses. Such employers, of course, do not put all the fleecings into their own pockets, but have to divide with land owners, bankers and other "gentlemen at large."

But the fact is — and on that it is we lay stress — that the *workers* receive only about half of what they produce, just enough to keep up life and strength and bring up a new generation of laborers, while the other half stealthily passes into the pockets of quite another class of men.

Now we can illustrate our "cakes," so that they present this appearance:

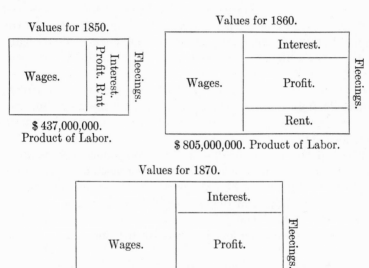

Values for 1850.

Wages. | Profit. R'nt | Interest. | Fleecings.

$ 437,000,000.
Product of Labor.

Values for 1860.

Wages. | Interest. / Profit. / Rent. | Fleecings.

$ 805,000,000. Product of Labor.

Values for 1870.

Wages. | Interest. / Profit. / Rent. | Fleecings.

$ 1,310,000,000. Product of Labor.

Values for 1880.

Wages. | Interest. / Profit. / Rent. | Fleecings.

$ 1,834,000,000. Product of Labor.

Here also is the place to note the answer to another question which the object-lesson may suggest: What is the average amount which the employing class fleeced from each worker during the respective census years?

In 1850 it amounted to $209.00;
" 1860 it was   327.50;
" 1870 it rose to   345.00;
" 1880 it dropped to   323.50.

By the way, we ought here to remark that it will not do to trust implicitly these or other calculations that might be made on figures in the Census Reports (remember it is the employers who have furnished all data); especially is a comparison of one census year with another liable to be very misleading, since one Report differs materially from another both in method and accuracy. But these Reports are of great service, when only, as here, a rough, approximate idea of the reality is required.

We then find that in 1880 — a fairly prosperous year, as all the above census years were, compared with our years of distress — the employer paid the worker on an average $346 in wages and fleeced, on an average, from him the sum of $324. That, perhaps, to many does not seem extravagant.

But he who employed 10 workmen gained $3,240
"   "   "   "   25   "   "   8,100
"   "   "   "   50   "   "   16,200
"   "   "   "   100   "   "   32,400
"   "   "   "   500   "   "   162,000
"   "   "   "   1000   "   "   324,000.

Three Hundred and Twenty-four Thousand dollars this latter employer gained, fleeced, "accumulated" (mark)! in one year! For what? what had the workers in return? The privilege each to earn three hundred and forty-six dollars! The privilege to use the soil, the machinery and all the resources of our civilization, which this employer possesses!

It is on purpose that we so far in our exposition have avoided to use the word "Capital." Political Economists have surrounded this category with such a hazy atmosphere that the word now denotes a good many things. Yet, the question: What is Capital? is of fundamental importance and relates to the whole structure of our present

Social order. We want that question answered, and the preceding pages, indeed, have been written for that purpose. But we are not concerned about the meaning of the *word* — throughout this work we care for the essence of things and not for the definition of words. By "Capital" we mean what in popular speech is meant.

He is called a "capitalist" who possesses wealth which brings him an income *without any work* on his part. True, many capitalists do some work of one kind or another, but the remuneration they receive for that work has nothing to do with their incomes as "capitalists"; these latter are something *over and above* such remuneration. We, therefore, mean by "Capital": that part of wealth which yields its possessors an income without work. But we are just as willing to adopt the definition of some Economists, that Capital is "the part of wealth which is employed *productively with a view to profit* by sale of the produce," for it is only by being thus employed, that it yields an income.

The question, then, which we are now intent upon finding an answer to is: What is the nature, the essence of that which we have agreed to call "Capital"? We want to *know* it, and therefore must learn the process of its origin. That is a comparatively easy thing to us who already know the origin of the "Surplus." Simply observe what our moneyed men, the operators of the cotton mill, are doing. They add their fleecings to what wealth they had already, and make that increased wealth pass through such another operation as we already have described. The oftener they do that and the more operatives they employ, the more surplus labor their wealth absorbs. *Now we have "Capital" and "Capitalists."* It is these fleecings which, absorbed by wealth, turns it into "Capital," and the pocketing these fleecings turns wealthy men into "capitalists."

Note, *"Surplus"* is the same as "fleecings," is *the difference between the price of Labor and the price of Labor's produce*, is the latter *minus* (−) the former.

Capital is the original little amount of wealth with which our employers start — which they may and may not have earned — *plus* (+) the sum of surplus values; is *accumulated fleecings — accumulated* WITHHELD WAGES.

Therein consists, really, the so-called "productivity" of Capital: in possessing the spongy capacity of steadily going on absorbing surplus labor. This capacity distinguishes it from all other wealth (which other wealth the old Economists called, very happily, *Revenue*). Far be it from us to deny the invaluable assistance which Capital renders to Labor. But Capital produces no Values whatever; it enables Labor to be immensely more productive, that is all.

We have now reached the very core, the grand secret of the present mode of production. This fact, that such a thing as "Capital" exists, that it is acquired and increases, legitimately, by fleecing those in its employ by the wage-system — a fact, unknown to all former periods — is the one characteristic mark of this era; wherefore it may with propriety be designated: *the Capitalist era.*

We took our illustration from the manufacturing industries. The same lesson however, might have been equally well drawn from agriculture, to the extent that the cultivator of the farm or plantation employs wage-laborers. And we arrive at the same results, if we direct our attention to the legitimate commercial enterprises. For commerce, — legitimate commerce — is an industry, and a productive industry. The labor of those engaged in causing the cloth of the cotton mills of New England to be transported to the heart of our continent and in their handing it out in small pieces to consumers creates an additional value in these pieces as fully as the labor of the operatives creates value. But here, also, the profits which swell the fortunes of our merchant "princes" are not the result of their labor, but fleecings, exactions, from the labor of their employees. The scores of millions of an A. T. Stewart were the result of the work of thousands of his fellow men — fleeced from them by the process, already described.

Thus in all industries, manufacturing, mining, agricultural and commercial, the legitimate fleecings which go to make up Capital, come out of the producers — we say *legitimate* fleecings, following naturally, as they do, from the wage-system. They are all fleecers, whether it be the capitalist who joins millions to his millions, or the workingman who brings his hard earned earnings to the bank for the sake of the interest. One is not better than the other. We do not blame either; they simply conform to the system we are living under. But we claim, that in this difference between wages paid and the proceeds of Labor, *in this little fold lies hidden the germ of all profit, interest* and *rent, of all pauperism and of nearly all modern crime.*

Now we can justly estimate the accounts which recent economists have given us of Capital. Some, with the evident design of drawing their attention away from the fleecing process, seek to confound men's minds with most reckless definitions. When in popular speech knowledge and skill are called "Capital," every one is aware that it is a metaphor. But when economists gravely apply that term to such acquisitions, to the wheel-barrow of the day laborer and the wooden horse of the wood-sawyer, then we have a right to dismiss them, somewhat contemptuously, with the remark, that in such case we are all, indeed a band of brother capitalists — since everybody has, at least, got a coat to his back — such as it is; — but then, also, we have amongst us a great many starving "capitalists." Then the German economist who claims the title of "capitalist" for the bear who goes into winter quarters with lots of fat on him is no wit after all, but a sober truth-teller.

Others, again, J. S. Mill among them, attribute capital to *saving*. The tendency of such an account is equally obvious. It insinuates, that capitalists are a highly deserving class of people, indeed, since it is due to their abnormal, unselfish "abstinence," that we have any Capital at all!

Well, all that we have is either consumable or inconsumable. The consumable goods like grain or meat — cannot be "saved" for any length of time; they must be consumed, or they spoil; the capitalists therefore only save here in the same way that soldiers "save" the chickens from being eaten by the enemy. The inconsumable things, like machinery, leather, coin — must be "saved" anyhow, since they cannot be devoured. And if it is any merit in capitalists, that they have "saved" *i.e.*, not devoured these, why — then it must be accounted them a merit, we suppose, that they have "saved" the very earth, or the moon, since they have not consumed these as yet! "Saving," therefore, is absolutely inappropriate here, as it properly means the accumulating such things which might have been consumed.

Much more to the point, therefore, is that other stereotypic definition of Capital, that it is "*accumulated* Labor." Yes it is; but why then do those who work most not "accumulate" Capital? Ah, nothing is so dangerous as a truth in a delusive dress. This definition omits to state, *who* does the laboring and *who* the accumulating. What a heaven-wide difference there is between the two activities, we have already noted. But the definition by that very omission, though it looks *so* innocent, insinuates that Capital at large is formed by wage-laborers laying up their earnings, and that in that way *they* become the capitalists. This insinuation is, to speak emphatically, a falsehood. The first thousand dollars may sometimes be formed in that way; the following millions — NEVER. It is simply impossible. Let us suppose a laborer earning $2.00 a day — a good deal more than the average wage — that he works steadily along, that he never loses a day's work, that he is never sick, that he lives like a Chinese, and thus is able to save up half of his wages: $1.00 a day. It will take him more than 3000 — *Three Thousand* — years to accumulate a million! It is this contemptible jugglery with words that the Socialist critique unmasks.

Now, furthermore, we can understand one very curious phenomenon, to wit: how it comes that the charging of interests was, until not so very long ago, considered infamous, while now it is considered the most natural thing in the world? A conscientious man, like Jeremy Bentham, wanted even to make it out to be one of the "natural rights of man." The reason of the change must lie in the nature of things.

The common arguments in favor of interest are transparently flimsy. They say, interest is a reward for abstinence. We have already seen what kind of abstinence that is, — that of not devouring gold coin and locomotives. But even if the capitalist were abstinent, why should he be especially rewarded for it by an increase? The apple which the boy abstains from eating before going to bed does not grow bigger during the night — the boy's "reward" consists in his having his apple the next morning. The German economist, Prof. Roscher, is honest enough to admit: "Rent is an appropriation of the gifts of nature, and interest, at best, a further fruit obtained by frugality, from older labor, already remunerated."

That other argument, that interest is the payment of a service rendered by the lender to the borrower is not better, for the service is reciprocal. The borrower preserves the capital for the lender; no slight service, since most capital will decay when not in productive use. Socialists give the only satisfactory explanation, and here it is:

The Roman Jurists used to say: "What is mostly done governs all other cases." In former times when people borrowed money, they generally did it, because they were in distress, and it was, very naturally, deemed disgraceful to take advantage of another's misfortunes. The law and the Church therefore, denounced all interest as usury. But now-a-days a person generally borrows money, in order to "make" money in the manner we have described. The "trouble" he is in, is the trouble how to get rich, — and the capitalists like to share that trouble with him. Interest, now, is nothing but a part of the fleecings, nothing but a fair division — therefore proper.

Now we can fitly characterize the "harmony," the "partnership" — compared to that of the Siamese Twins — between Capital and Labor, about which our comfortable classes talk so unctuously.

"If there be in this world a partnership between men which is natural, wise and useful" exclaimed lately Roscoe Conkling in one of his efforts, "it is the partnership between Capital and Labor."

Indeed, Capital and Labor are just as harmonious as roast beef and a hungry stomach. There is the most beautiful harmony, the most natural partnership, between the two — *when they are united in one hand.* But what another contemptible juggling with words we here have! As if there were no difference at all between *Capital* and individual "capital — *ists!*"

Labor, indeed, could not get along very well without Capital. But we are not so sure, that our workers would not get along tolerably well, if some beneficent spirit should take all our capitalists and carry them up to some other planet, say Venus; especially if they had to leave their Capital behind them. And, after all, they might take their Capital along with them — what they could carry away — for Edward Atkinson has told us that we should all be starving within one year, naked within three, and houseless within ten years, if Capital was not constantly being re-created by Labor.

The beautiful harmony between capitalists and laborers is happily illustrated by Carlyle in the address of Plugson, the manufacturer, to his workmen:

"Noble spinners! *We* have gained a hundred thousand pounds, which is *mine;* the three and sixpence daily was *yours.* Adieu, drink my health with this groat each, which I give you over and above."

There is, as a matter of fact, *dis*-harmony between Labor, reduced to a ware, and Capital, whether in the form of grain, or meat, or stone, or metal, or wood, or clay which is labelled: "hands off!" There is, as a matter of fact, *discord* between the worker — to whom nothing is coming beyond necessaries and decencies of life;

to whom even the most loathsome and irksome labor does not insure subsistence; who is not benefited by his own increased capacity of production; who is far from becoming richer the more he works — and the capitalist who, contrariwise, becomes richer the more the workers toil for him; who is constantly being immensely benefited by every increase in productive capacity. Instead of harmony there is, as a matter of fact, more than discord; there is a *chronic warfare* between Capitalists and Laborers, and as an evidence of it we point to — Strikes.

Capital and Labor Siamese Twins! *Are capitalists and laborers Siamese Twins?* Why? Because they are in contact with each other? So are the horse-leech and its victim.

Socialism has a serious dispute with Political Economy, or rather with its present teachers. The founders of the science taught many truths; truths which we acknowledge and on which Socialism, indeed, builds. But its professors claim that it tells *nations* how to become prosperous. It does no such thing. It tells *individuals* how to get rich: and it has found apt pupils in every civilized country. The wealth of the civilized world is incredibly large and increasing at an incredible rate. Its present magnitude may be appreciated from the fact, that the wealth accumulated in England during the present century is far greater than all the wealth accumulated during all previous centuries. Or to come down to figures: The wealth of the United Kingdom was:

> In 1800 Nine Thousand Million Dollars;
> In 1840 Twenty   "   "   "
> In 1860 Thirty   "   "   "
> In 1880 Forty-five "   "   "

Could human efforts have accomplished more? But is this enormous Wealth "*National* Wealth," as is pretended? What part have the beggars in the streets of London in it? What part have the British workingmen, who created this wealth, in it? We shall see.

The *income* of the United Kingdom in 1879 amounted to 5,325 million dollars, distributed as follows:

The working-classes (12 million persons) had 2,140 million dollars, or $178 to the person; while all others (3 million persons) had 3,185 million dollars; of the latter, again a little over 9,300 individuals had $100,000 apiece. One hundred and seventy-eight dollars a year — that, then, is the share of the British worker in the "National" wealth.*

Our Political Economists are yet more guilty. They make their science sanction our present industrial arrangements, instead of explaining them. They virtually teach that, because things are as they are, they will always remain, and ought always to remain so. Socialists, or Social — Economists, as they might call themselves, use the truths of Political Economy to prepare for a higher stage of development, show the workers that though now

> "The seed ye sow another reaps;
> The wealth ye find another keeps;"

it will not always be so, and urge that a Social Order which permits certain individuals to appropriate the withheld wages of generations of weary workers *ought* not to last.

The first lesson of Socialism, then, is that the *Wage-System*, the Profit-System, the Fleecing-System, is *utterly unfit for a higher civilization*.

"But you are not fair. You have entirely omitted to state that these individuals *do* contribute to the size of your 'cakes.' They *direct* all these enterprises, a work of considerable importance."

Granted. They do direct, or see to it that somebody directs. But is half the cake not a pretty dear price for overseeing its baking? Could not that work be done in some other way, just as well and somewhat cheaper?

---

* Do not jump at the conclusion, that because the British workingman is paid $178 a year and the American $346, that therefore the latter is twice as well off as the former. In England a given sum may go twice as far as here — for many reasons, one of which is that the "store-order" system, so extensively practised here, is in England sternly forbidden by law.

CHAPTER II

SOCIAL ANARCHY

"We all can see that there are all over our country energies which can find no employment or, at all events, minds which are cruelly compressed into duties far too narrow, and, on the other hand, work which remains undone for want of adequate energies, because no systematic attempt has yet been made to estimate the real needs of the social organism and to distribute its forces in accordance with them. — There is no organic adjustment anywhere." — The *Value of Life*," an American work, anon.

"Competition gluts our markets, enables the rich to take advantage of the necessities of the poor, makes each man snatch the bread out of his neighbor's mouth, converts a nation of brethren into a mass of hostile, isolated units, and finally involves capitalists and laborers in one common ruin." — *Greg*.

"It is not to die, or even to die of hunger that makes a man wretched; many men have died; all men must die. But it is to live miserable, we know not why; to work sore and yet gain nothing; to be heartworn, weary, yet isolated, unrelated, girt in with a cold universal *Laissez-faire*." — *Carlyle*.

The wage-system may be said to be of vital interest only to the wage-workers. They are a considerable part of the nation. They include not only the operatives in our factories and mines, but the whole army of railroad employees, all hired men on farms, all clerks engaged in stores and mercantile establishments; all, in fact, who help to create Values and receive a stated salary. And if not their numbers but the Values produced by them constitute the measure of their importance, they will be found very much to overbalance our independent farmers. The whole agricultural class (7,600,000 persons), indeed, did not create more wealth in 1880 than our manufacturing operatives alone (2,700,000 in number). But though the wage-workers are an important fraction of our population they, nevertheless, are but a fraction. If Socialism had regard to them only, it were nothing but a *class*-movement.

We claim there is a something-wrong in Society which vitally affects the whole nation and every individual of it. In prosperous years it may not obtrude itself on the attention of thoughtless people, but let "hard times" come on, and it makes everybody feel uneasy. What is this "something-wrong"? Socialists say that it is nothing less than the method, the policy, which governs all activities of the principal nations of our time. It is spreading itself in Catholic societies, and throughout the whole world, but it arose in Protestant countries. It is, in fact, simply the exaggerated form of one of the principles of Protestantism: the independence of the individual; which exaggerated individual independence we can properly call: *Individualism*. We can also call the policy: the "let alone" policy; its admirers give it a more euphonious name: *Private Enterprise*.

Let alone *whom — what?*

In the middle ages the feudal barons erected castles, from which they issued forth with their retainers, when they espied merchants and adventurers approaching on the contiguous highways laden with wealth, stopped them — and levied tolls. All that these barons desired was to be "let alone." In our age it is the spiritual descendants of these merchants and adventurers who have grown powerful, fattened on "fleecings." They in their turn demand to "be let alone;" they demand that society shall be an unrestricted hunting ground for their "enterprise." They *are* let alone; we shall now note with what results to the different classes of society.

Before our present industrial system got into full swing — that is, before the power of steam was utilized — the master-workman was an adept in his trade and owned his tools and the raw-materials he used. This is all now changed. The workman is now *divorced* from his implements and raw materials, which have got under the complete control of the capitalist class; he now has nothing left but his naked labor. This it is, again, which enables employers to buy labor in the market for a price much below the productivity of that labor; that is at a *value* much below its *worth*.

This monopoly has made employers into a class of autocrats, the laborers into a class of dependents — of *hirelings*. As Jesse Jones says in the "International Review," of October 1880: "A class is fixed, when nine-tenths of those comprising it can never get out of it. . . . Why mock workingmen by putting rare exceptions for a general rule?"

The laboring men are dealt with by our managers as mere tools. They are spoken of as tools, as things. This humanitarian age counts steers and sheep by "heads" and the workers by "*hands*." A pity God did not make them only "hands!"

It is a paltry evasion to say, that the workers are free to consent or to refuse the terms of the employer. It is an evasion worthy of the man who asked permission of the Virgin to rob her of her necklace — and then did it, taking silence for consent. The Laborers have to consent. If they refuse the terms, capitalists simply stop business; they can stand it. "Hard times" are really only hard on those whose subsistence depends on having work to do. The wives and daughters of capitalists do, as a rule, not leave off during "hard times" attending operas in their silks, satins and diamonds; do not, as a rule, quit their luxurious brownstone-fronts or dismiss their liveried servants.

Henry George in his "Progress and Poverty" epitomizes the position of our laborers as follows: "Compelled to more continuous labor than the savage, the laborer — a mere link in an enormous chain of producers and consumers, helpless to separate himself and helpless to move, except as they move — gains the mere necessaries of life, just what the savage gets, and loses the independence of the savage." And as to security he is not much better off. The irregularity of his employment, the frequency with which he is out of work, is the most alarming feature of the workingman's condition. And that irregularity is often, very often, purposely brought about by the employing capitalist class. For instance, in order to put up the price of anthracite coal, out of twenty-four working days of a certain month nine were made idle days by the coal companies of Pennsylvania. The mining was interrupted to limit supply and the miners were left to do the best they could with work for two days out of every three. This condition has been rendered yet enormously more precarious by the remarkable industrial inventions of the age.

These victories of man, of Society, over Nature's physical forces ought certainly to have been unqualified blessings to all.

Yet, how often have they proven instruments of torture to the working class! How many has the introduction of new machinery not thrown out of employment; how many existences have not thereby been destroyed!

We are familiar with the commonplace, that the outcry of laborers against "newfangled machinery" is a complaint born of ignorance; that in the end the working classes are as much benefited as other classes. This outcry is by no means nothing but an ignorant childish complaint. Machinery *would* be an unqualified blessing, if the temporary injury which it so often has caused to individuals and whole bodies of men were considered in a spirit of social justice and brotherliness. *That has never been done wherever the working classes are considered,* either in this or any other country. In their case our legislators persistently repudiate the duty to take care of the interests of those who are sacrificed for the benefit of their fellow citizens and of posterity. But whenever other classes have been thus affected there has never been the slightest hesitation to liberally compensate those, prejudicially affected. It is the action of *Society* that has made machinery an evil. This is the real meaning of the outcry against "newfangled machinery."

And we deny that working people hitherto have been essentially benefited by machinery and inventions at all. The sewing machine is a pointed illustration. That was thought, at all events, to be a blessing to the overworked, famishing needle-woman. Yet what has followed? That she is now still more overworked, more poorly paid and her health still more endangered.

But, to be sure — these inventions were not adopted by capitalists for the benefit of workpeople, or for the general benefit; no, indeed! For, of course, this machinery and these inventions have also gone into the hands of capitalists and are controlled by them for their exclusive benefit; and with admirable results. It has been calculated that two-thirds of all benefit arising from the use of machinery have gone to these "pushing" fellows and the remaining one-third to the consumers. Even our patent laws, with the *general* advantage for their primary idea, have become a means of enabling these capitalists, in no sense inventors, to levy heavy tribute upon the community for an indefinite length of time.

"Ah! but the workers are also consumers, we should think, and form the majority in fact of all consumers."

Hold on, sir! *Has machinery lightened the day's toil of any worker?* That is what ought to measure the benefits of machinery to him. Let us see, if it has.

Here is one picture: Massachusetts is a model state, we suppose. Well, a statute of that State in 1860 made *ten hours* a maximum working day for children under *twelve years* of age.

In 1867 her legislators became a little more humane and enacted that no child under *fifteen* years of age should work more than *sixty hours a week.* Go to Pennsylvania, and see children *ten years old* taken down every morning into the mines to work! Here is another picture: In England, two hundred years back *ten hours were a normal working day for strong blacksmiths and robust agricultural laborers.**

"But compare the comforts of our laborers two hundred years ago. What a wonderful betterment in that respect!"

What of it? What comfort is that to *our* laborers? You might as well compare their condition with that of a savage in Africa who does not *need* a coat, does not *need* soap. Just so the laborers of a former age did not need a good many things which now are necessaries or decencies of life. We say their condition has not improved, because it takes considerable more toil to procure the *needful* now than it did then, as testified to, among others, by Hallam: "The laborer is much inferior in ability to support a family than were his ancestors four centuries ago." Why! before the beginning of this "capitalistic" system laborers could in England live a *whole week* upon the earnings of *four days;* now in Massachusetts he often cannot live a week upon the earnings of a week of much more continuous toil. No, in many cases he is obliged to disrupt his family and send his wife and children to the factory.

For that is the greatest curse of machinery — or rather of *"individualistic" monopoly* of machinery — that capital can be and is coined out of women and even out of infancy; that women and children can be and are substituted for men. Thus, not alone are men turned into wares, governed by Demand and Supply, but *men are made to scramble for a precarious living with their wives, sisters and children.* In the cotton and woollen factories of enlightened

* Thornton: Over population and its remedy. Prof. Thorold Rogers: History of Agriculture in England. Hallam, 2nd part of 9th Chap. of "The Middle Ages."

Massachusetts women and children now compose two-thirds of the working force. The necessary result is a great reduction in wages. It is notorious that the wages thus earned by a whole family do not, on an average, exceed those of the head of the family in occupations where it has not yet become habitual to employ women and children.

And do not venture to compare the *independence* of our working classes with the artisans of England of a former age, who partly worked for themselves, and possessed a cottage and a cow and a strip of land to cultivate. Our ox-eyed, docile wage-workers, restrained by arbitrary shop rules prescribed by their lord — rules that forbid them to talk to each other or even to *laugh*(*!*) — will not for a moment bear comparison with the merry families of master and men of the despised Middle Age.

The first result of the "Let alone" System, thus, is that capitalists monopolize all the instruments of production, all the previous acquisitions of Society, all increase in the productivity of Labor, and therefore, *exercise an autocratic control of all industries and over the whole working class.*

The great weapon at the command of the capitalist is *Competition.*

"Competition," like most economical terms, is a very slippery word. At one time it means something which advances the successful, but leaves the unsuccessful on his former level. That kind of competition rouses the energy of both, of the unsuccessful as well as of the successful, and increases the capacity of both. We shall call that by a much more appropriate term: *Emulation.*

At another time "competition" means the advancing oneself at the cost of others; the pulling the many down, the elbowing the many aside, in order to advance the one. That "competition" is most cruel to the individual and, in the long run, most injurious to Society.

It deserves the name of "cut-throat competition" when the wage-workers are forced into a struggle *to see who shall live and who shall starve.*

But these are by no means the only sufferers. The small employers, the small merchants are just as much victims of that cruel kind of competition as the wage-worker. For every one of the fleecers lives in a state of nature with all of his brethren; the hand of the one is against the other, and no foe is more terrible than the one who is running a neck-to-neck race with him every day. The mammoth factory, the mammoth store is a most implacable foe. The fierce competition lessens the profit on each article, and that must be compensated for by a greater number of them being produced and sold, that is, the cheaper the goods, the more capital is required.

Precisely, therefore, for the same reason that the mechanic with his own shop and working on his own account nearly has disappeared in the struggle between hand-work and machine-work, the small employers with their little machinery, their small capital and their little stock of goods are being driven from the field.

Look at those queer *princes* of ours — vulgar men, far from possessing eminent faculties or high attainments; men having no more knowledge or mental capacity than is required in many mechanical pursuits — who by the employment and power of their capital yearly ruin multitudes of hard working merchants, and boast that they are selling more goods in a day than the whole "crowd" of other stores in a week! Scores of such small merchants, driven to the wall by an A. T. Stewart, had to be glad, if the "prince" would make them his servants and graciously allow them to help swell his millions.

In short, the smaller fortunes invested in productive or commercial enterprises are by this cut-throat competition attracted to the great capitals, just as iron filings are to the magnet. The great capitalist triumphs, the small capitalist becomes a clerk, wage-laborer or parasite of some kind or other; *the middle class disappears little by little.* Our social order may fitly be compared to a ladder of which the middle rounds are being torn away, one by one.

This, then, is another fruit of Private "Enterprise," that *the small employers are gradually being rooted out by the great capitalists.*

In former periods Society was tormented with plagues, caused, as we now know, by ignorance and consequent violation of the laws of health. Our era is cursed with *Crises,* occurring far more frequently than plagues and causing with each occurrence as much misery.

Economists say, that these crises are caused by overproduction. "Overproduction!" — a remarkable word, in truth, as long as one unfed and unclad human being, willing to work, roams the earth.

Would not our ancestors of any preceding age have considered anyone who would have talked to them of *overproduction* a lunatic? Could they, you think, have conceived of such an abnormity as that any nation could ever suffer from *too much* industry, *too much* commerce, *too many* tools and *too much* food? But we ought, in order to be fair, to take the word in the sense of these economists. They mean by "overproduction" a too large production, compared with the *effective* demand. But, then, what is the cause of the too large production?

Private Enterprise Socialists say. Private Enterprise compels every producer to produce for himself, to sell for himself, to keep all his transactions secret, without any regard whatever for anybody else in the wide world. But the producer and merchant — the small ones, especially — find daily out, that their success or failure depend, in the first place, *precisely on how much others produce and sell,* and, in the second place, on a multitude of causes — often on things that may happen thousands of miles away — which determine the power of purchase of their customers. They have got no measure at hand at all by which they can, even approximately, estimate the actual effective demand of consumers or ascertain the producing capacity of their rivals. In other words: Private "Enterprise" is a defiance of Nature's law which decrees that the interests of Society are *interdependent;* and Nature punishes that defiance in her own crude way by playing ball with these individualists, and what is worse, by rendering all production, all commerce chaotic. *Risk is Nature's Revenge.*

Just take a bird's-eye view of the way Private "Enterprise" manages affairs. Observe how every manufacturer, every merchant strives in every possible way — by glaring advertisements, by underselling others, by giving long credits, by sending out an army of drummers — to beat his rivals. Not one here and there, not a few do this; they all do it. We shall suppose the season a favorable one; all of them receive orders in greater number than they expected. These orders stimulate each one of the manufacturers to a more and more enlarged production far ahead of the orders received, in the hope of being able to dispose of all that is being produced. But mark! this production of all these manufacturers is and must necessarily be, absolutely *planless. It depends altogether on chance* and *the private guesswork* of these "enterprising" individuals, who all are guessing entirely in the dark. That means that all their production, all their commerce, *is in the nature of gambling*. To a thoughtful observer nothing will seem more inevitable, than that this *planless* production *must* end in the market being at some time overstocked with commodities of one kind or another; that is, that it must end in "overproduction" as to those goods. In that branch of production prices, consequently, fall, wages come down, or a great manufacturer fails, and a smaller or greater number of workmen are discharged.

But one branch of industry depends upon another; one branch suffers when another is depressed. The stoppage of production at one point, therefore, necessarily shows itself at another point in the industrial network. The circle of depression thus grows larger and larger from month to month, failure succeeds failure, the general consumption diminishes, all production and commerce is paralyzed. *We have got the crisis*. To those who were all the time planning and working in the dark everything seemed to be going on as usual; it has naturally come on them like a thunderbolt from a clear sky.

Vast quantities of stored up goods now have to be disposed of at great sacrifice, to the ruin not alone of their owners but of many others who thereby are forced, likewise, to sell under cost-price. Then it is we hear from everyone in every calling this the strongest of all condemnations of this Social "Order" of ours: "We have too many competitors; half of us must perish, before the other half can live." All the result of *planless* work.

When such a crisis has lasted for years, when such sacrifice of goods and standstill of production has finally overcome the "overproduction," then the inevitable demand at length calls for renewed production; and Society commences to recover slowly, but only to repeat the old story. Producers want to indemnify themselves for what they have lost and hope to "make" sufficient, before another crisis comes on. Because all producers act in like manner, each one trying to outflank the other, another catastrophe is invited. It responds to the call and approaches with accelerated strides and with more damaging effects than any of its predecessors.

These crises very much quicken the absorption of the smaller fortunes by the large ones, for the capitalist with large resources is the only one capable in the long run of withstanding this rough treatment of outraged Nature. The smaller capitalists the crises swallow up like veritable mælstroms.

These mælstroms: the crises, then, are the direct production of Private Enterprise.

Again, we saw how the workingmen were driven out of their employment as producers, how the small employers were pushed out of their business by this cut-throat competition. In nine cases out of ten they have only one refuge left: that of squeezing them-selves in between producers and consumers as shopkeepers, saloon-keepers, peddlers, "agents," boarding- and lodging-house-keepers; that is, of becoming *parasites*.

It may seem hard to speak thus of persons who by no means lead an enviable existence, who honestly try to make some sort of a living, whose life often is a tread-mill of drudgery and, if different from that of the workingman's, is only different in this, that while the latter struggles for the necessities of today, the former struggle for the threatened necessities of tomorrow.

They *are*, nevertheless, parasites, *unnecessary workers*. Going along our streets you observe one small store, one boarding-house crowding another, one saloon, and often several, in one block: you will have all kinds of men and women thrust their small stock into your face; in your house you will be annoyed by all kinds of ped-dlers and agents, socalled.

All these people live. *Somebody* must earn their living for them.

In the first place, they live by enhancing the price of provisions and all other goods twice and three times what the producers get. The difference between their prices and wholesale prices makes just the difference between healthful plenty and half satisfied hunger for the poor. It is a great mistake to suppose that competition al-ways, or necessarily, lowers prices. It often has just the contrary effect. Probably two-thirds of existing small shopkeepers can not make a decent living without extravagant profits. Or, if the prices can not be enhanced, then

In the second place, they live by depreciating the quality of their goods and by short weights and measures. Adulteration of provi-sions and merchandize is notoriously carried on in every branch of trade that will permit of it; has indeed become a social institution, against which no law can make any headway. A representative of a leading spice house lately said: "We sell to the trade more adulterated goods than pure. We cannot help it. We simply sell the retailer what he wants. It would ruin the trade to prohibit adulteration." Competition in drugs is now so hot, dealers, in order to live, are compelled to adulterate, to weaken and to substitute. It has gone so far, that manufacturers of "mineral pulp," now boldly importune respectable millers and grocers to mix rock-dust with their flour and sugar.

The laboring class, more than any other, is the natural prey of these parasites. Remember, that the laborer's ware, his labor, is never paid for till it has been used; that he must give his employer credit, always for a week, often for two weeks or a month; that he will have to wait for his compensation, even while the values he has created have been long since converted into cash in his employer's hands. It is a necessary consequence, that he, on his part, must ask credit from his shopkeeper. He becomes the prey, bound hand and foot, of that shopkeeper. He dare not murmur at the price charged, dares not be over particular as to weight or quality. He is pretty much in the same fix as the fly in the spider's web.

Thus the portion of the industrial cake allotted to labor is further considerably curtailed, and all on account of *Private "Enterprise;" for it,* also, *is exclusively responsible for these parasites.*

Let us pass over to our farmers. They, as yet the majority of our working population, are still the great conservative force, the brake, so to speak, on the wheel of progress. Is it likely that they will continue to be? We shall see.

Our farmers were half a generation ago considered and are still considered the most independent and prosperous class of the community.

True, the prosperity of the western farmer, especially, was and is not of a character to excite the envy of anybody. His whole life, and more particularly that of his wife, was one of toil. He had to break our lands and clear our forests. His family had to subject themselves to all kinds of privations for a lifetime of dreary years. The social life of the farmers' wives was a mockery of our civilization; their sisters struggling in the cities had, at least, the comfort of suffering in company. To the family of the farmer sugar, tea and coffee were, for a series of years, luxuries, especially when droughts and grasshoppers destroyed the fruits of his toil, generally as severe as that of his horse. And his reward? That of vegetating and "raising" a family, as we so expressively term it; yes — and of being the owner of his farm.

But his ownership is even now, frequently, one in name only. The capitalist has got hold of him also. Very many of the western farms are covered with mortgages, which their nominal owners have no hope of ever raising. This fact is so well known, that the N. Y. "Times" some time ago advised the farmers to prepare themselves for their fate. What fate? That of becoming tenant-farmers like their brethren of Great Britain.

It is, especially, since the commencement of the last decade that they are falling victims to "Private Enterprise."

There is in the "Atlantic Monthly" for January 1880 a most instructive article,* entitled "Bonanza Farms," containing many startling facts, which in the near future cannot but have an important bearing on the condition of our farmers. These "Bonanza Farms" are vast cultivated tracts of land in Minnesota, Dakota, Texas, Kansas and California, each containing thousands of acres of land owned by presidents and directors of railways, by bankers in St. Paul and New York, London and Frankfort-on-the-Main. They are conducted on purely "business," — that is, capitalist principles. On these farms there are no families, no women, no children, no homes. There is no need for them. But there is plenty of "Labor" in the neighborhood. There is such an abundance of unemployed men, that the managers of the farms can hire all the labor they want for $16.00 a month, during the busy seasons with thirteen hours of daily labor, and for $8.00 a month during the balance of the year.

This fact alone would render it absolutely out of the question for the surrounding small farmers to compete with the bonanzas. For the former have to support a family, and to feed, clothe and shelter, and altogether provide for the same number of persons throughout the whole year, while the latter only need to hire about one-fourth the number of persons, in proportion to the work to be done, and that for less than one-fourth of the year. But the small farmer has other and greater odds still to contend with: the discrimination

* Embodied in a book called "Land and Labor," published by Scribner and Sons. Mr. Moody of Boston is the author.

practised by other large corporations. Thus, the bonanzas obtain special rates from the railroad companies: for instance, they are charged for the transportation of their produce rates, fifty per cent. below those which the other farmers are obliged to pay; they buy their machinery and farming implements of the manufacturers and dealers at a discount of 33 1-3 per cent. from the published rates. We ought, therefore, not to wonder, when we are told, that the surrounding small farmers are hopelessly in debt, while the owners of these bonanza farms — the aforesaid bankers and railroad-presidents — are amassing colossal fortunes; that they even with wheat at only 70 cts. a bushel realize twenty per cent. the first year on their capital and the second year — fifty-five per cent.

The article concludes with the remark: "We are taking immense strides in placing our country in the position of Great Britain, and even worse." So it seems. For there the farms are practically homesteads, while the bonanza farms have nothing suggesting homes, except a building for the bachelor superintendent and the boarding house for the "hands."

There is no doubt that these bonanzas will in the near future increase greatly in number. Thus our public lands, which were intended for happy homes are in a fair way of becoming no better than penal colonies, and of being robbed of their rich soil for the benefit of capitalist pockets. What will then become of our farmer-"proprietors" but farmer-*tenants?* If they are already running behindhand *now*, how much time will it take for the bonanza farmers to put an end to their proprietorship, by means of Private "Enterprise?" Especially if our export to Europe, on account of good harvest there, should happen to cease. Bear in mind, that our country already now produces far more food than our population could possibly consume, and yet thousands of acres are yearly added to the area under cultivation.

Yes, the time will come, when our farmers will learn, that Socialism is the *only refuge* alike for them and the other working classes, and their eyes may be opened to the advantage of *the Cooperative Commonwealth.* The great dairy farms in New York State and elsewhere may also contribute their quota to this lesson.

Thus even our farmers, as yet the most splendid yeomanry the world has ever seen, *are becoming the victims of Private Enterprise to fully the same extent as our workingman and small employer.*

But our big capitalists have a still more powerful sledge-hammer than that of Competition ready at hand, to wit: *Combination.*

These gentlemen know practical dialectics. They know, that, though Competition and Combination are opposites, they yet may come to mean the same thing — to them. They have already found that while Competition is a very excellent weapon to use against their weaker rivals, Combination pays far better in relation to their peers. It is evident, that it is combination they mainly rely upon for their future aggrandizement.

Combination consists in one or several capitalists or corporations helping along a third, on the condition of participating in the fleecings. We have already mentioned one such instance. We saw how railroad officers united with bonanza farmers to crush out the small farmers. We read of another instructive instance in an article published in the "Atlantic Monthly" for March 1881, and headed: "The story of a great Monopoly."

It tells, how the Erie and Pennsylvania Railroads and Vanderbilt "pooled" their interests with the "Standard Oil Company," how they agreed to carry, and did carry its oil at much lower rates than the oils of other companies, and in many cases absolutely refused to carry the oils of the latter. It tells how, by such discrimination, the fleecings of the "Standard" swelled to such an extent that, starting with a capital stock of one million, it paid to its stockholders a dividend of one million dollars a month, and has now piled up in undivided profits and other forms a capital of Thirty Millions. Truly a "Great Monopoly," *a very dangerous monopoly,* one should think, for Pennsylvania and the public at large.

"By the same tactics," says the writer, "the Railroads can give other combinations of capitalists the control of the lumber, cotton, iron and coal of the United States."

In Europe such alliances between Railroads and corporations would be impossible. But in our country, where *Private "Enterprise" runs rampant,* where the "Let Alone" abomination is carried to its highest logical pitch, such alliances are certain to be a prominent feature of our future.

But the evils which flow from the something-wrong in Society is not confined to wage-workers, farmers and small employers. The at present existing relations of men constitute the comfortless mutual slavery of us all, as we shall find, wherever we turn. Professional men of every kind can, also, be divided into those who have and those who have not; and those among them who have not are fully as bad off as the wage-workers, indeed worse off, for their culture becomes an additional curse to them. We will suppose such a man has talents, that he has qualified himself by hard study for a responsible function in Society, yet this anarchical Society has no opening for him. He perhaps becomes a clerk, just as much dependent on his employer just as much a *hireling* as the wage-worker is; he likewise must hold his tongue, and constantly be on the lookout to preserve the favor of his august autocrat, while he all the while is doing the work of others who really receive the pay.

What a spectacle, for instance, does the medical profession present! One successful practitioner we find burdened with more work than mortal man can perform — in the surrounding streets twenty unhappy men, each of whom as laboriously trained, wasting their capabilities, starving, perhaps, for want. Under better arrangements these twenty would form a corps of subalterns under the really ablest physician — *and not merely the most successful impostor* — physicking people for headaches, while the latter treated only more difficult cases.

But now, even in all professions, the watchword is, "Every one look out for himself and the devil take the hindmost" — *all due to Unrestricted Private "Enterprise."*

Our era may be called the *Jewish Age*. The Jews have, indeed, had a remarkable influence on our civilization. Long ago they infused in our race the idea of one God, and now they have made our whole race worship a new true God: The Golden Calf; but, again, it is Jews — such noble Jews as Karl Marx and Lassalle — who have sounded the alarm for the most determined battle against this very Jewism. "Jewism," to our mind, best expresses that special curse of our age, *Speculation,* the transfer of wealth from others to themselves by chicanery without giving an equivalent.

If there is one species of gambling more despicable than another, it is gambling in grain. The sales of grain on our Produce-Exchanges are merely gambling transactions. Cliques of the wealthiest men in Chicago, Milwaukee and New York, having behind them banks and other moneyed corporations, make enormous combinations of capital to "corner" the market, locking up millions of bushels of wheat, and maintain famine-prices in the midst of plenty. Their profits are enormous. So are those of another clique who owns all pork. And where do those profits come from? From the workers, of course, from the bread-winners, who thus earn the support and the wealth, not only of their employers, their so-called "bread-*givers*," but of those *Vampires* who use their backs as the green table on which to play their games.

The Vampires are quite different creatures from the parasites we already have treated of. The latter are workers, though superfluous workers, the former are not workers at all. But then, they do not call themselves workers either, but — "business men." There is quite a difference between *work* and *business* as that word is now commonly used. "Work" is effort to satisfy wants, and may be either useful or useless; but *"business" is effort to benefit by the work of others,* and if that is to be called "work," it is at any rate *mischievous* work; in that sense our criminals, also, work and generally pretty hard. "Work" *is being busy in benefit;* "business" *being busy in mischief.* Our parasites are useless workers; our Vampires are not better than thieves and swindlers.

On a par with Speculation is much of our "Traffic." The "enterprise" of our mercantile "kings" and "princes" is very often but another name for chicanery and swindling. "Suppose," John Ruskin says, "a community of three men on an island. Two, the one a farmer and the other a mechanic, are so far apart, that they are wholly at the mercy of the third who travels between them, and effects their exchanges. He is constantly watching his opportunities, and retains the products of the one with which he has been intrusted and which are needed by the other, until there comes a period of extreme need for them and he can exact enormous gains from their necessities. It is easy to see that, while he may in that way draw the whole wealth of the community to himself and make his principals his servants, he also in fact diminishes the amount of wealth by cramping the operations of his two customers and diminishing the effective results of their labors. That is Wealth, acquired on the strict principles of Political Economy." And the millions which go into the pockets of these mercantile men of ours as "profits" are by them called reward for "enterprise," "compensation for risk," — Do we call the gains of the swindler or the robber "compensation for risks?" No, *commerce*, which is the interchange of commodities, is a most beneficial social activity; *Traffic, Trade,* which, as Herbert Spencer says, is "essentially corrupt," which partakes of the nature either of gambling or overreaching, is not.

These Vampires are the offspring of the "Let Alone" Policy.

"Laissez-faire," "Let alone" — leave the upright at the mercy of the cunning; leave the ignorant to teach themselves; leave everyone who profits by a corrupt system to make the most for himself; let Labor remain something wholesale out of which fortunes are made and which during that process yields such and such a per centage of Misery and Sin — what a grand "principle!" By adopting it for its guiding-star our Society has achieved — *Anarchy.*

Our comfortable classes talk much of "Social *Order.*" In ancient Greece and Rome there was Social "Order," such as it was; during part of the Middle Age, there was Social "Order," such as it was. But in our age there is, as we have seen, throughout our whole economic sphere no social order at all. There is absolute Social Anarchy. *It is against this Social Anarchy* that Socialism, chiefly, is a protest.

We have seen the various phases of this anarchy, all the legitimate outgrowth of private "enterprise:"

All instruments of production are monopolized. The evil of this monopoly does not so much consist in the plutocrat being the undisputed owner of that which he has acquired (the sum total of which is now so very inappropriately called *National* wealth.) Though formed out of fleecings and in no other manner whatsoever, he can claim these acquisitions as his property, because he has got hold of them by the express consent of Society. The evil lies in this, that he is able and permitted to use this property of his to *further* fleece his fellow-men out of the proceeds of their toil.

This private enterprise is responsible for our crises, the inevitable consequences of defying the natural law of *Solidarity* between all the members of Society.

It has produced our parasites and vampires.

It has given us Competition with all its baneful consequences.

Not *Emulation,* which no Society can afford to do without, the loss of which would check all advance and deaden all energy.

But *Cannibalism,* that poisonous tooth the extraction of which would immensely relieve society.

It has put into the hands of our Plutocrats a deadlier club than competition for them to use whenever it serves their purpose: *Combination* among themselves.

It has destroyed all the patriarchal, idyllic relations which formerly existed among men and left only the one relation: Cash-payment. It has drowned the chivalrous enthusiasm, the pious idealism which existed in previous ages in a chilly shower of realistic egotism. It has put exchange-value in place of personal *human* dignity and license in place of *freedom.* It has made the physician, the jurist, the poet, the scientist, retainers of the Plutocracy. It has made marriage a *commercial relation* and prostitution one of the established institutions of Society.

But let us be fair.

So far we have discussed only the evil workings of "private enterprise." We heartily admit that, on the other hand, it has performed wonders. It has built monuments greater than the pyramids. Its Universal Expositions have moved greater masses of men than the Crusades ever did. It has done mankind an immense service in proving by hard facts, that *wholesale manufacture* is the most sensible form of Labor.

But we contend that it now has done all the good it can, that the evils which *now* flow from "private enterprise" far outweigh the benefits it confers.

That is why we condemn it. We condemn it just as we condemn an old, decaying building, however useful it may have been in its time; or as Nature condemns the cocoon of a chrysalis, when a butterfly is ready to be born.

But we know full well that "private enterprise" will for some time yet go on working mischief. We know it must become a good deal worse than it is, before it can become better.

But we also know that in the fullness of time the *Logic of Events* will, imperatively, demand a change from this *Social Anarchy* to *true Social Order.*

CHAPTER III

THE CULMINATION

"Real history is a history of tendencies, not of events." — *Buckle*.

"Nothing would lead the mass of men to embrace Socialism sooner than the conviction, that this enormous accumulation of Capital in a few hands was to be, not only an evil in fact if not prevented, but a necessary evil beyond prevention.

"If such a tendency should manifest itself, it would run through all forms of property. A Stewart or a Claflin would root out small trades-people. Holders of small farms would sink into tenants. The buildings of a city would belong to a few owners. Small manufacturers would have to take pay from mammoths of their own kind or be ruined. . . . If this went to an extreme in a free country, the 'expropriated' could not endure it. They would go to some other country, and leave the proprietors alone in the land, or they would drive them away. A revolution, slow or rapid, would certainly bring about a new order of things." — *"Communism and Socialism," by Dr. Th. D. Woolsey*.

That Capital — not "Wealth," not "Property" but *Capital* — in private hands involves the dependence of the masses; that our Established Order is nothing but Established Anarchy are the conclusions we have arrived at. Will such a state of things last forever?

Here we meet with one of the greatest obstacles with which Socialists have to contend: the notion that whatever is, is the immutable order of nature. Because the wage-system and the "Let-alone" policy now prevail and have prevailed as far back as any one can remember, people, even well-informed people, fancy that this policy and that system constitute the necessary conditions for civilized society. Socialists hold that this is a fundamental error. They say, with all advanced scientists, that what is has grown out of something else that was, and that the present is the parent of the future. The history of our race is a series of preparations.

In the ancient states where the civilization of our race commenced there was no wage-system; there was *Slavery*. The master was lord of the persons of his slaves, lord of the soil and owner of the instruments of labor. We who have reached a higher stage of development look very properly back with horror on this ancient Slavery; and yet we should not forget that we are indebted to this same Slavery for our civilization.

Progress takes place, only, when either some individuals control other individuals, or when they voluntarily cooperate together. But voluntary cooperation is a hard lesson for men to learn; and, therefore, progress has to commence with compulsory cooperation; with control of everything, — with Slavery.

Look at our Indian tribes. They work, in their way, as well as civilized people do. Yet they are strangers to progress. Why? Because they never accumulated any wealth. And they accumulated no wealth, because they worked as isolated individuals; because they never have known any division of labor. Now *Slavery* was to our race, *the first division of labor;* it was the first form of co-operation; for it is too often overlooked, that division of labor is at the same time cooperation in labor. The ruling principle during Slavery was, of course, *Despotism,* the irresponsible will of the lord.

Feudalism, and *Serfdom* constitute the next great period in the history of our race, coming in contemporaneously with the ascendancy of Christianity and the dominion of the northern barbarians. Under it the lords of the soil were the dominant class; but the persons of the workers were free, though they were attached to the soil where they were born. This change conferred an immense gain on the working multitude. They were now invested with the most elementary right of all: that of creating a family for themselves. And their belonging to the soil was far from being altogether an evil, since it conferred on them the right to claim support from the soil.

The ruling principle during that period was *Custom,* which proved itself a most efficient protector of the workers. It fixed, strictly, and in many countries with the utmost particularity in details, the amount of work due to their lord for the use of the soil, and all other rights and duties of every class and individual. "Freedom" during the middle ages meant the enjoyment of those rights which Custom thus gave. It may well be a question, whether the workers of that long era were not a happier class than our wage-workers.

During those two stages of development "Capital" was unknown and unheard of. There was Wealth, there were Revenues, plenty of means of enjoyment. The great folks lived in splendor, certainly; but they did not, and could not *capitalize* their possessions.

Remember that best of economic definitions of Capital, which we adopted: "That part of wealth, employed productively, with a view to profit, by sale of the produce." During Slavery and Serfdom Wealth was not employed productively with a view to profit, by sale of the produce, but with a view to immediate, personal enjoyment. The lords could not make their possessions grow by "profit," by "fleecings," could not *invest* them. They could not levy tribute on anybody but their own slaves, their own serfs.

But the progress of mankind demanded that another step should be taken. The iron bands of Custom had to be sundered and that is done by an assertion of the independence of the individual in the form of *Unrestricted Private Enterprise;* which fructifies the germ of Capital, already found in the previous accumulations of wealth. Private Enterprise commences, in the closing years of the Middle Ages, by suddenly advancing commerce to an unprecedented degree and developing the Commerce of the World. It gives rise to the discoveries and inventions which now crowd upon each other; foremost among which are the discovery of America, the invention of the printing press and the steam engine. These in their turn nourish Capital. It becomes an infant, grows up to youth and manhood, bursts completely the fetters of the Middle Ages by the ever memorable French Revolution, and has developed in our days into a giant by division of labor being carried to an extent, not dreamt of before; or — what is the same thing — by a greater cooperation in production than was known before.

Thus we have arrived at the third stage in the development of our race: this era of Capital and Individualism. Wealth during all three periods governed the world, controlled the masses, but never before in the form of *Capital.* Our Plutocracy, our industrial, commercial and moneyed aristocracy, whom the French called "the Third Estate;" those who by the control of the instruments of labor have acquired the more advantageous position, are now our masters, the dominant power, who by laws and usages, enacted by themselves, have made this advantageous position of theirs a permanent one. The workers have hardly occasion to rejoice at the change. They are free to own land, but have not the means to buy it. They have personal liberty, yes. They are no longer bound to the soil; they have got the barren legal right to go where they please. But they have, at the same time, lost the right to claim support from the soil. Their liberty is one that benefits their masters, rather than themselves. The power of discharge and the advantage of having everywhere an army of proletarians to hire from, is vital to the growth of Capital. The workers have lost the power they as serfs possessed to labor to advantage for themselves, for in all branches of industry wholesale production has supplanted domestic industry. They have cooperation in production with a vengeance — think of Plugson and his spinners. The division and enjoyment of the products on the other hand, is entirely onesided.

The Plutocracy, the fleecing class and their retainers, is in this third stage of our civilization the really governing power all over the civilized world. But while it is checked, to some extent, in the European countries by the remnants of Feudalism: the nobility and clergy, it in our country is absolute, simply because this is a new country. Here its power is unquestioned and unrestrained. It is the easiest thing in the world for it to maintain its dominion here; for all it has to do is to command the government: "leave us alone!" Indeed our governments may be said to be merely committees of our Plutocrats, charged with watching over *their* common interests.

Now observe, that Socialists hold that each of these three periods, though together forming a long and weary road, was yet a necessary link in the chain of progress, was a preparatory step to each succeeding stage. We cannot accomplish the progress of our race by leaps but must do it by growths. We cannot dispense with any of these stages. We could not dispense with the present reign of Individualism and Capital. If a magic wand could restore the mode of production in vogue two hundred years ago, it would require another two centuries to mature the conditions for that New Order which lies in the womb of time. And we also hold, that history is radically incomprehensible without the conception, that the social state of each epoch was just as perfect as the corresponding development of our race permitted. The evils, therefore, of the "let alone" policy which we described in the preceding chapter are to be considered the legitimate workings of a principle to which humanity in times to come will find itself greatly indebted.

This conception ought to guard us against feeling any ill-will towards the individual members of our Plutocracy. Passions directed against the system are most proper; for it is only passion that can nerve us sufficiently to overthrow the system. But our capitalists are as much the creatures of circumstances as our paupers are. Neither should we forget, that there have here and there been employers and capitalists who would willingly have sacrificed their all to right society. Robert Owen was the more noble a man for being rich.

Having noted the principles and factors which thus far have shaped the destinies of our race, and having seen how the "Let-alone" policy has worked, and how it is working at this very day, the next inquiry naturally is: What will be the outcome? How will this policy work in the future?

Dr. Theodore D. Woolsey is a very cautious man, as benefits his profession and his position as a representative of our luxurious classes. He admits in his *"Communism and Socialism,"* that "there is some reason to apprehend, that the 'free use' of private property must end in making a few capitalists of enormous wealth, and a vast population of laborers dependent on them," — *if not prevented.* This conclusion is not due to any flights of fancy or unseemly rashness on the gentleman's part, for he goes on to say what we have quoted at the head of this chapter. If such a tendency "should" manifest itself, then he thinks, a Stewart "would" root out smaller trades-people; small producers "would" be ruined by mammoths of their own kind and the land and houses of a city "would" be more and more monopolized. We should say, that Dr. Woolsey is, if anything, over-cautious. Most people would be ready to say outright, that those things *are* daily taking place; and that, thus, the tendency of the "free use of private property" is manifest. Private "Enterprise" will, evidently, work in the future, as it has done in the past — ay! it will gather greater and greater momentum — if not prevented.

That is to say: Concentration will be the order of the day along the whole line of production, transportation and exchange. The small farm will give way to the large one; the small producer to the wholesale-producer. The wholesale trade will be more and more concentrated. All retail trade of any consequence in our larger cities will be gathered together in huge *bazaars*, after the Wanamaker pattern in Philadelphia; they will soon attract to themselves the customers of the country-stores just as the hardware factories already now do much of the work, formerly done by prosperous cross-roads blacksmiths. The contract system of erecting buildings will soon constitute, and constitutes now to a great extent, all engaged in the building-trades a movable, disposable force, to be hired now by this contractor and now by that. A few years hence the entire production and sale of the anthracite coal of Pennsylvania — that is, of the whole country — will be in the hands of four companies: the Reading; the Lehigh Valley; the Delaware, Lackawanna and Western and the Delaware and Hudson. In other words four persons will practically decide, how much the producers shall be paid and how much the consumers shall be bled. Probably it will not last long before the whole output will be controlled by one corporation.

The sugar-refining business will in a few years be in the hands of a couple of houses. We shall not have to wait long, before the whole railroad-system of the country is in the hands of, say, four companies. The Standard Oil Company already controls the oil business, and a few magnates now control in one corporation the whole telegraphic system of our country, so there the concentration is almost complete.

The last census report demonstrates conclusively that this concentration of manufacturing industries commenced in good earnest during the last decade; while, as we already have seen, the number of workers and values created considerably increased, the number of establishments was in 1880 almost exactly what it was in 1870.

Such complete centralization of all activities of Society will, evidently, render the working-classes more dependent on their masters; will make it more and more impossible for the workingmen to control their own conditions. They will have individually, less and less, if any, control as to what shall be their hours of labor and what their pay. That is clearly the tendency of the working of "unrestricted private enterprise" — if not prevented.

It will perhaps be objected, that our own figures do not support such an inference. The wages of labor it will be said, rose steadily from 1850 to 1880; to wit: $248, $310 and $346.

This objection would be a good instance of the bad uses to which the census-figures could be put. This rise in nominal wages can be accounted for on the hypothesis of Ricardo. While laying it down that wages are determined by the cost of living, he took occasion to observe that wages would probably steadily rise, because the prices of provisions had a tendency continually to rise. It is impossible to say whether there has been a real rise in wages before we know how many of the necessaries and decencies of life a given sum would buy in the respective years.

But note that our figures in the 1st chapter for the year 1870 were all reduced to a *gold basis*, as the value for the three other census-years were gold-values. The workman, then, who in 1870 received the average yearly wage of $310 in fact got $388 in currency. Now if provisions and many other commodities were not dearer in 1870 than in 1880 — as we think is the fact — then, comparing these two fairly prosperous years with each other, there has been an absolute fall in wages.

Again, we do not suppose that this complete dependence of the working-class on the employing class will take place before the concentration of the social activities is complete. When that time arrives, the workingmen will have the screws applied to them quickly enough, and they will find out the fact by themselves.

That consummate advocate and retainer of our fleecers — we again use this word simply as a term of description, to emphasize a fact, — Wm. M. Evarts, saw the point clearly when serving them in the office of national Secretary of State, and coolly said in an official document:

"The first great truth to be learned by manufacturers (*sic*) and workingmen is that the days of high wages are gone. In the near future the workingman of New York cannot expect twice or three times the wages of his fellow-worker in Europe, nor can the coal-miner of Pennsylvania expect twice the wages of the Northumberland miner."

Thus there is not a shadow of doubt that the enormous accumulation of wealth in the hands of a few capitalists, and a vast population of laborers dependent on them will be "an evil in fact — if not prevented." But *can* it be prevented?

One of the proposed "remedies" is the extension of our foreign markets.

This is a "remedy" which our fleecers, our plutocrats, guarantee as an infallible cure for Dr. Woolsey's "evil," in other words for the discontent of the working-classes. It must be admitted that they seek for that "remedy" with a remarkable zeal and pertinacity; and not alone our plutocrats, but the plutocrats of all capitalist countries as well. To get hold of the panacea their governments, *i. e.* their governing committees, write bushels of diplomatic notes and protests (remember the American protests against prohibiting the importation of American pork into Germany and France,) annex or conquer half-civilized countries, shake up by the roar of cannon the sleeping Chinese, encourage the building of railways in Mexico and incursions into the heart of Africa; in brief, penetrate into and ransack with feverish and frantic energy every nook and corner of the globe, where human beings are found that can be coaxed or driven to — trade.

Our own Evarts spent much of his time and energy as Secretary of State in hunting after these foreign markets. Whatever motive our plutocrats may pretend in pursuing their object — and we shall soon see that they have an excellent motive on their own account — Mr. Evarts cannot very well pretend solicitude for the working-classes after the "advice" he gave them — and our manufacturers — which we just now quoted. It was also Mr. Evarts who, to fortify his advice, caused our consuls in other countries to prepare reports for the State Department about the wages paid to foreign workers, which were mis-leading, and afterwards were published to show our workingmen that they were altogether too well off.

But no matter what the motive was and is, this cry: Foreign Markets, is very characteristic, indeed, of the "statesmanship" of these plutocrats who rule us — of these "Rulers who are no rulers," in Carlyle's language. It, like all their other public measures, proves them the veriest quacks, in this that it shows that they are satisfied with some temporary advantages, without considering the ulterior consequences. For to anybody who takes into account the immediate future these efforts to secure foreign markets must on a little reflection appear, as a writer in the *Atlantic Monthly* for Oct. 1879 calls them, "the maddest of all follies."

Because, supposing we could secure them, we could not possibly hold them. The nations whose custom we are soliciting, even China, Japan and Hindostan, are even now adopting all our inventions and improvements, and are fast learning to manufacture for themselves.

Because to secure them, we have to manufacture cheaper than any other nation; that is, we have to lower the wages and lengthen the working day of our operatives. Well, that, of course, does not disconcert Mr. Evarts. But now comes the point. England and all other competing nations will, on the same principle, try to oust us by manufacturing still cheaper. It is, thus, only by *continually* lowering the remuneration of our workers, even below the starvation wages of Europe, that we could possibly hold on to our "supremacy," even temporarily. And then how contemptible a supremacy! Carlyle's words should be a fitting rebuke: "Sad, indeed, that our national existence depends on our selling manufactured cotton a farthing cheaper than any other people."

Because, lastly, it is anyway a losing business. As the wages of our operatives decrease, their power of consumption decreases. Foreign markets can, therefore, only be obtained at the cost of losing our home-trade. The writer, mentioned above, computes, that thus far, we have lost ten dollars in domestic trade to every dollar gained in foreign trade.

Foreign markets, thus, truly mean: grasping at a shadow, even to our plutocrats. And that it is worthless as a "remedy" against Woolsey's "evil" is *ipso facto* apparent.

A second "remedy" is the voluntary individual cooperation, advocated by the English economist, Prof. Cairnes, and which has become almost a hobby of so many reformers.

Prof. Cairnes is a man we must respect. He has got a clear conception of the condition of the laboring classes:

"The conclusion to which I am brought is this, that, unequal as is the distribution of wealth already, the tendency of industrial progress — on the supposition, that the present separation between individual classes is maintained — is towards an inequality greater still."

And unlike Evarts he is anxious to raise them:

"The first and indispensable step toward any serious amendment of the laborer's lot is that he should be, in one way or another, lifted out of the groove, in which he at present works, and be placed in a position compatible with his becoming a sharer in equal proportion with others in the general advantages, arising from industrial progress. . . .

"The laborer shall cease to be a mere laborer."

But the way he indicates, "that the workmen contribute of their savings towards a common fund which they employ as capital and cooperate in turning to profit," is, decidedly, not the way to solve the problem.

In the first place it should be apparent to a man like Prof. Cairnes, that it is like mocking the laboring classes to suggest to them, to start *productive* enterprises, in competition with capitalists. Fancy them contemplating the millions needed to build factories, to buy machinery and lay in raw materials, and then feeling in their own pockets and finding them empty! How can workmen save anything, when their wages vibrate around the point of necessaries of life? And suppose, that they by adding together their pennies do start some factory or other, how can they, possibly, succeed in enterprises that require more and more capital; where Capitalists with experience fail?

But admit that such associations here and there have succeeded and that others therefore likewise might succeed, it yet leaves the kernel of the Labor-question untouched. These successful associations are brilliant examples of workingmen raising *themselves out of* their class, not raising *their class*. They are not truly cooperative but virtually joint-stock companies. They compete among themselves just as ordinary concerns do. They (the Rochdale Pioneers, for instance, who of late are an industrial as well as mercantile association) hire and fleece laborers after the approved fashion of the age, and experience teaches that they are indeed the hardest taskmasters. The interest of the members of these associations becomes identified with Capital, and if ever circumstances should make it easier for the smarter laborers to start such companies successfully, that fact would create a *Labor-caste*. In a general dispute between Labor and Capital these associations, instead of being a vanguard of Labor, will go over to the side of Capital. The sons of Rochdale Pioneers, living in luxury and imitating the airs and fashions of the wealthy of all times, point the moral. Where is, then, the gain to the laboring classes to come in? No, instead of advising workingmen to save, and to invest their savings in such risky enterprises, it would be much better to advise them to put their savings into their own flesh and bone, where they of right belong on account of their more efficient labor.

Voluntary Cooperation in enterprises of *consumption* is quite another thing. Such have in many instances succeeded. They can succeed, because they require no very large amount of Capital. And Socialists very often advise workingmen, wherever and whenever they can, to start cooperative stores and thus get better goods and save the profits, otherwise going to the middlemen. It is in other words, a very prudent thing to do for *the individual.*

But how will it help the body of workingmen? Evidently, it could only do so, when the whole body, or at least a large majority of them became the beneficiaries of such cooperation. It is curious, that an economist like Prof. Cairnes does not foresee the necessary consequences.

In such case, of course, the average wages requisite for a given standard of living and comfort would become less and consequently — for Prof. Cairnes admits the law of wages of Ricardo and the Socialists — would fall to the new level. The workmen thus would be no better off than before. Next, what would become of the small traders and shop-keepers, thus displaced? They, naturally, would be ruined. They either would have to become a burden on the community, or fall into the ranks of the wage-workers, and thus contribute to lowering the rate of wages still more by their frantic competition. The writer of this once heard a small trader in a western town bitterly upbraiding the grangers, who had started one of their cooperative stores at his place, because of their meanness. They ought to "live and let live." Was he so very unreasonable?

Such voluntary Cooperation may be very excellent for the individual, just as long as it is a sporadic phenomenon — no longer.

A third "remedy," firmly relied upon by another class of Labor-reformers, to check the increasing power of the capitalist and employing class is the formation and strengthening of Trades-unions and the legal enactment of a normal working-day; two objects which may be said always to go hand in hand.

We and all Socialists, indeed, have nothing but commendation for and active sympathy with every effort that is made to bind all the workers of the various crafts together, and to gather these crafts again into greater unions. These Trades-unions and Trades-assemblies are powerful instruments for educating their members for the coming Social Order, whether they are aware of it or not; in another connexion we shall have more to say on that point. They impress vividly on their members the fact, that their interests are mutual, and that their employers, far from being identified with them, are diametrically opposed to them in interests. They open the eyes of their members to the fact, that their masters are not wage-*givers* but *take* wages from them; that their masters do not support *them* but that *they* support their masters.

Again, while we do not recommend strikes — what the Trades-unions, indeed, are also far from doing — we accept them as necessary evils. We claim that as a matter of fact (what we have already stated) there is an existing warfare between capitalists and laborers, and that strikes are simply the skirmishes in that warfare. Strikes are the efforts of *wares* to act like *men*.

We also hold as a matter of course, that eight hours of hard daily work, is a sufficient, more than a sufficient, task for a mere living.

But we are at the same time convinced that Trades-unions and all these efforts of theirs are absolutely impotent to counteract the workings of "unrestricted private enterprise."

The Trades-unions of England have indeed succeeded in raising the wages in various trades and shortening the daily toil — yes, *they* and they *only*, have succeeded in procuring for the English working-classes the great boon of a nine-hours working day, — but only because the masters have not combined sufficiently. Strikes must necessarily fail, if due resistance be made, because the immediate effect of them is to deprive the worker of his means of subsistence, and the capitalist of his profit simply. When "wares" try to act like men, they naturally fail, for *wares are only things.*

And suppose the Trades-union movement of England to accomplish its ultimate object: that of uniting all the workers of all the trades of Great Britain into one compact, comprehensive body, the result will evidently be, that the employers and capitalists will be compelled to follow suit; that is, such a union of workingmen will call into existence a Power, that can crush them at the first trial of strength.

The writer of this is, furthermore, decidedly of the opinion that the efforts to establish in our country by law a normal working day of eight hours will prove equally futile.

We shall not enlarge upon the point, that one state of the Union cannot afford to establish it, except all states do so; that therefore *national* legislation is the only object worth striving for. But what sort of legislation? Our Congress and some local legislatures have passed laws which fix eight hours as a working day for government employees and which provide, or at least imply, that the same wages shall be paid for the eight as formerly for the ten hours. All friends of an eight-hour law agree as to the propriety and expediency of these statutes, and claim, that if honestly enforced, they will by the example they set lead — nay, compel — private employers to follow suit.

Have they done that so far? Some of the noblest and most unselfish of martyrs witness by their gray hairs or the broken hearts with which they have gone to their graves, that these statutes have had no such effect, that they have had no effect at all; that they have, indeed, been nothing but dead letters. Ah, but if they had been enforced, it would have been different, it is said. May it not be that there is one underlying reason, why they have not been enforced and why they could not have affected other laborers if, perchance, they had been enforced? The point is, that the less does *not* include the greater. Under the Established Order our national Government and all state governments are on exactly the same footing as private parties and the employment they give is but a small part of all employments. It is therefore the rate of wages paid in private employments and the hours of labor obtaining there which, as long as this system lasts, will regulate public employments, and not reversely. To hope that it will be otherwise is Utopian.

There are more radical eight-hour men, among them many Socialists, who agitate for an enactment to the effect, that all private employers who work their men more than eight hours a day (and presumably, that all wage-workers who work more than that number of hours) shall be punished in a certain way. They do not care whether anything is provided about wages, arguing that, if eight hours become a normal work-day, wages will soon rise to their former level, all other things being equal, — in which we agree with them. But it seems to be entirely overlooked in all discussions on such an enactment of a national character, that it requires a constitutional amendment. We for our part believe that we might just as soon expect to have this nation changed into a Socialist Commonwealth by a constitutional amendment, passed in the constitutional way, as such a *compulsory* eight-hour law. But we need say nothing further here, for we are discussing the workings of *unrestricted* private enterprise, of the "*free* use" of private property.

Only one word more. It may be objected that we admitted that the Trades-Unions of England did obtain a nine-hour work-day in England; and that in many of our states a ten-hour law prevails and is obeyed. There is perhaps a misapprehension here. There is neither here nor in England any *legal* normal working-day for *men*. Whatever legal restriction exists applies to women and children exclusively, and as to them even only, when they are working in factories. The English Trades-Unions did succeed, for the time being, in wresting from their employers their consent to a nine-hour workday, simply because at the time the market-demand exceeded the supply.

A fourth "remedy," advocated by the Greenback-party — of whose doctrines we shall have more to say in another place — is that the Government should advance to its citizens all the capital they may be in need of, at a very low rate of interest, say one per cent. This "remedy," which was also the hobby of Proudhon, we can dismiss with a very few words. Even if it were not impossible, which it is as we shall afterwards see, it would not help the *masses* in the least. The proportion between wages and fleecings in our "cakes" remains the same, whether interest is large or small. The reduction of interest would simply increase the *balance* of fleecings which go to profit and rent. Such a measure, if practicable, would thus only benefit the employing class, the small producer and merchant, and, possibly, the landowners.

But then, the Greenback-party is a middle-class-party, that is to say: a *reactionary* party, as Proudhon was a reactionist; for the middle-class (what we in America call the "middle-class" and the English the "lower middle-class") is doomed to extinction.

Thus it truly seems. Dr. Woolsey! that "this enormous accumulation of Capital in a few hands" *is* to be a "necessary evil, beyond prevention!" It, undoubtedly, *will* "run through all the forms of

property." Our manufacturers, our merchant "princes," our transporters, our money lenders, and, finally, our land owners will go on
dwindling in numbers, as they swell in size. The millionaires *will*
gobble up the Capital of the whole middle-class, and the more their
own possessions grow, the wilder will be their chase after the
smaller game. Our working classes, on the other hand, *will* go on
being gathered into larger centres. There is no "if" at all about the
matter and there is, absolutely, no patent medicine in the market
that can prevent it.

But is it philosophical to call that "an *evil*," Dr. Woolsey?

When a child is growing its teeth it is, we know, a season of
misery to it: yet we do not therefore call the process of teething an
"evil." What if the present and future workings of "capitalism," that
is of the "free use" of Capital were the teething period of Society?
We know, of course, that the parallel is imperfect; for there is this
terrible difference, that in the latter case the suffering of myriads of
sentient beings is involved, for which reason the agitation for shortening the daily toil and all other efforts to alleviate the condition
of the working-classes are worthy of all our sympathy.

Just as the teething process runs its course according to the physical laws of our organization, and must run its course, so the centralization of all social activities goes on according to laws indwelling
in our social organism, and to stop it, if we could, would be turning
back the wheels of progress. This is the consolation left to the self-
sacrificing eight-hour agitators for the failure of their efforts. For
there is no doubt that, if they could succeed, the wage-workers
would be rendered almost satisfied with their lot as wage-slaves, be
reconciled to the wage-*system*, just what the partial success of the
Trades-Unions in England, unfortunately, seems to have done with
the British wage-workers.

When the culmination is reached, *then* comes the dawn.

And what will be the culmination?

That the Established Order will be dying of exhaustion. This
conclusion lay indeed, potentially, in our exposition of "Value" in
chapter I, wherefore we also there called it the "mother-idea" of
Socialism. Since all real Values are the results of Labor, and since
Labor under our wage-system, our profit-system, our fleecings-sys-
tem, only receives about one-half thereof as its share, it follows that
the producers cannot buy back that which they create.

Now we can see, that this wage-system concerns the whole Nation, and *not* merely the wage-workers, as we for argument's sake granted at the commencement of Chapter II. For the more Capital is being accumulated in private hands, the more impossible this wage-system renders it for the producers to buy what they produce. The more necessary it becomes for capitalists to dispose of their ever increasing fleecings, the less the ability of the people to purchase them will, relatively, become. The greater the supply the smaller the consumption. The more Capital, the more "overproduction."

This is a fatal contradiction. This "Individualism" which has created and nourished Capital and is making it bigger and bigger, is at the same time digging the grave of Capital.

The logic of the upholders of the present Social Order, when they fancy it will last forever, or hope, that it, like its predecessors, will last for a thousand years, is sadly at fault. Slavery and Serfdom were long-lived, because they rested on broad endurable foundations, so that they had a chance to petrify; their nature, in other words, was *stability*. But our Social Order cannot exist without repeated industrial revolutions: *its very nature is insecurity and movement*. It can be fitly compared to a spinning top which only is saved from toppling over by being made to turn swiftly about on its apex. It is unrestricted Private Enterprise which imparts to our Social Order this wild movement. But just as the top is sure to finally topple over, so is this Social Order of ours.

That is the "Logic of Events." That events have logic simply means, that "statesmen" and "leaders" have none.

And we have no need of trusting to logic; we need only trust our senses. Any one who has eyes to see can perceive this Social Order tottering, not alone in our own country, but in all industrial countries. Do we not hear from *everywhere* the cry of the fleecers: "Foreign markets! We *must* have foreign markets!?" Did we not say that the fleecers had excellent reasons of their own for hunting for them? *This cry is the first frantic death-gasp* of Capitalism, showing it is dying of inanition. What better evidence need we? Socialists might simply fold their arms and calmly await its dissolution. Thus our plutocrats, who a hundred years ago untied the fetters that bound all industrial and social relations in their unyielding embrace, now find themselves in the position of the magician who unloosed the elemental forces of Nature, and afterwards, not being able to control them, was overwhelmed by them.

We are approaching the culmination with giant strides, with railroad speed, in fact. Every invention that renders production on a smaller scale more unprofitable, every bankruptcy, every so-called "crisis" brings us nearer to the end.

Then will come the real "*crisis*." We do not say it will not come before; but, if not before, it will surely come with the culmination.

And then, what?

Well, Political Economy cannot tell us; it came in with the present Social order, and it will go out with it; its whole scope is to bring the present social arrangements into a system.

Only Socialism can lift the veil of the future, for it only contemplates this Social Order and the whole previous history of our race with a philosophic eye. Therefore it can predict with the same claim to certainty, with which the Signal Service Bureau predicts to-morrow's weather.

There are two alternatives. Barbarism may be the outcome. But we do not believe it will.

Thoughtful men observe that there never before was diffused through society so large a sense of unhappiness. Our large accessions and acquisitions of comfort have enhanced and aggravated our ideas of poverty. Capitalists, for their own purposes, have taught the masses a thousand needs, and at the same time rendered it impossible for them to satisfy these needs. Society is from top to bottom seized by discontent — next to hope the greatest gift from the gods to man.

There is an old saga of a King and Queen to whom a fair son was born. Twelve fairies came to the christening, each with a gift. A noble presence, wisdom, strength, beauty — all were poured upon him until it seemed he must excel all mortal men. Then came the twelfth fairy with the gift of discontent, but the angry father turned away the fairy and her gift. And the lad grew apace, a wonder of perfect powers; but, content in their possession, he cared to use them for neither good nor ill; there was no eagerness in him; good-natured and quiet, he let life use him as it would. And at last the King knew that the rejected had been the crowning gift.

Again, the masses are becoming more and more intelligent, too intelligent to submit to a new slavery, or a new serfdom. The work-ing-masses now feel themselves human beings and have become conscious of their power; their concentration in large centres of industry has given them that consciousness, which, perhaps, will make them too impatient to await the final crash.

And then — *we Socialists have now been born into the world,* a guarantee, that Society will go forward, not backwards.

The other alternative is Dr. Woolsey's: "that a *revolution,* slow or rapid, *will certainly bring about a new order of things."* There we agree with him.

Whatever is, is *not* the immutable order of nature. It is very natural that our well-to-do classes should believe that arrangements which suit them have been settled by some law of the Medes and Persians! nevertheless when these arrangements have done their work they are destined to disappear. But whatever is, is *rational.* It exists, because, and so long as it fulfills some useful office.

Private Enterprise has done civilization excellent service, but after having run this Social "Order" into the ground it will be sup-planted by a new principle: *Social Cooperation,* up to which the whole Martyrdom of Man during his whole previous history has been training us. "Individualism," a rhythmical swing of the human mind, will then commence its backward movement and find its compensation in due time.

The divorce between Capital and Labor will cease. Capital will no longer be the *master* of Labor but, as true National Wealth, the invaluable *hand-maid* of Labor.

The steward of that National Wealth will be the *State;* it having, as we shall now see, a title to all Capital, *paramount to that of either capitalists or laborers.*

CHAPTER IV

THE SPHERE OF THE STATE

"It is only by being citizen of a well-ordered State, that the individual has got Rights." — *Hegel.*

"Not State-action in itself, but State-action exercised by a hostile class it is that ought to be deprecated." — *Matthew Arnold.*

"Look to the State! From that you can expect the highest experience and skill, real and efficient control, a national aim and spirit." — *Frederic Harrison.*

We have concluded the Socialist critique of the present order of things. In a nutshell it is this: The Fleecings increase in our country and in all industrial countries at a very great rate. In order that Capital (the sum of these Fleecings) may be simply *maintained,* (mark that!) it must be constantly employed in production and a market must be found for the products which it enables Labor to create. Foreign markets will soon dry up; our autocrats, therefore, will be confined to their respective home-markets. But the masses at home are more and more becoming wage-workers from the operation of "Individualism;" wage-workers receive in wages only about half of what they produce; the masses, consequently, are becoming more and more unable to buy back the Values they create. Thus for lack of consumption, Capital will be more and more threatened with depreciation. The more Capital, the more "overproduction." The Wage-System and Private "Enterprise" *will,* indeed, involve capitalists and laborers in one common ruin.

This is the foundation for what may be called: "constructive" Socialism. We are not under the delusion, that Nations can be *persuaded* by the grandeur, excellence and equity of our system. The Future is ours, because the present system will soon be *unbearable;*

because, as we said, we might fold our arms and calmly wait to see the Established Order fall to pieces by its own weight. Our conception of Value, therefore, truly comprises the *whole* of Socialism.

When the culmination has been reached, the reins will drop from the impotent hands of our autocrats and will be taken up by an impersonal Power, coeval with human nature: The STATE.

It is a pity that we must commence by guarding ourselves against the corrupt American use of the term "State;" but, writing mainly for our American countrymen, we cannot help ourselves.

The "State" of Pennsylvania and the other thirty seven "States" are not, and never were, *States*. By State we mean with Webster "a whole people, united in one body politic." That is the meaning of *State* in all languages, English included — except the American language. Now, not one of our American "states" was ever for one moment a "whole people." They either were subjects to the crown of England, or parts of the Confederation, or of the Union. The Union then is *a State*, just as France and Spain are States, and it is emphatically so since the American people commenced to call themselves a Nation with a big N. This, however, by no means excludes local centres of authority, what we are wont to call "local self-government."

"The State" is a stumbling block to many very worthy persons. They apprehend — a fear very honorable in them — that State-supremacy would be prejudicial to Freedom. We hope to make it apparent, that State-action and individual Freedom, far from being antagonistic, are really complementary of each other.

The reason why "the State" is now-a-days such a bugbear to so many, is that this word has quite another meaning in the mouth of an individualist, wherever you find him, than when used by a Socialist. Indeed, the fundamental distinction between "Individualism" and Socialism must be sought in the opposition of these two conceptions.

Individualists, and foremost amongst them our autocrats, cherish this degrading notion of the State: that it is merely an organ of Society, synonymous with "Government" — with the political machinery of Society. We claim — to quote Webster once more — that the State is "a whole people, united in one body politic," in other words, that

The State is the organized Society.

We cannot better contrast these two conceptions than by comparing the views of Herbert Spencer when he was a young philosopher
with his present views now that he is a mature one.

Young Spencer wrote a book, called "Social Statics," which to a
great extent, has become a manual to our "let-alone" politicians. In
that work he starts out with a "first principle" from which he proposes to reason out, deductively, the whole science of government
— a method, by the way, that is thought rather precarious by
scientific men of to-day. This assumed axiom which, undoubtedly,
looks very captivating at first sight, is that "every man has freedom
to do all that he wills, provided he infringes not *the like freedom* of
any other man." From this "principle" — of which we shall presently have more to say — he proves with flawless logic, that Society is simply a *voluntary* association of men for mutual protection
and the State merely its organ to that end. The business of the
State, therefore, is only to secure to each citizen unlimited freedom
to exercise his faculties. Then, to be sure, the State has no right to
tax men of property for educating other men's children, or for feed-
ing the poor or even for looking after the Public Health. In taking
upon itself these functions the State is acting the part of an aggres-
sor instead of that of a protector.

The State is a policeman — nothing more. By and by, when the
millennium arrives, the State will lose even that function; it will
become a rudimentary organ. The State will then disappear altogether. As long as it exists, it is nothing but a necessary evil; only
instituted for the bad, and only a burden to the good. If the facts
do not verify that conclusion, so much the worse for the facts. If the
State's activity does spread more and more, even in Spencer's own
country — in response to the pressure of the "Logic of Events,"
and in spite of the frantic struggles of its ruling class: the wealthy
middle-class — so much the worse for the State.

Such was the reasoning of Spencer in 1850; and these views are
accepted and practiced by the ruling powers of our country, as far
as in them lies. Our capital-holders cry out: "You, State! You Government! Your whole business, you know, consists in securing us
unlimited freedom to exercise our faculties. That is all we are doing
here; the whole crowd of us are exercising our faculties, each to the
extent of his ability. It does not concern you a bit whom or how
many we are able to fleece or how much we fleece them; or how

many fall and are trampled upon. Let us alone, then, and simply see to it that we are not interfered with! That is what you are paid for, you know. 'Every one look out for himself, and the devil take the hindmost,' is our and your rule of action." And the "government" lets them alone. That is to say, it allows itself to be made into a peace-officer of a singular sort. For suppose a police-man should see a bully attack a weaker man, and should say to himself: "It is not my business to protect that weak man or to interfere with the combatants at all. I take it to be my duty, just to see to it that no one interferes with them. So I will make a ring round them and let the best man win." That is what our so called "Governments" virtually do, and so the shrewd greedy individuals who can exercise their faculties do so to their heart's content and grow fat at the expense of other individuals. Probably in no other age did individuals have such a power over their neighbors as they have now in consequence of this "let-alone" policy. Every factory, mine, workshop and railroad shows the working of it. The indi-vidual Vanderbilt has acquired two hundred millions, while another individual — perhaps the producer of part of his fortune, — is sent to prison as a tramp.

But that is all in order. For hear young Spencer: "The shoulder-ing aside the weak by the strong, which leaves so many in shallows and miseries, is the decree of a large, farseeing benevolence, re-garded not separately, but in connection with the interests of univer-sal humanity. To step in between weakness and its consequences suspends the progress of weeding out those of lower development" — and Vanderbilt and Gould, of course, are the "strong," and men of "*higher* development!"

Why do not those men of property — of "higher development" — abolish this good-for-nothing "State" altogether? Would it not be a good speculation for them to let Courts of Justice to the highest bidder, and farm out the prosecution of wars to stock-companies? Can they not buy protection against violence, as well as insurance against fire, and more cheaply too, on the glorious free-competition plan? Why do they not do it?

Well, perhaps the State is something else than *an organ* after all.

Herbert Spencer, the *mature* and profound philosopher, pursues the far more scientific method of studying Society, as it is, and the process of its development, instead of evolving it, as young Spencer did, out of his own inner consciousness.

His results now are, that the body politic, instead of being a "voluntary" association is, what Socialists claim that it is, an *Organism*.*

Beside arguments in his other works he devotes a very able and ingenious essay to the drawing of parallels between a highly developed State and the most developed animals, and sums up:

"That they gradually increase in mass; that they become, little by little more complex; that at the same time their parts grow more mutually dependent; and that they continue to live and grow as wholes, while successive generations of their units appear and disappear — are broad peculiarities, which bodies politic display, in common with all living bodies, and in which they and other living bodies differ from everything else."

In several striking passages Spencer further shows with what singular closeness correspondences can be traced in the details between the two kinds of organisms, as, for instance, between the distributing system of animal bodies and the distributing system of bodies politic, or between our economic division of labor, and that prevailing in organic bodies, "so striking, indeed, that the expression 'physiological division of labor' has been suggested by it."

And some of the leading contrasts between the two kinds of organisms, he shows, are far less important than appears at first glance. Thus, the distinction that the living elements of Society do not, as in individual organisms, form one continuous mass, disappears, when we consider that the former are not separated by intervals of dead space, but diffused through space, covered with life of a lower order, which ministers to their life. And thus with this other peculiarity, that the elements of a social organism are capable of moving from place to place, is obviated by the fact, that as farmers, manufacturers and traders, men generally carry on business in the same localities; that, at all events, each great centre of industry, each manufacturing town or district, continues always in the same place.

There is then but one distinction left that may be deemed ma-

* [Spencer had in fact first suggested the analogy of the Social Organism in *Social Statics* (1850). He greatly amplified the idea in a paper, "The Social Organism," of 1860. Gronlund corrected this passage in his revised edition. — Editor's Note.]

terial. In the Social Organism the living units are conscious, while in the animal organism it is the *whole* that possesses consciousness.

But then those other highly developed organisms, — to wit: the vegetable ones, — have no consciousness at all. Society could then be considered a mighty plant whose units are highly developed animals.

Again, though the social organism has no consciousness of its own, it certainly has a distinctive character of its own; a corporate *individuality*, a corporate "oneness." As a unit of that organism every individual certainly displays a wholly different character from that of the organism itself. Every Nation has its own spirit, which the Germans call the *"Volksgeist;"* a spirit which has its life in the national history, which produces specific traits of nationality, differing from the common traits of humanity. It generally lies deep, hidden, unsuspected until such a moment arrives as that with us, when Fort Sumter was fired upon; then rising, as it were, out of an abyss it urges thinkers and actors resistlessly on to pursue, unwittingly, the loftiest ideal of the race. This corporate individuality is far from being identical with average "Public Opinion." It is *sui generis* and makes the Social Organism an organism *sui generis.*

We therefore insist, with even greater force than Spencer did, that the State is a living Organism, differing from other organisms in no essential respect. This is not to be understood in a simply metaphorical sense; it is not that the State merely resembles an organism, but that it, including with the people the land and all that the land produces, literally is *an organism*, personal and territorial.

The "Government" — the punishing and restraining authority — may possibly be dispensed with at some future time. But the STATE — *never*. To dispense with the State would be to dissolve Society.

It follows that the relation of the State, the body politic, to us, its citizens, is *actually* that of a tree to its cells, and *not* that of a heap of sand to its grains, to which it is entirely indifferent how many other grains of sand are scattered and trodden under foot.

This is a conception of far-reaching consequence.

In the *first* place, it, together with the modern doctrine of *Evolution,* as applied to all organisms, deals a mortal blow to the theory of "man's natural rights," the theory of man's "inalienable right" to life, liberty, property, "happiness" &c., the theory of which mankind during the last century has heard and read so much; the theory that has been so assiduously preached to our dispossessed classes, and which has benefited them *so* little!

Natural rights! The highest "natural right" we can imagine is for the stronger to kill and eat the weaker, and for the weaker to be killed and eaten. One of the "natural rights," left "man" now, is to act the brute towards wife and children, and that "right" the State has already curtailed and will by-and-by give it the finishing stroke. Another "natural right," very highly prized by our autocrats, is the privilege they now possess of "saving" for themselves what other people produce. In brief, "natural rights" are the rights of the muscular, the cunning, the unscrupulous.

These so-called "natural rights" and an equally fictitious "law of nature" were invented by Jean Jacques Rousseau (who followed Luther and the other Reformers in the work of making breaches in the old petrified system of the Middle Ages) as a metaphysical expedient to get some sanction to legitimate resistance to absolute authority in kings, nobility and clergy. He derived them from a supposed "state of nature" which he and his disciples as enthusiastically praised as if they had been there and knew all about it. Now, modern historical comparative methods prove conclusively that this "state of nature" never existed. A man, living from the moment of his birth outside organized society, if this were possible, would be no more a man than a hand would be a hand without the body. *Civil society is man's natural state.* This "state of nature," on the other hand, would be for man the most unnatural state of all, and fortunately so, for in it we should not have been able to make the least headway against our conditions, but must have remained, till the present moment, hungry, naked savages, whose "rights" would not procure us a single meal. And as to a "law of nature," if it is proper to use that term at all, it is nothing but the conscience and reason of civil society.

No, Rousseau did say several things worth notice — as any author who is being refuted a century after his death must have done. These speculations of his are indeed worth notice, to us Americans especially, since they formed the logical basis of our own "epoch-making" Revolution — as a German might happily call it — though we cannot help remarking that the conclusion here justified the premises, rather than the reverse. And, further, they also furnished the justification, the steampower, for the great French Revolution. The incidents of the latter event, however, showed that Rousseau could, under certain circumstances, be a very unsafe guide; they demonstrated that the "Natural Rights of Man" were good tools to tear down rotten systems with, but sandy foundations on which to erect new systems.

We have been out-spoken on this matter, because it is so important that thoughtful people should know that philosophic Socialists repudiate that theory of "natural rights," and insist that the lesson taught by Rousseau and repeated (why not say so outright?) in our own Declaration of Independence must be unlearned before any firm foundation can be reached. Unfortunately nearly all our "reformers" — men with the noblest and often truly Socialist hearts — cling to it and build on man's "God-given Rights" as if they were the special confidants of God.

But Carlyle is emphatically right when he says "Nothing solid can be founded on shams; it must conform to the realities, the verities of things."

Here is such a reality:

It is Society, organized Society, the State that gives us all the rights we have. To the State we owe our freedom. To it we owe our living and property, for outside of organized Society man's needs far surpasses his means. The humble beggar owes much to the State, but the haughty millionaire far more, for outside of it they both would be worse off than the beggar now is. To it we owe all that we are and all that we have. To it we owe our civilization. It is by its help that we have reached such a condition as man individually never would have been able to attain. Progress is the struggle with Nature for mastery, is war with the misery and inabilities of our "natural" condition. The State is the organic union of us all to wage that war, to subdue Nature, to redress natural defects and inequalities. The State therefore, so far from being a burden to the "good," a "necessary evil," is man's greatest good.

This conception of the State as an organism thus consigns the "rights of man" to obscurity and puts *Duty* in the foreground.

In the *second* place, we now can ascertain the true sphere of the State. That is, we now can commence to build something solid.

We say *Sphere* on purpose; we do not ask what are the "rights," "duties" or "functions" of the State, for if it truly is an organism it is just as improper to speak of *its* rights, duties or functions towards its citizens as it is to speak of a man's rights, duties and functions in relation to his heart, his legs, or his head. The State has rights, duties and functions in relation to other organisms, but towards its own members it has only a sphere of activities.

The sphere of the State simply consists in caring for its own welfare, just as a man's sphere, as far as himself is concerned, consists in caring for his own well-being. If that be properly done, then his brain, his lungs and his stomach will have nothing to complain of.

So with the State. Its whole sphere is the making all special activities work together for one general end: its own welfare, or the *Public Good*. Observe that the Public Good, the General Welfare, implies far more than "the greatest good to the greatest number" on which our "practical" politicians of today base their trifling measures. Their motto broadly sanctions the sacrifice of minorities to majorities, while the "General Welfare" means the greatest good of every individual citizen.

To that end the State may do anything whatsoever which is shown to be expedient.

It may, as it always has done, limit the right of a person to dispose of himself in marriage as he pleases.

The State is, in the words of J. S. Mill, "fully entitled to abrogate or alter any particular right of property which it judges to stand in the way of the public good."

The State may tomorrow, if it judges it expedient, take all the capital of the country from its present owners, without any compensation whatsoever, and convert it into social Capital.

In Chapter 1 we showed that the whole wealth of the country (*i.e.* not natural wealth but the sum of all Values) is the result of Labor. As against capitalists the producers, therefore, would clearly be entitled to it. But as against the State, the organized Society, even Labor does not give us a particle of title to what our hands and brain produce.

One need not be a Socialist to acknowledge that.

Wm. B. Weeden, a manufacturer in Providence, R. I., says in a criticism on Henry George's book in the *Atlantic Monthly* for Dec. 1880:

"The axe you use is not yours, though you may have made it, instead of buying it in the market. The idea of the axe, its potentiality, which enables it to prevail over nature, does not belong to you. This is the result of long generations of development, from the rudest stone-tool to the elegant steelblade which rings through the pine-woods of Maine. This belongs to Society. Neither the laborer nor the capitalist owns that principle. So everywhere. Neither Labor nor Capital employs the other. It is Society which employs both."

To whom does the telegraph belong? To Society. Neither Prof. Morse nor any other inventor can lay sole claim to it. It *grew* little by little.

With still greater force the State may reclaim possession of all the land within its limits, all laws, customs and deeds to the contrary notwithstanding.

We say "with still greater force," not because the ownership of land is on a different footing from that of other Capital. Its Value, like that of other Capital, is partly real, arising from the labor of this and former generations, and partly unreal, due to the monopoly of it and the constantly increasing necessities of the community. It therefore is the creation of Society as much as other Capital. We say so because the Common Law of Great Britain and our country has always claimed, and still does claim that the State is the sole landlord:

"The first thing the student has to get rid of is the absolute idea of ownership. Such an idea is quite unknown to the English law. No man is, in law, the absolute owner of lands; he can only hold an estate in them." Williams: *On the law of Real Property.*

When, therefore, the Trinity Church Corporation of New York City claims to *own* city property of sufficient value to pay all the debts of the State of New York, its cities and villages, a value mainly created by the tenants who have covered that tract of land with buildings, graded and paved the streets and built the sewers, it is simply a glaring usurpation.

When, therefore, the increased values of Real Estate, due simply to the progress of the country, are permitted, in the form of increased rents "to drop into the mouths of landowners as they sleep instead of being applied to the public necessities of the Society which created it" in the words of Mill, it is only because the too "enterprising" individual has got the better of the State.

For the same reason the landowner has been permitted to possess whatever treasure may be hidden in it, even treasure of which no man knew anything, when the owner entered into possession — an allowance, than which no one more foolish or absurd could be imagined.

For the same reason the splendid opportunities which our country had, both in the reconstruction of the Southern States and in the settlement of our public lands, for making the Nation the sole Landlord, were not so much as thought of.

Our landowners ought to admit with Blackstone: "We seem to fear, that our titles are not quite good; it is well the great mass obey the laws without inquiring why they were made so and not otherwise."

But there is no need to devote more space here to discuss the supreme title of the State to the land since the appearance of Henry George's book: "Progress and Poverty," which we hope all our readers have read. The main criticism which Socialists have to make on this work is that it pushes the land question — in our country a secondary question in importance — so much into the foreground, that sight is entirely lost of the principal question: Who should control the instruments of production and transportation? Furthermore, George seems to have written his book for Englishmen, Scotchmen and Irishmen, rather than for Americans. To start the solution of the social problem in our country, where as yet the great majority of farmers own the land which they cultivate, with a proposition to divest all landowners of their titles, is to commence by making a very large portion of the workers to be benefited hostile to all social change.

The State is thus fully entitled to take charge of *all* instruments of Labor and Production, and to say that all social activities shall be carried on in a perfectly different manner.

Undoubtedly the whole fleecing class will interpose their socalled "vested rights." That is to say because the State for a long time tacitly allowed a certain class to divide the common stock of social advantages among themselves and appropriate it to their own individual benefit therefore the State is estopped, they say, from ever recovering it. And not alone will they claim undisturbed possession of what they have, but also the right to use it in the future as they have in the past; that is, they will claim a "vested right" to fleece the masses to all eternity.

But such a protest will be just as vain as was that of the Pope against the loss of his temporal sovereignty. The theory of "vested rights" never applies when a revolution has taken place; when the whole structure of Society is changed. The tail of a tadpole that is developing into a frog may protest as much as it pleases; Nature heeds it not. And when the frog is an accomplished fact, there is no tail to protest.

This whole doctrine of "vested rights" moreover, has its reason in the fact that from the dawn of history to the present time we have had and have *privileged* classes. Henry George remarks very pointedly: "When we allow 'vested rights' we still wear the collar of the Saxon thrall." The only "vested right" any man has is the right to such institutions as will best promote the Public Good. A man has no other right whatever in a civilized community. If he is not satisfied with that, he may exile himself to where there is no civilization, and even there his descendants will necessarily grow up into a State.

Observe further, that the Public Welfare means more than the welfare of all the living individuals composing it. Since the State is an organism, it is more than all of us collectively.

It would be absurd to say, that a man is nothing but an aggregation of his cells. Burke said rightly of the State, that it includes the dead, the living and the coming generations. We are what we are far more by the accumulated influence of past generations than by our own efforts, and our labor will principally benefit those who are to follow us. The Public Welfare thus includes the welfare of the generations to come. This comprehensive conception places the pettiness and impotency of our "individualism" in the most glaring light. For how can it ever be the private interest of mortal individuals to make immediate sacrifices for the distant future?

"But if the State's Sphere is to be extended to everything that may affect the Public Welfare, why! then there is no stopping to what the State will attempt."

We let Professor Huxley reply ("Administrative Nihilism.")

"Surely the answer is obvious, that, on similar grounds, the right of a man to eat when he is hungry, might be disputed, because if you once allow that he may eat at all there is no stopping, until he gorges himself and suffers all the ills of a surfeit."

Does it not now seem more profitable, especially to our dispossessed classes, to lay stress on *Duty* rather than on *Rights?*

Does our conception of the State not furnish a very firm foundation, firm enough to build a New Social Order on?

Let us then give due credit to Herbert Spencer for his profound speculations on the Social Organism. He has indeed, in them laid the foundation for constructive Socialism, as far as the Anglo-Saxon peoples are concerned, just as Ricardo by his speculations on Value did it for critical Socialism. True, Spencer is still the apostle of "Individualism;" he exhibits still a morbid aversion to all State-activity, but we have a right to call his present utterances on that point mere crotchets, since they do not receive the least support from his splendid arguments in favor of the organic character of Society.

That is also Professor Huxley's opinion. He says: "I cannot but think, that the real force of the analogy is totally opposed to the negative (individualistic) view of the State-function.

"Suppose that in accordance with this view, each muscle were to maintain, that the nervous system had no right to interfere with its contraction except to prevent it from hindering the contraction of another muscle; or each gland, that it had a right to secrete, as long as its secretion interfered with no other; suppose every separate cell left free to follow its own interests and be 'let alone.' Lord of all! what would become of the body physiological?"

This negative view of the State-function is a very modern one. No thinker or philosophic Statesmen up to the 18th century anywhere dreamt of it. Not until the exaggerated form of the Protestant doctrine of the independence of the individual had taken possession of men's minds; not until the great delusion had become prevalent, that we have been brought into this world, each for the sake of himself, did it come into vogue. Then it was that William von Humboldt (who may be said to be the father of the doctrine) deliberately degraded the State below a peace-officer or a watch-dog.

But even ultra-Protestant nations that adopted this view in theory have constantly been impelled by an inward necessity to repudiate it in practice. It forbids the State, as we have seen, to concern itself about the poor, and yet the Poor law of Elizabeth (still in force in Great Britain and our country) confers upon every man a *legal* claim to relief from funds obtained by enforcing a contribution from the general community. It forbids the State to concern itself about schools, libraries, universities, asylums and hospitals, and yet it concerns itself more and more with them. England is to this day proud of having spent a hundred million of dollars in abolishing slavery in her colonies, and in these latter days she is spreading her activity over railroads and telegraphs, without the least apparent compunction of conscience. And our country, (especially under democratic control the champion of this "let alone" abomination) finds today her chief glory in having torn slavery up by the roots with its strong national arm.

But let it, in the *third* place, be emphatically understood, that when we insist that the State ought to extend its sphere over all social activities, we do not mean the *present* State at all.

Our Republic is a State. Parliamentary Great Britain is a State. Imperial Germany, autocratic Russia and bureaucratic China are all social organisms. But not one of them is a *full grown* State, a fully developed organism. In all of them, our own country included, CLASSES *exercise the authority* and direct all social activity.

Do not here bring forward the insipid commonplace that, properly speaking, we have no "classes" in our country and that the "people" govern here! No classes? Indeed!

Roam around in New York, Boston, Philadelphia or any of our towns above a country-village, for that matter, and you will find them all mapped out into districts strictly according to the poverty or wealth of the inhabitants. Those who live in the poorer districts along neglected dirty streets in badly arranged and badly furnished houses constitute a lower *caste* in fact, since nine-tenths of them cannot *by any possibility*, under our Social system, get out of it. They and their children after them *must* remain in their poverty, squalor and degradation as long as this system endures. In the healthy, beautiful and comfortable quarters we find those who arrogate to themselves the name of "Society," our "best people," "prominent citizens."

Which of these two classes govern — the majority living in tene-ment-houses, back-alleys and ill-smelling neighborhoods or the mi-nority in the aristocratic districts?

It is frequently remarked that "our best people" have withdrawn themselves from politics. Suppose that is so — though it is also noticed that men of wealth lately have secured seats in Congress to such an extent that our national Senate, to a great extent, consists of very rich people — still that is very little to the point. For, since the State is the organized Society, "politics" constitute but a trifle of the social activities, compared with the various forms of industry. We have seen that it is our "prominent citizens" who control our manu-factures, transportation and commerce, who indeed exercise an *auto-cratic* control over these, and that they are destined to do the like in agriculture within a short time. Their control over the transporting interests of the country, — interests so dominant that it has been justly said: "He who controls the highways of a Nation, controls the Nation itself" — is indeed so supreme that Vanderbilt is reported to have observed with refreshing candor: The roads are not run for the benefit of "the dear public." No matter, whether he has been so candid or not, they certainly are not.

Politics then form but a very small part of our social activities. The people are said to govern these; their "government," in fact, consists in choosing on election day between two sets of men pre-sented for their suffrages. What that amounts to we shall see in another chapter, and shall here simply remark, that as soon as the one or the other set of men have been elected they pass entirely out of the control of the voters. Who then control the actions of those thus chosen?

We shall entirely pass by the ever-recurring charges of bribery of legislators and whole legislatures; we shall pass by another reported candid admission by Vanderbilt: "When I want to buy up any politician I always find — the most purchasable;" we shall pass by the solemn declaration of a committee of the legislature of the State of New York, that no bill could pass the Senate without Vander-bilt's consent. We let all these things pass as perhaps *non proven*.

But one thing is so evident that no one will dream of disputing it, as soon as its meaning is fairly understood: these *autocrats* of our industrial affairs *dictate the policy of the government* to legislatures and Congress, to presidents, governors and judges, and have dictated it since the establishment of our government. What we mean is simply what we have all along insisted upon, that both our national and local governments throughout profess allegiance to the "let alone" policy; that all executive, legislative and judicial officers are trained from the day they enter school or college to look on public affairs through capitalistic spectacles. We simply mean to say that not one so-called statesman of any influence in either of the two great political parties ever dreams of interfering with the "business"—interests of our plutocrats, if he can help it. They all echo the sentiment of Judge Foraker, the Republican candidate for governor of Ohio: *"Capital is sensitive; it shrinks from the very appearance of danger."*

What need then for them "to go into politics" when they already have their devoted retainers in every place of authority?

They need have no fear ever to be interfered with as long as they retain their preeminent position in industrial affairs. The ruling class industrially will always be the ruling class politically.

Therefore we say it is Utopian to hope to have a legal normal working day of eight hours, much more so one of six hours, as Moody proposes in his *Land and Labor*, as long as the Established Order lasts.

Therefore it is Utopian to hope to have land nationalized as George advocates, as long as we have the wage-system.

Therefore capitalists will very likely succeed in their strenuous opposition to the proposition made by a late Postmaster General, that the Nation shall take possession of the telegraphs of the country. But if they should at last be compelled to yield — because the necessities of the Social organism command it — they are sure to demand and receive extravagant compensation for their "property," for the "vested rights" of capitalists have always been appreciated, while as we already have noted the working-classes have never been thought entitled to compensation when new machinery drove them out of old employments.

While now our autocrats generally are satisfied, and well may be satisfied, with their *veto* on all proposed public measures, prejudicial to their sinister interests, and with interdicting all legislation in favor of the masses, they never have objected to any State-action that would put money into their pockets. They have been, and still are to a great extent, beneficiaries of the Nation, another proof that *they* really govern, even politically.

We all know that the National Government has presented six railroad companies with an empire of land as large as Great Britain and Ireland and half as much more, and in addition has guaranteed bonds of theirs, which with accrued interest at the maturity of these bonds will amount to more than 180 million dollars.

We have already seen, how the whole machinery of Government has been set and kept in motion to acquire foreign markets for our autocrats and to prepare our working-classes for the requisite reduction in wages, simply that this wage-system might secure a new lease of life, however short and precarious and however injurious the effect which this policy would have on the condition of the workers.

We see to-day, as our forefathers have often seen, how agitated the two great political parties of our country are on the questions of Free-Trade or Protection. This issue makes it so very plain how paramount the influence of our autocrats is in political affairs. It is our *manufacturers* who want protection; it is our *commercial* men who want free-trade. The former undoubtedly pretend, that protection benefits the laboring classes; but that this claim is a mere sham is evident from the fact that they never have proposed to discourage the immigration of foreign laborers; that they would violently oppose a proposal to that effect; that they, on the contrary, always have done all they could to encourage foreign laborers to come here, that they even send agents over to Europe to coax them by false pretences over here. Our protectionist fleecers want *protection for the results of Labor, but free-trade in Labor.* The commercial men, on the other hand, whose interest it is to have free-trade in all things, never have objected to handsome gifts from Government for their ships in the guise of subsidies for the performance of mail-services.

Class-rule is always detrimental to the welfare of the whole social organism, because classes, when in power, cannot help considering themselves pre-eminently the State. They, furthermore, cannot help being biased in favor of their special interests and therefore are necessarily hostile to the rest of the Nation, and as we daily see in our free-traders and protectionists, hostile to each other. Matthew

Arnold speaks truly when he says that State-action by a hostile class ought to be deprecated.

Our Republic, therefore, just as all other modern States, may properly be compared to some imaginable animal organism, where the blood, proceeding from the collective digestion, is principally diverted to the stomach or the brain, while the arms and legs are stinted as much as possible.

This *Class*-State will develop into a *Commonwealth* — bless the Puritans for that splendid English word! It will develop into a State that will know of no "classes" either in theory or practice; in other words into a State *where the whole population is incorporated into Society.* In the place of the present partially evolved organism in which the arms and legs, and to a great extent the brain, are stinted in blood as much as possible, we shall have an organism "whose every organ shall receive blood in proportion to the work it does" in the language of Spencer.

That is to say: *the Commonwealth will be a State of* EQUALITY.

It is said that "we already have equality," and when we ask the meaning of the phrase we are told that all are "equal before the law." If that were really the case — what it is not — it would be but a poor kind of equality. The cells of the root and of the flower in a plant are "equal;" the cells of the foot and of the heart in an animal are "equal," for they are all properly cared for; the organism knows of no "higher" and "lower" organs or cells. And so it will be in the future Commonwealth; there "Equality" will mean that every unit of Society can truly say to any other unit: "I am not less than a man, and thou art not more than a man."

Again, our Commonwealth will put *Interdependence* in the place of the phrases of our Declaration of Independence, which claims for every citizen the "right" to life, liberty and the pursuit of "happiness." This declaration was evidently adopted by "Individualists," as the French Revolution was a revolution of "Individualism," for of what use is it to possess the "right" to do something, when you have not the power, the means, the opportunity to do it? Is this "right to the pursuit of happiness" not a mocking irony to the masses who *cannot* pursue "happiness"? We saw how the millionaire and beggar would be equally miserable outside of the State, and behold, how much this Rights-of-Man doctrine has done for the former and how very little for the latter!

The future Commonwealth will *help* every individual to attain the highest development he or she has capacity for. It will lay a cover for every one at Nature's table. "State" and "State-*help*" will be as inseparable as a piano and music.

Do not now object, as *young* Spencer did in "Social Statics," that this means "transforming every citizen into a grown-up baby;" for the objection is not to the point at all.

State-help is not to do away with a man's own efforts. I do not do away with a man's own efforts, when I hand him a ladder. I do not set aside his own exertions in cultivating a field, because I give him a plow. Our State does not render useless the powers of a boy, when it furnishes him schools, teachers and libraries. Our Commonwealth will relieve none of self-help, but make self-help possible to all. *It will help everybody to help himself.*

That is to say: this Commonwealth will be a Society all of whose units have a sense of belonging together, of being responsible for one another; a Society, pervaded by a feeling of what we, using a foreign word, call *Solidarity,* but what we not inaptly may in English term Corporate Responsibility.

It is worth noting that our modern Insurance companies, particularly those of Life-Insurance, are teaching us that responsibility, for do they not make the strong and temperate of us use their prolonged lives to pay up premiums which go to the progeny of the weak and reckless?

"But what about *Liberty?*" the reader may ask.

Many worthy persons, as we said commencing this chapter, entertain the fear which shines forth in Mill's famous essay on "Liberty;" the fear lest freedom should be drilled and disciplined out of human life, in order that the great mill of the Commonwealth should grind smoothly. To ascertain whether this fear is well grounded or not we must first know, what we are to understand by the words: "Freedom" and "Liberty."

Everybody calls the not being oppressed: "Liberty." That is, undoubtedly, an indispensable and yet, as has been said, a most insignificant fractional part of human freedom. Then, again, we mean by "Liberty" the not being restrained, being "at Liberty" to do this or that. Now, that may be a good thing or otherwise. Whether it is the one or the other depends entirely upon the answer to the question: to do *what?*

To be "at liberty" to be a tramp or to die of starvation, or to steal, or to be lodged in a jail are not good things. We sometimes find a great lout in a railroad car who thinks he is "at liberty" to spread himself over four seats, but occasionally he finds out, that he is not; that he must take his feet down and sit along. The liberty of this lout is the "liberty" which our shrewd, grasping, vulgar autocrats glorify, for it means the predominance of their interests over everybody else's interests, over the General Welfare. It is in the name of that "liberty" that all fleecing is done.

Of that kind of liberty there always has been too much in the world — somewhere. That kind of liberty means slavery to somebody; means as the Yankee defined it "to do what he liked and make everybody else."

Every struggle for real liberty has been a struggle against that sort of "Liberty," entrenched in classes. Progress demands the curbing of that kind of "liberty," and our Commonwealth will use no gloves in handling it.

The fact is, there is a radical difference between liberty to do the right thing and liberty to do the wrong thing. That is why young Spencer could not draw any sound conclusion from his so-called "principle:" "that every man has freedom to do all that he wills provided he does not infringe on the like freedom of any other man," because no one can do any wrong act, without doing harm to other men; or as Professor Huxley puts it: "The higher the state of civilization, the more completely do the actions of one member of the social body influence all the rest, and the less possible is it for one man to do a wrong thing without interfering, more or less, with the freedom of all his fellow-citizens."

As Liberty is such a hazy term, why use it at all, when we have such a glorious word in the English language as *Freedom?* There is the same difference between "Liberty" and "Freedom" as between "Right" and "Might," between "Fiction" and "Fact," between "Shadow" and "Substance."

"Freedom" is something substantial. A man who is ignorant is not free. A man who is a tramp is not free. A man who sees his wife and children starving is not free. A man who must toil twelve hours a day, in order to vegetate, is not free. A man who is full of cares is not free. A wage-worker, whether laborer or clerk, who every day for certain hours must be at the beck and call of a "master" is not free. As Shelley says in the Apostrophe to Freedom.

"For the laborer thou art bread."

Right so far. But Freedom is not alone bread, but leisure, absence of cares, self-determination, ability and means to do the right thing. Restraint very often is just requisite to develop that ability; indeed, Restraint is the very life of Freedom.

Freedom is something the individual unaided can never achieve. He is as drift-wood in a flood. It is something to be conferred on him by a well organized body politic.

Now certain people have altogether too much "liberty." Our Commonwealth will evolve that priceless good: FREEDOM.

This is by no means a finished Humanity, but there is a constant unfolding, a steady advance towards completeness and perfection. True, this or that Nation may decay, but some other Nation then comes to the rescue. All that Socialists undertake to do is to ascertain the several stages so far reached by Humanity on its onward march, therefrom to infer the next advance that will be made by some one of the social organisms in the van of progress, and then they reverently propose to help Humanity in taking the next step. They full well know that all that individuals can do is to aid or check that onward movement, but that to stop it is even beyond a Czar's control.

We have observed that it is round the working-classes that the battle of progress has been waged; their condition has determined the stage of civilization, though history has given but scant account of them. During the two great periods that lie behind us: Slavery and Serfdom, they were in fact and in law subject to their lords who took the lion's share without disguise, as a matter of right. Based on that subjection, however, there was an intense feeling of *Unity* which pervaded the whole of Society; a Unity that made these systems so strong and so lasting, and without which Unity no social system can be enduring. But men rebelled against the subjection. Luther was fortunate enough to start that rebellion in the religious sphere, for it is always at the top that all radical changes commence.

Then was inaugurated the era in which we are living, which really is nothing but a *transition period* between the two great systems of the past and another great system of the future, *for it possesses no unity*. It corresponds exactly to the transition-period between Slavery and Serfdom, when Christianity was striving for mastery. It is an era of anarchy, of criticism, of negations, of opposition, of hypocrisy, as this was one. Instead of Slavery or Serfdom and *Subjection* we now have the wage-system and *contracts.* That is to say, while formerly the lords appropriated the results of labor openly, they now do it underhandedly. The wage-worker, if he will live, must *agree* to relinquish one-half of what he produces. There is, in fact, fully as much subjection now as formerly, but it has taken on a softer, a more hypocritic form. That is why the rebellion not only continues, but has reached down into the material sphere and is shaking the very foundation of Society. It will not cease before all slavish subjection is done away with.

Then this "Individualism," this re-action against unquestioned submission, will find its compensation in *another Unity.* Everybody will again feel a dread of living for himself only. We shall have *Corporate Responsibility, Equality, Freedom,* all three combined in INTER-DEPENDENCE, SOCIAL COOPERATION. It is with the Social organism as with a harmoniously developed man, who has three stages of growth: implicit obedience, then restless self-assertion, at last intelligent, loyal cooperation with what has a rightful claim to his allegiance.

This Inter-dependence will find its practical expression in THE COOPERATIVE COMMONWEALTH, which in the following chapter will be seen to be *now* expedient, *for the first time in human history.*

CHAPTER V

EXPEDIENCY OF THE COOPERATIVE COMMONWEALTH

"The relations of structures are actually such, that, by the help of a central regulative system, each organ is supplied with blood in proportion to the work it does." — *Herbert Spencer.*

"No thinking man will controvert, that associated industry is the most powerful agent of production, and that the principle of association is susceptible of further and beneficial development." — *J. S. Mill.*

"All human interests, combined human endeavors and social growths in this world, have at a certain stage of their development required organizing; and work, the grandest of human interests, does now require it." — *Carlyle.*

We now have reached our objective point: the Cooperative Commonwealth.

The previous chapters were mere stepping-stones, leading us to where we are, but as such indispensable, for it is their reasoning, rather than its own reasonableness, which will determine whether the Socialist System is to be, like Thomas More's imaginary island, a "Utopia:" an *un-reality*, or not.

The observation in our Declaration of Independence "that mankind are more disposed to suffer while evils are sufferable than to right themselves by abolishing the forms to which they are accustomed" is true of changes in forms of government, but much more true of alterations in the structure of Society. To these, in fact, Nations must be *driven* by an inward necessity.

For this reason we had to show that the present chaotic system, with all instruments of Labor in private hands, will soon become unbearable and renders a change of some kind inevitably impending. For this reason, further, we had to point out the significance of the recent factory and educational legislation and State-action in regard to railroads and telegraphs, accomplished or proposed in our country and Great Britain, and to show that this extension of the State's activity was a sign that Society is approaching a crisis in its development; an indication that this transitory state in which we are living, after having lasted about as long as that other transitory state between Paganism and Christianity, is on the point of crystallizing into another enduring Social Order.

These reflections will make it clear — and we cannot lay too much stress upon it — that Modern Socialists do not pretend to be *architects* of the New Order. That is to say; they do not propose to demolish the present order of things, as we tear down an old building, and then compel humanity to rear a new edifice according to any plan that they have drawn. They have no such absurd idea, just because they know that Society is *not* an edifice at all, but an organism; and men are not in the habit of "planning" the development of a dog or a rosebush.

Right here is the radical distinction between us, Socialists of the German school, and such Socialists as St. Simon and Fourier. These had the same faults to find with the present social order as we have; they were, indeed, capital critics, but as reformers they were miserable failures simply because they wanted to be architects — inventors. They entirely ignored all social and political conditions and wanted mankind to don their ready-made systems as men do ready-made clothes. Fourier fancied that he had only to publish his system and all classes of Frenchmen would eagerly embrace it and in the twinkling of an eye transform all France into "phalansteries." St. Simon went even to the length of having his first scheme patented.

They and all the old-style socialists represent the childhood of our movement, stand in the same relation to it as astrology and alchemy do to physical science. All great changes that have taken place in the world have had to pass through a "Utopian" phase. These primitive Socialists were true "Utopists:" they invented Systems; we are intent on discovering the laws of development. They framed universal precepts; we ascertain universal sequences.

For what is "the Cooperative Commonwealth"?

Extend in your mind Division of Labor and all the other factors that increase the productivity of Labor; apply them to *all* human pursuits as far as can be; imagine manufactures, transportation and commerce conducted on the grandest possible scale, and in the most effective manner; then add to Division of Labor its *comple-ment:* CONCERT; introduce *adjustment* everywhere where now there is anarchy; add that *central regulative system* which Spencer says distinguishes all highly organized structures, and which supplies "each organ with blood in proportion to the work it does" and — behold the COOPERATIVE COMMONWEALTH!

The Cooperative Commonwealth, then, is that future Social Order — the natural heir of the present one — in which all important instruments of production have been taken under collective control; in which the citizens are consciously public functionaries, and in which their labors are rewarded according to results.

A definition is an argument.

It shows that our critics, when they style Socialism a Utopia, do not know about what they are talking. We can imagine a caterpillar, more knowing than its fellows, predicting to another that some day they both will be butterflies, and the other sneeringly replying: "What Utopian nonsense you are talking there!" Our censors are just as ignorant of the groundwork of Socialism. For our definition makes it evident that the Cooperative Commonwealth is not to be regarded as a product of personal conceit, but as *an historical product,* as a product in which our whole people are unconscious partakers. When the times are ripe for Social Co-operation, it will be just as expedient, as Feudalism was, or as Private Enterprise was, when each, respectively, made its appearance. It will prove its right to control by virtue of its own superior fitness.

Or is there anything Utopian in predicting that Division of Labor will go on increasing? Has not wholesale production already vindicated its right to be the ruling system, and is it Utopian to assert that Private Ownership of Capital, so far from being necessary to production in wholesale, will prove a greater and greater obstruction to its inevitable development? Is it Utopian to expect that all enterprises will become more and more centralized, until in the fulness of time they all end in *one* monopoly, that of Society? Are not, indeed, *Anti*-monopolists — as far as they believe that they can crush the big establishments or even prevent their growth — the real Utopists?

But that is by no means all. We have not yet sufficiently emphasized the *central* fact of Society of *to-day*. Not alone is the necessity
which we claim will drive the nations into Socialism steadily growing, *but all civilized Societies are being driven into Socialism under
our very eyes* — if we may apply the word "driven" to an inward
impulse. Not alone are the conditions for the establishment of the
New Order fast ripening, but the New Order is amongst us and
asserting itself vigorously. Not only is the social organism growing
from the circumference by Society multiplying and subdividing its
activities and again concentrating them, but the central regulative
system *has* silently put in an appearance and *is* irresistibly organizing one social activity after another. This is a *fact,* of *transcendent
significance;* and yet our politicians, the gentlemen of our "editorial
staffs," our would-be-wise leaders and statesmen, all, indeed, except
Socialists, seem not to have the smallest inkling of it. They all look
upon the factory legislation across the ocean and here and the
agitation for nationalization of the land and national control of the
telegraphs as isolated, rash expedients, and those who have adopted
the accepted theories forthwith condemn this legislation and agitation and loudly proclaim that Society — is going astray!

But the fact is, that our modern civilization mainly consists in this
that the State — that is, Society in its organized form — has of late
been constantly expanding its jurisdiction, and has more and more
contracted the sphere of individual ownership and control. Why,
nearly everything the State now manages for us, was once entrusted
to private individuals.

Consider, criminal jurisprudence was once in private hands, and
was the first in time to be taken in charge by the State. There was a
time when the customs and national finances were farmed out to
private persons, but that time is long passed by. Then the State
turned its attention to postal affairs, and they are now everywhere
under national control. The world has entirely forgotten that these
affairs once were private enterprises, simply because the State has
managed them so much better than was formerly done. The whole
struggle between State and Church is also here in point; the principal consequence of that struggle has been that nearly all civilized
States have taken charge of education, which undoubtedly will also
soon in our country be a matter of national concern. There are still
other matters, in which the older States of Europe in this develop-

ment are ahead of us: national control of railroads and telegraphs. And in proposing that the State shall insure workingmen against accidents and against want in their old age, Bismarck is virtually impelled by the same spirit, rather than by any concern for the welfare of the working-classes.

This fact of "the centralization of Power in the National Government," as it is called, is the central fact of Society everywhere *now*. You may deny everything else, but you cannot deny that. You cannot look at a democratic paper without seeing a lament over the fact. The Democrats, though, are giving undue credit to the Republicans in charging it to their account, for they were but humble instruments in the hands of the laws of the Universe; if the Democrats should come into power, they would have to be "centralizers" to the same extent. The social organism has once for all got the impetus in that direction, and the movement is gathering greater momentum. That is why it is now everywhere in the air. That is why this fact is *the true rationale of Socialism.*

The cry: "Beware, it is *Socialistic!*" will have absolutely no effect. The State will go on expanding its jurisdiction, hurry on to its destiny, without asking or caring if it is "Socialistic." The workingmen and grangers will continue to importune the State to come to their relief, without knowing anything about Socialism. Henry George has written a book that has enticed very many persons very far out on the road to Socialism, protesting all the time that he is not a Socialist. Frederic Harrison abominates Socialism, and yet preaches "Look to the State! From *that* you can expect the highest experience and skill, publicity, concentration of power, real and efficient control, a national aim and spirit and far more true responsibility."

But it is evident that the process of placing all industries and all instruments of labor under collective control will be carried on with far more energy and directness, when once the true leaders learn that the State is not some power outside of the people, but that it is the social organism itself, and that, as an organism, it is destined to grow until it embraces all social activities. Hitherto the State has acted from impulse, in opposition to accepted theories. But a logical foundation of some sort is necessary to all great movements. Rousseau's theory of a "Social Contract," though false, did in that way a great service to Humanity.

The New Social Order to which we look forward is thus, certainly, the very reverse of Utopian. As a historical product from every point of view we consider it, it will be a *natural* product, hence RATIONAL. "Whatever is, is rational" Hegel said; that is, it necessarily conforms to the innermost nature of things; and so: whatever is to be is rational. As soon as the people learn not to be scared by the word "Socialism;" as soon as they learn the true nature of the State and see whither they are drifting, the Cooperative Commonwealth will be the only *expedient* system. But it certainly was not expedient when Plato wrote his *Republic*; it was not expedient, but it *was* a "Utopia" in the times of Thomas More; it was not expedient when St. Simon "invented" his system, for Private Enterprise with the steam engine and other inventions had first to increase the productive capacity of man a thousand times, and thus to prepare the way for it. And when it becomes expedient, it will be so for the first time in human history.

When the Cooperative Commonwealth becomes an accomplished fact we shall have the full-grown Society; the *normal* State. That commonwealth — whose citizens will, *consciously* and avowedly be public functionaries — will not know of a particle of distinction between the terms "State" and "Society;" the two ideas will come to cover each other, will become synonymous. It will be a social order that will endure as long as Society itself, for no higher evolution is thinkable, except Organized Humanity, and that is but Social-Co-operation extended to the whole human race. It will effect a complete regeneration of Society: in its economic, politic and juridic relations; in the condition of women and in the education of youth (indeed its chief concern, its true starting point;) in morals and, we may add, in religion and philosophy. The remainder of this treatise will draw in barest outline this normal State in these various relations, in the order above named, for the economic features are the foundation of every social system, out of which grow all the others, morals and religion last of all. It is, as we once observed, at the top: in morals and philosophy, that all changes from one Social Order to another commence, from whence they insinuate themselves down to the material conditions; *there the change of base takes place* and the new superstructure is then gradually built up. Therefore, also, we defined our system in economic terms alone.

If now Social-Cooperation is that to which we are certainly drifting, it is undeniably the wiser course, instead of calling it names, to inquire if not that which is "socialistic" may also be good, and to try to find out the character of that New *Regime*. We shall therefore here suggest the most notable respects in which its *economic* features are likely to promote the social welfare.

It must be evident to every fair-minded man that this New Order — where every worker will be remunerated according to *results* — is in no sense *communistic*. Socialism and Communism are, in fact, two radically different systems; and yet they are constantly confounded, even by well-informed people. We wish we could in a serious work like this entirely ignore the vulgar conception of Communism: that it proposes "to divide all property into equal parts," but when a man like Prof. Fawcett of England gives currency to this vulgarism in these very words and then proceeds to lecture us, saying: "if the State divided all lands among the inhabitants, there would gradually arise the same inequality of wealth which exists now," we must notice it sufficiently to say that now-a-days no one outside of a lunatic asylum proposes any such thing, and that Prof. Fawcett ought to know it.

The Communism we refer to is that practised by the Shakers and similar bodies, bound together by some form of religious belief or unbelief. Their peculiar method of giving practical effect to their doctrines is different from ours; we believe that to retire from the world, as they do, is a poor way of reforming the world; we believe it is with reformers as with yeast: it must be mixed with the dough to act upon it; if kept to itself, it spoils. But their *principles* — in which they agree with political communists — are diametrically opposed to ours. Communists make *all* property common property, while our Commonwealth will place only the *instruments* of *production* — land, machinery, raw-materials &c. — under collective control. They require every one to do his share of labor, and allow him to consume as he needs. Our Commonwealth leaves everybody at perfect liberty to work as much or as little as he pleases, or not at all, but makes his consumption exactly commensurate with his performances. Adam Smith observed that "the produce of labor is the natural recompense of Labor" and St. Paul laid it down: "whoever does not work, neither shall he eat" and the New System — as our definition points out — will put these doctrines into practice.

In short, the motto of Socialism is: "Everybody according to his *deeds;*" that of Communism is: "Everybody according to his *needs.*" The communist motto is undoubtedly a very generous one, more generous than ours; but our motto is more just, taking human nature as it is, — and the fact that Socialists take human nature as it is, is just their merit. Indeed, if we define Capitalism as the fleecing of the weak by the strong, Communism might be said to be a fleecing of the strong by the weak, an observation already made by Proudhon; though the "strong" under our system simply means those buoyed up to the top, while under the latter system they would mean the truly, physically or intellectually, strong.

Communism must therefore plead guilty to the charges: first, that it means to abolish the institution of property and, next, that it must result in crushing out all individuality. Socialism not only will do neither of these things but the *very reverse.* Instead of taking property away from everybody, *it will enable everybody to acquire property.* It will truly sanctify the institution of individual ownership by placing property on an unimpeachable basis: that of being *the result of one's individual exertions.* Thereby it will afford the very mightiest stimulus for individuality to unfold itself. Property will belong to its possessor by the strongest of all titles, to be enjoyed as he thinks proper, *but not to be used as an instrument of fleecing his fellow-citizens.*

Next let us pass in review one of the chief industries after another and note the most obvious advantages that will flow from Social Cooperation. But especially here will our motto apply: that "our purpose is not to make people read but to make them think." For the experience of our readers will naturally supply them with innumerable other cases in point.

Take, first, *manufactures.*

Suppose there are at present in a given city a hundred black-smiths, who together employ four hundred men. The hundred bosses spend necessarily a great deal of their time in seeking jobs. In this pursuit they are constantly thwarting each other's purposes, and trying to beat each other. When in their shops, they have directions to give, estimates to prepare, letters to write and bills to make out. They all perform a laborious and necessary work, and yet the productive result of their work is very insignificant.

Again, these hundred employers have a hundred different shops, a hundred different fire-places, which take up very much space and use up very much fuel. The money spent in renting these shops, in constructing these fireplaces and bellows and for the fuel which is thus wasted, would be sufficient to build a most magnificent cooperative factory in which these bosses and wage-workers might, as cooperative workers, find steady and remunerative employment.

Again, in these hundred shops there are a number of tools and machines that might be reduced immensely, if these five hundred blacksmiths worked in common; while, on the other hand, a good many machines and implements could be introduced into such a cooperative factory which at present even the richest of those employers is not able, or at least not willing to procure, because even his business is not large enough to warrant the outlay.

Add to this that very seldom a man is a good artisan and a good man of business, and it will be evident from this example, that if all manufacturing enterprises were concentrated to the same extent that we might imagine this smithing business concentrated, the dispensing with much useless, and therefore unproductive work, the reduction in operative expenses and especially the most fruitful division of Labor which could be inaugurated would immensely enrich Society. Every large factory which arises on the ruin of the shops of the small artisans we consider an advance in civilization, simply because the more production is being organized on a large scale, the easier it will be for the associated workers, by the authority of the Cooperative Commonwealth, to take charge of it, and secure to themselves the utmost benefit of inventions, machinery and division of employments.

Further: At present our hundred bosses are frequently in financial embarrassment; but few of them accumulate a competence for their old age; many succumb to competition and crises, while their workmen are nothing but wage-slaves, having violent periods of overwork, followed by long and terrible stagnation. The working in concert under the Cooperative Commonwealth will reduce all risk, all crises, all production beyond the effective demand, to a minimum.

Peter and Paul run risks, because the cannibals John and James stand ready to eat them up at a given opportunity. But the whole production of a country in any given branch need run hardly any risk at all. Do away with the secrecy which now obtains in our manufacturing establishments, shut up those gambling shops: the stock and produce-exchanges; let scientific statistics be taken of the demand and supply in all parts of the country, and elsewhere if practicable; in other words: introduce *systematic* work instead of *planless* work, and crises and "overproduction" will be next to impossible. Whatever losses may occur from inaccuracies in statistics or unavoidable mishaps will be almost inappreciable, being borne by the whole country. Thus, our Commonwealth will be what a Commonwealth ought to be: the General Insurance Company; but of that more hereafter.

The advantages of the Commonwealth being *the sole Merchant* are evident: they will be all that our grangers and voluntary co-operationists are in the habit of expecting from their schemes and not include one of the disadvantages, which, in a previous chapter, we saw necessarily resulting from these. Under our Commonwealth the small shopkeepers, pedlers, commission-merchants and all of that sort will disappear. No more need for bribing newspapers for puffs; no longer any temptation to use lying labels or sell adulterated goods. A bale of cotton will not as now have to be sold ten times over to get from the producer into the hands of the consumer; nor will the people of Philadelphia be bled to the extent of $6.50 for a ton of coal which only costs, all expenses and outlays included, $1.50 at the mouth of the mine. Nevermore shall we find twenty drugstores in a little town that only needs one.

No, indeed! In place of that we shall have great permanent bazaars, embracing all possible articles of consumption, of which stores like that of Jordan Marsh & Co., in Boston, or still better the one, once mentioned, in Philadelphia are only insignificant miniature models — but thanks to their chiefs for furnishing us those models!

The salesmen and saleswomen in those bazaars will be quite different beings from those of the present day, who are very often slaves from morning till late at night. They will, like all other citizens, be independent human beings, with plenty of leisure at their command.

The greatest gain to Society, however, in taking control of commerce, will perhaps be found in the suppression of that talent, so peculiar to our Plutocrats and seemingly acquired by them with their mother's milk: the faculty of speculation; a talent which contributes nothing to production, but whose only end and aim is the transfer of wealth from one pocket into another. Nearly all workers are devoid of that talent. The New Regime will, like the Man of the New Testament, lash the howling lunatics, the brokers and cornerers, out of our stock and other exchanges, which will be devoted to nobler uses; for Cooperation and Speculation are strangers.

"Trade" — as far as it means the buying and selling of goods for the sake of *profit* — will at home be changed into distribution of the produce of labor among the workers, and as to foreign countries into genuine *commerce i.e.* the exchange of such home-products we do not need for such foreign products we may need.

These changes in manufactures and Commerce will naturally affect *Transportation* in a remarkable degree. While now our mails, railroads, ships and wagons do business for innumerable private concerns, in the New Commonwealth they will do business for *one,* only. What a colossal concentration and simplification of Transportation does that, in itself, imply! Bear in mind simply the mass of drays and wagons of every sort, which now in every one of our populous cities choke up our streets and distract most people's nerves! Think of the amount of human and animal labor now absolutely wasted in this way! It might, indeed, be difficult for those now living to recognize the aspect of our cities, to be brought about by this simplification, alone, under the new order of things. Even *New York* may thereby become a clean city.

Transportation itself, of course, will be taken under collective control, and thus the radical wrong undone of granting public concessions to individuals for the express purpose of making our highways subservient to private interests. For what are now our railway corporations but a clique of persons empowered by law to use these highways, in the *first place,* for their *own benefit,* and only incidentally for the public convenience?

It is just as easy to demonstrate the vast superiority of *social-cooperative farming* over the present style.

The prevailing isolated mode of Agriculture wastes an immense amount of human and animal labor, of time and of materials. What an economy would there not be in having one large stable, one large yard, one large barn, in the place of one hundred stables, yards and barns? Any one can estimate for himself what an enormous sum of money could be saved in one single item, when he learns that the fences of Indiana alone, if extended in a single line, would go around the globe nearly 14 times, and cost no less than $200,000,000. How many wagons and horses will not be rendered superfluous, when the Cooperative Commonwealth takes charge of Agriculture? How many persons will not be made available for manufacturing and other productive pursuits? And as to time, these words of Professor Fawcett are suggestive: "It has been calculated, that a steam-cultivator would plough a square field of ten acres in half the time, occupied in ploughing two fields of five acres each, and with two-thirds the expense."

But why waste any words in abstract demonstration? Do not our "bonanza farms" teach us practically the lesson? And will not the hundreds of "bonanza farms" of the near future, eventually knock the lesson even into the heads of our country-cousins? Do they not already practically demonstrate, that there are a hundred things requisite for thorough farming, that only can be had by cultivation on a grand scale? Do not the "creameries" that everywhere are springing up show that butter and cheese can be made much better and more cheaply in one dairy than on a hundred farms?

Our farmers cannot help finding out by and by, that social-cooperative farming will prove to them an immense benefit, simply in a *financial* point of view.

It is certainly easy to comprehend that association, in Mill's words, "is the most powerful agent of production" — few words ought to suffice to prove that. It ought, indeed, to be easy to see, that Social Cooperation will increase the total production of our country at least as much beyond the capability of the present system as the latter surpasses that of the Middle Ages in proportion to population. This it will do by adding, simply, Concert; by inoculating into the Social Organism that central regulative system which Spencer finds in all other high organisms, but of which he apparently sees no need in the Social Organism, the highest of all. For this Concert, this Regulative System, will reduce immensely all operative expenses, in Manufactures, in Exchange, in Transportation, in Agriculture; it will prevent waste; it will do away with nearly all risk; and, lastly, it will permit, the most advantageous Division of Labor.

He is said to be one of the greatest benefactors of mankind who makes two blades of grass grow where one grew before. What then is to be said of the men who are determined to develop society, as quickly as possible, up to the adoption of a system of production, demanded by the conditions of the age, and which will increase, to an unprecedented degree, the net results of all our industries, and evidently lead to innumerable technical improvements in all their branches?

This fructification of Labor, will on the first view readily make Social Cooperation appear highly desirable. But the objection, that this increase of the means of subsistence and enjoyment really means a far greater "overproduction" than has yet confronted us, lies very near. It is precisely the principal excellence of the Cooperative Commonwealth that it will create an *effective* demand for even the greatest imaginable production.

We said in the preceding chapter that the full-grown State will *help* every one of its citizens *to help himself.* That, first of all, means that it will furnish employment, *productive* employment, and such employment as they, respectively, may be best fitted for to all citizens; thus enabling them to pay for anything they may want or wish for — which is what is meant by "effective" demand.

After what we already have remarked in regard to "natural rights," it cannot be supposed that we lay any stress on the socalled natural "right to Labor." And yet more can be said in favor of that claim than for any other "natural right." Of course "right to labor" is a very inapt phrase; nobody really complains of not being sufficiently burdened with toil. But all know well enough that it is meant to assert a claim to a decent livelihood, to be gained by profitable Labor. Now, if it be once admitted, what even Herbert Spencer affirms, that land is the common heritage of all, then there is very great force in the argument of such philosophers as Fichte and Considerant that "those who are not proprietors of land must, *as a compensation for the common property which they have lost,* be guaranteed the right to labor." And communities have, as a matter of fact, recognized the force of that claim. The Poor-law of England is a recognition of it. And, though it seems unknown to even professional lawyers, a Pennsylvania Statute provides as follows: "If such poor person be able to work, but cannot find employment, it shall be the duty of the overseers *to provide work for him*

according to his ability, and for this purpose they shall procure
suitable places and a suitable stock of materials."

But it should be distinctly understood that we do not think the
Coming Commonwealth will base its action on this ground, but on
quite another.

Malthus says bluntly, in his "Essay on Population," that the man
born into the world whose family cannot support him and whose
labor is not in demand must take himself away. "For him there is no
cover laid at nature's table."

Now we affirm that in our Commonwealth *there will be a demand for the labor* of *every citizen.* This is a proposition that every
one on a little reflection will assent to.

Mark! we speak of *productive* labor, and mean thereby labor that
creates anything which men desire. This desire is absolutely unlimited. The desire for certain staple articles of food or for this or that
manufactured article or for a given means of enjoyment may be
limited, but the desire for the products of human labor and skill *in
general,* physical, artistic or intellectual—*never.*

The desire for — that is, the power of — consumption in the
body of the citizens is thus boundless. And they will have the
means to pay for all there is to consume. Under the New Order all
will be productive workers; they will be paid an equivalent for
what they produce — not merely one half of it as now under the
wage-system — in some form. Consequently their *purchasing power*
will in all cases balance the total production.

There *is* a demand for the labor of every man under any well-
ordered Social system. If there is a waste of men now, it is the fault
of the Wage-System. A slave was actually worth what he would
fetch, and there were very few slaves who would fetch nothing.
Why, in a free Commonwealth, should men be of less account?
Cattle are valuable; why not men? Carlyle remarks: "a white European man, standing on his two legs, with his two five-fingered
hands at his shackle bones and miraculous head on his shoulders, is
worth, I should say, from 50 to 100 horses."

By giving all the idle employment; by putting all our parasites
and superfluous workers where they can work productively, the
Commonwealth will create the needed effective demand, and more
than that: The stock of the good things of this life *will thereby be
very much enlarged,* perhaps doubled.

But do not believe, that when we say that the State will furnish all profitable employment, that we mean that every one will have to do manual labor. Labor undoubtedly will then come to honor; work will then be a beneficent law, and not an oppressive rule as now, but brain-work will have its due weight: the New Commonwealth will not be a state of mechanics. In all States that at present pretend to give its citizens educational facilities, it seems to be entirely overlooked that education and aspiration go hand in hand. Our country, in particular, which gives such of our young men and women who can afford to improve themselves free access to high-schools, colleges and universities, afterwards leaves them to scramble for a precarious existence, for which their very education has unfitted them; yet an educated pauper is the most pitiable subject of all. Our Commonwealth, on the other hand, will nourish the aspirations it has awakened; it will use for its own good the talents it has matured and enable every man and woman to develop his or her peculiar aptitudes, whether it be in brain-work or hand-work. This fact, that every citizen will be able to follow his or her peculiar bent, will also itself vastly increase the productive result of all social activities, for it is well-known that a person accomplishes most when he works in the line of his greatest inclination.

We may note here that the enlargement of the purchasing power of the masses will also contribute considerably to increase the wealth of Society by materially changing the *character* of the demand from what it is at present. That is to say: articles of use and beauty will more and more crowd out the costly goods, which at present are principally in demand because, and only because, they are costly and by that quality enable our money-aristocracy to display their wealth.

It has been computed that if everybody now worked at some useful calling, everybody could live in comfort on four hours' daily labor. There is some good reason for believing that this computation is not so very far from being correct. But who can doubt that in the Coming Commonwealth, with all objects of desire thus increased, the hours of Labor could be very much reduced, and yet everybody, willing to work have everything that heart could wish?

Why should anybody then object to being restrained from working more than six or four hours a day? That very many workingmen should object to such a check on their liberty *now*, when they often are reduced to absolute want by seasons of enforced idleness, is natural enough and may be noted as the immovable stumbling-block in the way of those who agitate for a compulsory eight-hour law under the present system.

In our Commonwealth all men and women can be endowed with that supreme good — *Leisure,* the mother of Culture. Observe, there is the greatest difference in the world between Leisure and Idleness. The idler, whether poor or rich, has no leisure, for it means the delightful hours reserved from some regular employment, of not too long duration, and which secures the satisfaction of all material wants.

Under the New Regime "Charity" and "charitable institutions" will be things of the past. By-the-way, is it not a pity that the noble word: "Charity" has in this hypocritical era come to mean — *alms-giving?* In our Commonwealth no alms will be given; indeed, *nothing will be had gratis.* Everybody will get the full produce of his labor in direct revenues or in public benefit. Every citizen will be *entitled* to the use of all public institutions: be it of libraries, of schools for his children, of hospitals, asylums, or assistance in his old age, on the same principle as the insured is entitled to the amount named in his policy, on the happening of a certain event. This makes it clear how our Commonwealth is to be the General Insurer; and our various companies that insure against so many forms of risk point out the right road to pursue. They, indeed, embody whatever of corporate responsibility there is left in this chaotic age.

We should therefore say that the Cooperative Commonwealth will be highly promotive of social welfare by securing to all its citizens abundance; by furnishing them leisure; and by enabling them to follow their natural bent. Work will no longer be a tribute to physical necessity but a glad performance of social office. It will for the first time in human history establish harmony between personal Egoism and the Public Welfare, by, simply, distributing the forces of the social organism in accordance with its real needs.

We make a distinction between the soil of cities and towns and agricultural lands. The former will have to be taken under collective control simultaneously with other Capital, while the nationalization of the latter, in a country like ours especially, may be postponed for years. That this change will prove highly beneficial to our city population is not difficult to see.

The greater a city is, the worse are the "homes" — as they are still by courtesy called — of the masses that inhabit it, mainly because the ruling class, the moneyed aristocracy, becomes the more exclusive. There was a time when this aristocracy formed one class with the masses: called in England the "Commons," in France the "Third Estate." For a long time after the settlement of our country we had only this *one* class. As long as this state of things continued, the chiefs of industry and commerce lived over their shops, near their offices among their people. Now they have deserted their posts of social duty. They live in separate districts, in the suburbs and only come into town to spend a few hours in their places of business on week-days. This modern fashionable suburbanism and exclusiveness *is a real grievance* of the working-classes. Had the rich men continued to live among the masses, they would with their wealth and influence have made our large towns pleasant places to live in, especially as they are almost the exclusive owners of the ground and buildings.

It is evident that when the Community assumes the ownership, all kinds of improvements can and will be carried on in a far grander and more systematic manner than now when many a measure, imperatively demanded even by the Public Good, is met and often checked by some opposing private interest. Then the many unsightly vacant lots in the very heart of cities will disappear. Then, and only then, we can hope for the introduction of such sanitary measures, both in dwellings and factories, as the present development of Public Hygiene recommends and as the aggregation of workers imperatively demands. Compare now the public institutions in any city: schools, asylums or even jails with the factories found in the same place and note the difference in the workings of corporate responsibility, on the one hand, and private greed and indifference, on the other. Every community owning the soil on which it lives, can be made responsible for the death of nearly every person who may fall a victim to the Yellow Fever or any other epidemic. For all the conditions of epidemic diseases, like foul air, stagnant pools, alleys filled with garbage, can be brought wholly within the control of an energetic administration, as General Butler conclusively proved in New Orleans.

But this subject leads up to another problem. The present relation of city to country is an abnormal one. Every civilized country, with its overgrown cities may fairly be compared to a man whose belly is steadily increasing in bulk, out of all proportion to the body, and whose legs are constantly growing thinner. This evolution is as yet perfectly legitimate. Our large cities and towns are the necessary fruits of our industrial system, and are destined to become the needed and inevitable centres for the coming changes; in their hands will chiefly lie the threads of destiny. But then their purpose will have been fulfilled. Then the evolution will necessarily have to go back in the contrary direction: population will have to take its march back into the country. It will become a life-problem.

Why do the sons of farmers now flock into our cities? Because their fathers and especially mothers lead a life of drudgery and privation that no mechanic in the city would wish to undergo; because they want to get rid of the prosy, stunting, isolated, barbarian life on a farm. The working masses stay in our overcrowded cities because such a farm-life has no attractions for them. They are not going to leave the cities before they can carry with them the civilization in which they have been reared; and well it is that they cannot be made to do it. Only our Commonwealth and collective control of all land can bring the pleasures and comforts of city life, the blessings of our civilization, into the country. This consideration, beside the financial one we already have suggested, may in time make our farmers see the beauties of Socialism.

But the nationalization of the land and Social-cooperative farming will not prove beneficial merely to the agricultural class and our surplus city-population, but also preeminently to Society at large. It may, indeed, in a short time, be imperative on Society to adopt it.

Our present mode of farming impoverishes the soil; "bonanza" farming does so to a still greater extent. Every bushel of wheat sent to our large cities or abroad, robs the soil of a certain amount of nutriment. And next to nothing, — in fact, on the bonanza-farms nothing at all, — is done to reimburse the soil for that loss. The object of the bonanza-farmers is simply to plunder the soil as much as possible in order to fill their own pockets. When it becomes no longer profitable to work the lands with even the most extensive machinery, they will be left mere deserts.

Manure is just as requisite for the soil as food is for a human being. Our large cities, constantly growing, are the especial consumers of the substance of the soil, without returning to it their refuse: this manure which is so all important to it. Evidently the result must be that our agricultural production will be paralyzed, if an end be not put to this system of plunder.

Nothing but Social Cooperation will put an end to it. Only that can institute a wise system of gathering and of distributing this invaluable refuse of men and animals. This is evidently a matter in which Society at large is vitally interested. And there are other measures, that only yield in importance to this matter of manure, which only Social Cooperation will know how to deal with properly: as a comprehensive system of drainage, without which land cannot be cultivated to its highest degree; and the preservation and culture of our forests, which even in our days call loudly for the interposition of national authority.

However, volumes would be requisite to give an adequate conception of all the benefits to be conferred by the Cooperative Commonwealth in detail, for as has been truly observed by the reputable German Political Economist, Prof. Schaeffle: *"it requires years to think one-self into it."*

But all this will not satisfy people who pride themselves on being *practical.* "Practical people are people whose knowledge is limited to what is going on under their eyes" — this is Buckle's definition, not ours. These nearsighted gentlemen will say: "Your Commonwealth may be ever so much in harmony with the conditions of this age; it may be able to create ever so great an abundance and even to furnish the most effective demand for it; it may be able to establish the most perfect social adjustment; yet it is *impracticable;* it cannot be made to work for many reasons."

Now, we are not here concerned about how to institute that New Order, — when the time is ready, when we reach that brink, a bridge will grow before our way, *somehow* — but it may be worth our while to notice some of these reasons.

"It is a stupendous scheme! That is enough to make it impracticable. It is an insane idea to propose to make fifty or a hundred million people work in concert."

Yes, the Philistines of the Middle Ages, likewise, undoubtedly would have scorned, as insane, the idea, that a city like London could possibly be provided with the necessaries of life under any system of *free competition*. And now, when it is daily done, our modern Philistines consider the fact as an evidence of "the beautiful harmony between private interests and public necessities." Yet it is a far greater wonder, that we get along under the present system as well as we do, than that our Commonwealth should work without the least friction. We have, indeed, every reason to expect, that it will be a Social Order, as regular and unobtrusive as if it were a Law of Nature.

"But how are you going to nationalize the land? How would you go to work to bring these innumerable private enterprises under collective control? Even Herbert Spencer, who, like you, condemns private ownership in land — in that very *Social Statics* that you criticized — sees no means of overcoming the difficulties in the way of making land collective property."

It would be easy enough. Suppose our national constitution were tomorrow amended to this effect:

"All titles in fee in private persons to any Real Estate are hereby abolished; all such titles shall henceforth vest in the United States, exclusively."

What then? Not anything like the overturning of existing relations which followed the abolition of slavery would be caused by such an amendment. *Not a single person* would need to be ousted from the premises he uses, still less from the dwelling he inhabits. The tenants of private parties would simply be turned into tenants of the Nation; the payments of the present proprietors to the community would be changed from "Taxes" into "Rents."

Undoubtedly in other respects the change would be tremendous. The occupants of lands and buildings could no longer sell them, no longer mortgage them, no longer rent them. Land as *Capital* and as source of Capital would evaporate into thin air like mist before the morning sun, but would remain as Social Wealth. It would lose its speculative, unreal value, but would retain its intrinsic, real value. Then an "enterprising" individual could no longer one day acquire a piece of land for twenty five cents an acre, and, without spending a day's work or one dollar for improvements on it, ten years thence dispose of it for ten or a hundred dollars an acre; this way of fleecing the community would be stopped. In short, Land held for speculative purposes would be dropped like a hot potato, to be sure, but occupants in good faith could use it precisely as they do now. The difficulties of such a measure would be reduced to absolutely nothing, if the amendment proposed, instead of taking effect at once, were made operative, say, twenty five years from the date of its adoption; for then values and relations would have ample time to settle themselves.

This is Henry George's "Remedy." Now, from the very moment when we read the title-page of George's book we did not think well of his being ready with a *remedy* at all. This fact shows that he considers Society sick and thinks it must have some medicine. Afterwards he seems to recoil from the drastic operation of his medicine, the confiscation of land — it might shock the preconceived notions of people — and proposes, instead of that heroic treatment, the confiscation of rent.

We admit that either of these two remedies would have two results, highly beneficial in themselves: the revenues of the community from land would be largely increased, and the vast sums, now squandered as purchase-money and rents for purely fictitious values, would be saved.

But after having shown our men-in-spectacles that it would be easy enough to nationalize the land, we must emphasize that to do so would be, especially in our country and in Germany and France, *commencing from the wrong end*. Society is not sick; but Society may be said to be suffering the pangs of child-birth. Now, to assist her deliverance by touching agricultural lands with the Socialist wand would be as inexpedient as to help a woman in travail by forcing the feet of the infant out first, and inexpedient *everywhere* — even in Great Britain where only a comparatively few owners would have to be expropriated — for the simple reason that the evolution in agriculture is everywhere far behind the evolution in all other industries. This objection, of course, would not apply to land used for manufacturing and mining purposes or to that of towns and cities, as we already have remarked. But the nationalization of such land should not be considered as a measure by itself, but as an adjunct to the taking our Manufactures, Distribution of products and Transportation under collective control.

What practical difficulties would there be in the way of doing that?

Why! If our "statesmen" were less blind to the Logic of Events, which is pushing us with railroad-speed toward a total and abrupt revolution, they might from to-morrow bring it about gradually and peaceably by a series of measures, each consistently developing itself out of the previous ones. They might begin from the two poles of Society at once.

See how! It is now proposed to take the Telegraph-system of our country under government control and incorporate it in our Postoffice-department. The latter *is* already essentially a Socialist institution, though to make it such fully, will require some important changes that we shall refer to in the following chapter. Suppose this measure realized as it is sure to be sometime. Then do likewise with our Railroads, our Express-business and thus onward: absorb one great enterprise after another, as quickly as practicable.

And so from the other pole. We now speak of those interests which so vitally affect the inhabitants of different communities, but which are confined to them. Why could not our cities commence by furnishing to their citizens fuel in winter and ice in summer? Are not these things just as essential to the Public Health as water? After that let them furnish all the milk needed. Then let them take under their control and operate their gas-works and horse-railways; their bakeries and drugstores. Yes, and let them take charge of the liquor-traffic, so that the number of saloons may be restricted to the wants of their respective populations and be conducted as the beer-selling cooperative stores of England — not the least beneficial of her many cooperative establishments — are conducted.

Now please observe, we do not say, — or even think — that the social question will be solved in that manner, but that it seems to us the most *practical* way in which to solve it for "practical" people. And mark further! that to carry out one or a few of these measures (as the nationalization of Land, or collective control of the Telegraph system, or communal control of the coal-business) and *then stop there*, will not solve the question at all. These measures, *standing alone*, will be almost worthless to the working-classes. They will benefit the small number employed in these enterprises; they may benefit all by the resulting public improvements, but they will not help the great body of the workers in any material respect, for to the same extent, that the price of their necessaries of life and rents may fall, their wages are sure to come down. That is the final answer to George's proposition. Even if he could possibly persuade the Social organism by his insinuating periods to swallow his medicine, she would not be a bit less restless than before. That child, the New Social Order, is going to be born.

"But whence will your Commonwealth take the money to indemnify the present owners?"

Oh! that matter of compensation will not worry us so very much. Socialists, indeed, claim, that it is Society, to whom our Plutocrats owe all their wealth, and that, therefore, Society has the right at any moment to take it back. Besides — a fact to which we already have once called attention — Society has *never* yet compensated the laboring classes when *their* interests have been sacrificed to the gain of their fellow-citizens and posterity, as they have repeatedly been during this century by the introduction of new machinery and the adoption of new inventions. But they are, also, ready to admit, that, if our Plutocrats are willing *peaceably* to give up their possessions to the Commonwealth, they ought to be fairly compensated, on the *sole* ground that these possessions were acquired by the sanction of Society. But what of that?

All the wealth of the country in the year 1880 is estimated at $40,-000,000,000. Much of that is composed of speculative, unreal, values. All that Socialists wish to expropriate, is only the most important instruments of production, a fractional part of that wealth. If, now, this nation could spend six thousand million of dollars to deliver a foreign race out of slavery, could it not spend, say, twenty thousand millions of dollars to make all its citizens free? Compare such a debt with the incumbrances of so many modern wars, waged in the interests of a few persons or of a small class, and remember, that in this case the consideration will be bequeathed with the debt; for the land and machinery will remain intact, or rather will multiply itself in course of a few generations. On this point we shall have more to say in the next chapter.

But should our Plutocracy choose to make the Revolution a violent one, then — we suppose they will be dispossessed without compensation. Read history, and you will find, that the dominant class has furnished us with plenty of precedents.

The various privileges of the nobles and clergy were "property;" they are so no longer. Germany, Italy, Spain, and France have repeatedly confiscated the estates of nobility and clergy. England has done the same thing with the soil of Ireland. It is worth while for capitalists to bear in mind Carlyle's words: "Who can be hood-winked into believing that *loyalty* to the *money-bag* is nobler than loyalty to nobles and clergy?" But we need not go away from home: *our country confiscated the slaves of the South;* that is a splendid precedent for us.

"But it is certainly granted, that Government never can do business as well as private individuals, simply because the latter are personally interested in their affairs."

This is decidedly *not* granted. It is only a commonplace, manufactured to order by interested parties; a stigma, ingeniously fastened on State-activity by individuals who profit by the absence of it. The fact, that our government carries a letter for us promptly and safely across the continent for two cents; the fact that the English telegraph service sends a despatch to any part of the United Kingdom for twenty five cents; the fact, that the Belgian railway management only charges thirty-six cents for every thirty miles, these prove, that the State, *even as now constituted,* can and does manage national interests better than any private parties could do it. Or, to clinch our argument: suppose a proposition was submitted to the people to relegate our mail-service back to private corporations, can any sane man doubt, that it would be overwhelmingly defeated, even if all Star-route frauds were brought to light?

There is one particular State-activity that has proved the eminent fitness of the State to direct the work of Society — and that is its scientific labors. Look at the exceptional efficiency of our Coast-Survey, Light-House-Service, the labors of the Naval Observatory, Signal Service, Patent Office, Geological Surveys.

And, in point of fact, is the management of any of our big corporations better entitled to be called management by the "persons interested," than the administration of a public office? The State can evidently be far more efficient than the most efficient private company to-day, simply because it will have in its service the best capacities that the country contains, and can organize the greatest possible Division of Labor.

"But what an unbearable omnipotent centralization! Unbearable to a degree unheard of before in history. Your Commonwealth will have the supreme power without appeal, to domineer over all the social and industrial interests of the country at its pleasure, even to the extent of saying how many hours a man shall work or how much money he may earn. That is a tyranny, a slavery, that certainly will never be submitted to by the strong individuality of our people. And what an enormous crowd of officials? If corruption is now everywhere cropping out in our Civil Service how will it be when that service is increased a thousandfold?"

One thing at a time, friend, though it is very well to have these objections noticed. Civil Service increased, you say. Then you are truly nearsighted. What else are now our merchants, our foremen, our superintendents, our bank-presidents, cashiers — yes and all our workers but persons who serve *us*, or pretend to serve us; what else but functionaries of *Society*, though they are so in a private capacity? Is there not an immense number of men now, occupying private positions intent only on their interests or the interests of their employers and *yet to all intents and purposes officials of Society?* The only change, then, which our Commonwealth will bring about in that respect, is to change these *private functionaries* into *public officials,* but far from increasing the "Civil Service," this change will, actually, vastly decrease the number of those who now spend their time as mere overseers, managers or middlemen.

And why should a change from private into public functionaries tend to make these officials corrupt? Public Service always lends dignity to the servant, and if our Civil Service is corrupt, it is evidently due to the uncertain tenure and the fact that political adventurers have the inside track. If, for instance, the Gas Trust of Philadelphia is poorly managed, it is only because it is used for political purposes. But politicians will not have much to say under the New Order, as we shall see later on.

And centralization! Well, what of it? There are people who pronounce that word with unaffected horror, as if it signified something exceedingly execrable. And yet every healthy man is an instance of the most perfect centralization in his own person. Indeed, the moment that perfect centralization ceases, suffering is the result. And as with the human organism, so with the social organism. Division of Labor *demands* centralization or anarchy is the result.

We, however, can very well appreciate the cause of that outcry. The centralization of industries that we witness around us is not altogether good; our *monopolies* are not altogether good things — that is exactly what we took pains to show in our second chapter — for the simple reason that they are centered in private, *irre-*

sponsible individuals, bent only on private gain. And so whenever any one advocates the centralization of industrial or political activities in the State, everybody thinks of the present State, which, as we have seen, is as yet only the representative of certain classes; everybody thus has in mind a private party, a power outside of the people.

It is no wonder that people shudder at the thought of giving unlimited, supreme control over all our social, political and industrial affairs to a lot of politicians of the sort that now sit in Washington and our State-capitals and rule us. They think of the princes of the Middle Ages who arbitrarily *interfered* with and domineered over the private affairs of their subjects and imagine that Socialists propose to introduce similar tyranny on a far greater scale. This must also have been in George's mind, when he wrote: "it is evident that whatever savors of regulation and restriction is in itself bad," for he certainly cannot mean that order and method are bad.

It must therefore be borne in mind, that we contemplate the fully developed State; the State that has incorporated in itself not only all social activities, but also the *whole population;* the State where every citizen is a part of the Administration, not in a Pickwickian sense as now, but a *real, integral* part, performing his share of it in the place where he is put; a State where, according to our definition, every one is a public functionary, where therefore all State-help is really and truly Self-help.

Such a State, of course, will require quite other machinery than any present State has got, and perhaps it is difficult to grasp the idea of such a State, without considering the kind of machinery that will be necessary to work it; but that we must defer till the eighth chapter.

In order, however, to dispel the notion that centralization of all social activities in the Cooperative Commonwealth implies any domineering whatever or anything whatever analogous to the arbitrary interference of medieval princes, we shall call attention to the parallel between that normal State and a human organism. The latter possesses a central regulative system, which is not the man, but quite distinct from the man: which is but an organ, on a footing with the other organs. In like manner the normal State will possess its central regulative system and will exactly thereby distinguish itself from the present State, which has no such system or a but very, very imperfect one. But this regulative system will not be the State, but simply an organ, on a footing with the other organs: the associated workers of each branch of industry or social activity. It will, we suppose, have three essential functions: that of being *Chief Superintendent*, *Chief Statistician* and *Arbitrator*. Each of the other organs may manage their own affairs, subject simply to the supervisory control of what we, temporarily, call the central regulative organ. That is the Socialist idea.

Suppose for instance the cotton-workers to control the whole manufacture of cotton. They settle among themselves the rate of remuneration which shall be paid to unskilled labor and to the various grades of skilled labor; they, further, calculate for themselves how much labor will be embodied in their products and from these data the remuneration to be paid to each worker is a simple matter of figures.

But the *prices* of the products is a matter that vitally concerns the whole people; wherefore, most naturally, the central regulative organ will claim the right to have the annual price-list laid before it for its approval.

The rate of remuneration and the hours of labor of these cotton-workers, on the other hand, only concern these workers themselves. There need be no fear, that they will not be able to settle these matters among themselves, for if they do not come to an agreement they will have to starve. It will not pay to "strike" in the Coming Commonwealth and there will be no reason for striking. Moreover, if any of the workers should feel himself aggrieved by the action of his fellows, there will be the recourse to the Courts of the country left him; that is, recourse to the central regulative organ as Arbitrator.

With such an arrangement we fail to see where the "unbearable" centralization will come in. Will it not rather be an ideal sort of self-government?

Now we can see why Socialists put such a value on *Trades-Unions* as they do. It is not that these Unions are always models of associations — though even the most faulty unions are better in every way than no unions; — it is not that they always materially benefit their members, but that these Unions are destined to form the skeletons of these industrial departments of the future of which we, in another chapter, shall have more to say. Especially will these Unions prove invaluable during the transition period. In places where they are well organized and embrace all the best workers of the trade, they may, on the establishment of the Cooperative Commonwealth, take possession of the industrial plant of their trade and go right to work as if they never had known any other arrangement. And that the artizans of England are already thus strongly organized is just a reason why we should think, that England may be nearer the realization of Socialism than is generally supposed. *Organization is only second to sound ideas.*

"But, then, don't you know the Malthusian law? Don't you know, that if your Commonwealth succeed as you expect; if four hours of daily labor will provide the laborer and his family with all comforts, that then this country will very soon not have standing room for its population? Do you not know, that your Commonwealth cannot last a generation, unless it commands its people when to marry and how many children they may have?"

Yes, Socialists know Malthus very well, that English clergyman, himself the father of not less than eleven children, who told the poor, that they have themselves to thank for their miseries, because, forsooth, they marry too early, and beget too many children! But they also know that this doctrine of his is a vicious monstrosity, hatched in the saloons of the wealthy and flattering to the conscience of the ruling classes and that *therefore* it has been so widely accepted. Just as well say, that if you crowd millions of people into a city and besiege it for months, that it, also, is Nature's fault, when they die of starvation and plagues.

No, neither England nor Ireland had at the time of Malthus or has had at any time since too large a population. It may be safely said, on the contrary, that Great Britain even now has too small a population for a really high civilization. If the smart fellows of the Stone Age had been Malthusians and had been able to prevent increase of population beyond the supply of the then existing *caves*, we never should have had brown-stone-fronts or architects.

Again, it is not true that the better fed and better off people are, the more they will propagate. The reverse is the fact. Hopeless poverty makes men reckless and only intent on animal gratifications. Facts prove that the increase of any class is in inverse ratio to its social position and wealth.

In England it is a matter of common observation that the families of the nobility and gentry constantly tend to die out. Here in our country it is even so. In the beginning of this century families with from ten to fifteen children each were not rare in New England; now one with more than six is found only among the poor. In the Cooperative Commonwealth there will rather be reason to fear that the population will tend to decrease than that it will ever be too redundant.

The best service that Henry George has rendered to Socialism with his "Progress and Poverty" is, that he has laid bare the utter absurdity of the Malthusian philosophy. All we now have to do, when any body brings it forward as an objection, is to tell him to go and study the second Book of his work.

If the misery of the world were caused by overpopulation, as Malthus would have it, then, indeed Socialism, or any other progressive movement, would be a Utopia. Fortunately the reverse is true: it is

Misery that causes Overpopulation.

CHAPTER VI

SOCIAL ECONOMY

"The principal narrowness of Political Economists is that of regarding their present experience of mankind as of universal validity, mistaking temporary phases of human character for human nature itself." — *Auguste Comte*.

"The best state of human nature is that in which, while no one is poor, no one desires to be richer, nor has any reason to fear being thrust back by the efforts of others to push themselves forward." — *John Mill*.

"The citizens of a large nation, industrially organized, have reached their possible ideal of happiness, when the producing, distributing and other activities are such, that each citizen finds in them a place for all his energies and aptitudes, while he obtains the means of satisfying all his desires." — *Herbert Spencer*.

Political Economy pretends to be a science. Proudhon, on the other hand, remarks that the merit of Malthus — not dreamt of by his admirers — is that he has reduced Political Economy to an absurdity. When we think of the dogma of the "wages-fund," which, divided by the number of laborers, is said to determine the current rate of wages, Proudhon's observation must strike us as pat. A philosophy which turns the labor-question into a question in long division is certainly a counterfeit-science. But if *legitimate* Political Economy be a science, it is at all events a very modern science. We do not find a trace or promise of it in the former historical periods as we do of the other sciences. Like Athene it came into the world suddenly and full-fledged about 100 years ago. Curiously enough nobody seems ever to have asked for the reason for this phenomenon, and yet there must be a reason for it. We think we have found it in the fact that Political Economy concerns itself with the production and distribution of wealth *under the wage-system, exclusively;*

for this explanation of course, includes that it would have no *raison
d'être* — no reason for being — under a system of slavery or
serfage. But in order to maintain the nimbus of a "science" it has to
inculcate that this Wage-System is a permanent system, the normal
condition of effective production, and thus it has come to pass that
a philosophy which was legitimate if it limited itself to its proper
sphere: that of *explaining* the working of the present system, has
been prostituted by being made to *justify* the present social arrangements, as having universal validity.

But if, as we maintain, this wage-system is nothing but a temporary phase of the evolution of Society, then it follows that Political Economy is destined to be superseded by a new philosophy, a
true science, as soon as the new conditions arise. Under Social-
Cooperation we shall have a perfectly different Philosophy of the
Production and Distribution of wealth, which we, not inaptly, may
call *Social Economy*.

But do not for a moment suppose that we here intend to elabo-
rate that new science, we are all of us too much the children of our
own age to make such an attempt. Yet we also know that both
Americans and Englishmen cannot be expected to cooperate consciously with the natural development of the New Social Order
before they have learned to know its leading features and have
found them on the whole desirable. Such an attitude is decidedly
commendable, but may easily degenerate into a disposition to pro-
pound conundrums, and such we are not disposed to try to solve.

Do not forget, that Socialists are not willing to be taken for
architects. He is a bad architect who cannot plan the building he is
required to erect, to the nicest details; who is unable to tell the size
of this drawing-room, or the exact location of that closet. Do not
demand such details from us.

Rather may we liken ourselves to naturalists: a botanist ought to
be able to tell what plant will develop out of a certain seed, but he
cannot tell how many leaves it will have.

And in like manner we ought to be able to indicate the most
striking economic consequences which with logical necessity will
flow from collective control of the instruments of labor.

We can say, that Interest, Profit and Rent, being nothing but the
spoils which private monopoly of the instruments of production at
present enables individuals to exact, will become things of the past,

as soon as the Commonwealth takes possession of the whole industrial and agricultural plant.

Interest will, for the first time in human history, be given a fatal blow. All laws against Usury have proven worse than useless. When under the Roman Republic Usury was punished with death, it flourished the most — at the rate of a hundred per cent. We have already seen, how in this capitalist era the taking of interest has become a normal and legitimate feature of our system, even one of "the inalienable Rights of Man," in Bentham's words. All Usury-laws limiting the rate of interest are set at defiance, simply because they clash with the prevailing mode of doing business.

The Coming Commonwealth will be the effective destroyer of both Interest and Usury. For when all enterprises have been taken in hand by Society, Wealth will no longer be used — and consequently will no longer be borrowed — as Capital; in the words of our previous definition: it can no longer be "employed productively, *with a view to profit.*" Thus with the reason for it, with its *raison d'être*, Interest itself will cease to be legitimate. Interest and Usury will once more be convertible terms; that is, it will become, as of old, infamous to charge interest for sums of money loaned to persons in embarrassed circumstances. And who will need to be in such circumstances?

As a matter of course, that which now is called *Profit* will disappear. It will be added to the reward of Labor.

Rent as Rent, as a tribute levied by individual monopolists of land, will be no more. All land used for agricultural or industrial purposes, will have become a part of the collective plant. Land used by citizens for homes or other private purposes will yield rent or taxes — whatever you choose to call it — to the Commonwealth; which rent will probably be regulated by Demand and Supply, for there is no reason, why the more desirable sites should not then as now be the more valuable.

The Commonwealth will derive whatever revenues it needs for collective purposes from two sources: Rent and, probably a percentage on every article sold, added to the cost of production, which then will mean, what "Cost of production" should even now always, but does not always, mean: the Value of the article, the sum total of Labor embodied in it. Everybody will thus bear his share of the public charges in proportion to his consumption. And his consumption will in all likelihood be pretty nearly equal to his income. He will not be able very well to go beyond his income, as is so frequently the case now — by-the-way, this system of "living upon credit" is responsible for a very large proportion of the miseries by which modern society is afflicted; — and he will be, at least, under very great temptation to spend all he earns. It will be public policy to encourage him in doing so. It is not for the individual citizen to save, but for Society. The best interests of Society require that a taste for comforts and enjoyments should be widely diffused and, if possible, interwoven with national habits and prejudices, as Mc-Culloch remarks.

From this it will appear, that the Cooperative Commonwealth will have an immense advantage over all modern States in the matter of taxation. Not alone, that assessors and tax-gatherers will be dispensed with; that there will be no possibility of evading one's contribution to the collective expenses; that they will be distributed in the most equitable manner, and cannot be burdensome to anybody: but the Commonwealth will at all times have the whole wealth of the Nation at its command. Suppose the rate of percentage for the ensuing fiscal year, as estimated, be found to be too low, or any sudden emergency to arise! There are the warehouses! No need any more of issuing bonds, to be bought for half their face-value by greedy capitalists.

Next, we can affirm, that *money* — by which we understand Gold and Silver-coin and their representatives — will become entirely useless in the Coming Commonwealth. We do not say that Society may not go on for an indefinite period using it for various reasons of convenience, but that not a trace of the necessity which makes money play such important role in our present system will remain.

Money is now the quintessence of Capital, or "Capital *par excellence*," as Lassalle called it. The manufacturer or merchant cannot make a move without Money. They may have their warehouses filled with merchandise, but they cannot pay their drafts with them. Yet many, even men of the acutest intellect, do not sufficiently appreciate the important function which Money performs in our present social system.

Thus John Ruskin compares people with partiality for money to children who would tear furniture to pieces and fight each other for brassheaded nails.

And an economist and logician like John S. Mill speaks of Money as "only (!) a contrivance for saving time and labor."

Very *naive*, indeed! As if that were not enough! He might just as well dispose of railroads by remarking: "Bah! they are only contrivances for saving time and labor."

Money is precisely so precious, because it, under the industrial system which we have now, is the greatest of all labor-saving instruments. People are separated by their interests, by a multiplicity of interests. Money brings them together; is, as it is termed, a *medium of exchange* between them. That is the vital function of Money. *That* medium of exchange is the best which brings people together in the easiest and quickest way; and that is just what Money does better than any other commodity. Just as a railroad is a more efficient contrivance than a stage-coach, and this again than a lumber-wagon, so Gold and Silver are better media of exchange than wheat or tobacco or oxen or any other commodity that has been tried. Money was invented, as any other labor-saving instrument has been invented: to save time and labor; to escape the deadlock of Barter.

But what is it that makes a railroad at all useful? The fact, that men are separated in space. Imagine, however, that distance were annihilated, then there would certainly be no earthly use for a railroad.

In the same manner, whenever men's interests cease to be adverse; whenever these interests become identical, as they will become under our Commonwealth by perfect association, then evidently, the business of Money will be gone. Gold and Silver will then become absolutely worthless as Money, as far as the internal affairs of Society are concerned — they will have, of course, to be used as Money in all intercourse with other Nations who have not yet embraced Socialism. Then John Ruskin may assert, that they are not worth much more than brassheaded nails — but not till then.

How will Exchange then be carried on? By Account, facilitated by some such contrivance as labor-checks. The current of development is running in that direction: first we have Barter, then Money, and even now Account is more and more supplanting the latter, the more and more closely we are becoming associated. When in the Cooperative Commonwealth Money has been superannuated we shall have nothing but checks, notes, tickets — whatever you will call them — issued by authority.

"Ah! So you Socialists are half-Greenbackers."

You are mistaken, sir! It would be more correct to say, that Greenbackers are *half*-Socialists; and because they are only that "half" we maintain they are wholly wrong, even on the money-question. We have already seen that on the broader question of social development they are absolute reactionists; that they have no fault to find with individual ownership of the instruments of labor, but war against its inevitable natural development.

By the way, there is really something curious about this greenback movement in our country. How shall we account for it? May not the reason for this abnormal phenomenon be sought in the fact that the "almighty Dollar" is peculiarly the American *fetish?*

But to return to the distinction between Socialists and the consistent Greenbackers: the *fiat*-men. The latter propose, that the State shall issue its notes, tender them to its creditors and give them to the People saying: "Take this! With this dollar-note you can go anywhere within my jurisdiction and buy one dollar's worth of goods with it."

The great trouble, however, is that the State of these fiat-men is the present State. They want to abolish Money — that is the precious metals as Money — and yet to retain the present system of production, which is just as irrational as a scheme would be to abolish the Pope and still to preserve the Catholic church. For what does an assertion like the above by the present State amount to? It is a promise, without any possible performance, for the simple reason that this State has absolutely no title to the goods which it thus disposes of. These belong, by its own sanction and concession, to individual citizens.

Now note how much more logical the Socialist position is. We claim that the state shall first take possession of and own the warehouses and the wares, and thereafter issue its notes. Then, and not till then, the State will be so conditioned, that it can perform what it promises. For then it can say: "Go into any of *my* warehouses, and I will sell you a dollar's worth of *my* goods for this dollar note of mine."

The distinction on the money-question then is, not alone that Greenbackers are but half-Socialists but that it is the *latter* part of the Socialist program which they have appropriated; they have put the cart before the horse.

It will further be seen from this, that we differ from the Greenbackers, and agree with Political Economists in holding, that "money is the tool we use for effecting exchange by the help of two half-exchanges of commodity for commodity;" that Money, therefore, is a *commodity*, and could not be Money, if it were not a commodity, and that this commodity, like all other wares, derives its Value, partly from its scarcity, but mainly from the labor crystallized in it; and that our present paper-money is but a representative of Money.*

But we agree with the Greenbackers in holding that Money is destined to be "superannuated," if we may use the term, as payment in kind has long since been, and that the Credit of the Nation will take its place.

We shall here make a digression to state definitely our position in regard to compensation to the dispossessed owners of property, which we left somewhat unsettled in the last chapter.

We suggested there that, if the final change were accomplished by force, the State would possibly expropriate our men of wealth without any compensation whatever. *Their existing rights are such which the law gives and what the law gives law can take away.* That would be done without any compunction of conscience, seeing that much of that wealth is obtained by questionable methods, and very much of it by the trickery of buying and selling, which never can create value, and, indeed, ought not to furnish the manipulator mere subsistence. But as a matter of policy the State may see fit to give the proprietors a fair compensation for that property which Society took under its control. But there are two important "buts" to note.

They will not receive any interest on the sums allowed them. When all interest has ceased to be legitimate throughout Society, Society itself will hardly charge itself with that burden.

They will not be paid in Money, but in goods, in articles of

---

* We may here remark, that we also, with Political Economists, consider our fractional currency, not Money at all, but mere counters, tokens; just what our labor-checks will be.

enjoyment, furnished in annuities to those whose claim is sufficiently large.

Suppose we owe Vanderbilt a sum equal to one hundred million of Dollars. We pay him a million a year for a hundred years, and cancel the debt. Vanderbilt could then take his one million in labor-checks, or whatever products he chose, and ninety-nine millions in non-interest bearing U. S. certificates of indebtedness, and use them in Europe or elsewhere just as he pleased. We should say that this would be acting *very* generously with him, when we remember — what it will not do any harm once more to call attention to, — that Society *never yet* has acted in a like spirit of social justice towards *the working classes,* whenever *they* suffered injury, and grievous injury, by new machinery and new inventions.

Socialists of old used to insist upon the abolition of the Right of Inheritance and Bequest. Now we can see, that there absolutely will be no need for that. And it is well. For if that which I gain by my own labor is rightfully my property — and the Cooperative Commonwealth will, as we have seen, exactly sanction that claim — it will be decidedly inexpedient in that Commonwealth to destroy any of the essential qualities of propertyship; and I can hardly call that my property, which I may not give to whom I please after my death. Further, to deny me that right is undeniably to lessen, by so much, my incentives to effort.

There will be no need to do away with that right, for when property can no longer increase from interest, and fleecings; when it no more confers *power* on its possessor, then Private wealth will become harmless.

Take even a Rothschild. Suppose him compensated in full for all he is "worth." — How abominable this phrase is! so *very* significant of our age, to call a man whose body and soul may not be worth a farthing to Society "worth" millions of dollars — well, he will be paid in bread and meat and luxuries and wine and theatre-tickets. Let him enjoy these things. Let him fill himself to repletion! Let him give away and squander the rest! Do not be afraid, that the State will be burdened for many generations with these charges; his very next heirs will see to it, that it will not. These immense accumulations will not last so very long, when they cease to be prolific.

But our present laws of inheritance may very likely experience great modifications. It, certainly, is absurd, that a second cousin of mine who does not know himself related to me, until there is some-thing to be gained by it, should have any claim to my property after my death. But that is a matter foreign to our purpose.

"But, to return to the money question, how will you dispense with the other function which Money now performs: that of measur-ing values?"

This function of Money as a *Measurer of Values* is really but an *incidental* one, while that of acting as a *Medium* of *Exchange* is its principal and *true* function. There are abundant reasons why the precious metals should be the media of exchange, as long as we need any, but absolutely no reason can be given for either gold or silver being a better measurer of values than any other commodity. They have, in fact, always performed that function poorly; gold and silver have fluctuated nearly as much as most of the wares whose values they had to measure.

We saw in the first chapter, that it is really the amount of labor, crystallized in an article, which determines its value; that it is labor which determines the "level" value of even gold and silver; that is, the value round which their market price vibrates. Why, then, would not a definite amount of labor be a far more appropriate, constant and convenient measure? The change would have the great advantage of enabling the worker to know for certain what returns he receives for his work. He does not know it now, for Money obscures the transactions of all buying and selling; it serves as a mask, which this change will tear off. Instead of saying, that a coat is worth so many "dollars," we shall in the New Common-wealth discard all mystery and call it *worth so much work*. We, therefore, apprehend, that, just as one of our greenbacks promises to pay one dollar on demand, these labor-checks of which we spoke will promise to pay on demand anything of the value of, say, one day's labor or fractional part thereof.

"Well, but a day's labor by one person, and a day's labor by another are, certainly, very different things. To talk of a day's labor as a measure is about as definite as the boy's comparison: 'long as a string;' is it not?"

Yes, but it would make some difference, if the boy said: "long as this string" and showed it to you, without allowing you to measure it exactly. The unit: "a day's work" will mean *the simplest work of average efficiency of a normal working day*. We would here recall to our readers what was said on *Value* in the first chapter. It was there stated, among other things, that all skilled and professional work is nothing but multiplied common, or unskilled, work. We once more cite the words of Ricardo: "The estimation of different qualities of Labor comes soon to be adjusted in the market with sufficient precision for all practical purposes." While therefore we grant that "a day's labor," as a unit of value, has not the scientific precision of a foot-rule as a unit of length, we claim, that it is well fitted to supplant the dollar-unit. When five days' labor is demanded for a coat, it will not be at all difficult for the buyer to compare that with the amount of common work, contained in his own day's labor.

The distinguishing economic traits of the New Order, considered so far in this chapter, were of a negative character: they consisted in the elimination of features that we now everywhere meet with; yet this change alone would make it a different world from ours. In passing over to the positive characteristics of the Cooperative Commonwealth we should keep in mind that it is not an imaginary picture drawn on a blank tablet, but that it will bear the same relation to the Established Order that the full-blown flower bears to the green bud. This relationship, indeed, will make us feel quite at home, if we in imagination take a bird's-eye view of its economic workings, though we should find ourselves irretrievably lost in its labyrinths, if we attempted to tread our way through its details. For its grand industrial processes will be carried on pretty much as they now are, or might be, conducted in some of our best managed manufacturing or retail-selling establishments. Or it might perhaps suit our purpose better if we take the present State-management of our postal affairs as an illustration, and compare that with Socialist management of *all* our industries.

The Postoffice Department was self-sustaining, before the two-cent rate was introduced, and will beyond doubt be so again in a short time. That is to say, its expenditures in salaries for all in its service, and in paying for transportation of the mails and printing of stamps equaled, at the end of the fiscal year, its receipts. That is the summit of success, for to have a surplus, to make any "profit," is contrary to the end for which it is instituted.

Let us now see how this most important matter will stand in our

Commonwealth. Its receipts, — not the "revenues" of which we spoke a few pages back but — its *gross* Receipts, the National Income, will consist of the total results of the productive labor performed in a given year; — by "productive labor" is of course not meant merely agricultural and manufacturing labor, but also the labor of transporting and handling the goods, of writing books; every kind of labor, in short, that creates values-in-exchange. Its Expenditures-Outgoings — will consist of *these very receipts less* all buildings and machinery, constructed during the year, and all that is reserved as addition to its Capital. As the products were received or as services were rendered, labor-checks will have been issued, (or perhaps such money as we use now, which then, however, will have no other function than the checks: that of being tickets, tokens,) each check will represent so and so many normal days of common labor, and there will during each fiscal year have been exactly as many checks issued as will correspond to the days of labor, productive or unproductive, *actually performed.*

The outgoings will be distributed at the various depots or bazaars of the Commonwealth to the holders of these checks, "sold" there, in other words. These check-holders may be those to whom they were originally issued, or strangers visiting the country or citizens who have parted with something valuable for them. These bazaars will be *one price* establishments. The wares will have their value, real, "natural" value, as Ricardo termed it, which is — as we saw in *Chapter I,* — the amount of human labor embodied in them; that determines their value now, has always done it, and will determine it under the New Order. The wares will be sold for a price equal to that value, with possibly a percentage added.

For it will be noted that the checks issued represent and call for more days labor than are contained in the products, destined for distribution. There are, first, the checks issued to those citizens who have performed unproductive labor: physicians, judges, teachers, clerks, domestic helpers &c. and, next, checks for the labor contained in what is set aside as Capital. There are thus a good many legitimate claims which must be extraordinarily provided for. The Commonwealth has already a fund on which it can draw considerably for these purposes: its *rent-fund.* In all probability, however, an impost will, in addition, have to be laid on the sales; that is, goods representing 20 days of Labor will be sold for checks, representing, say, 21 days of labor. This, though really plain, may seem intricate to many, but if the social transactions of to-day were similarly analyzed, they would appear far more complex.

But it is of the highest importance that the Commonwealth shall dispose of all the products it thus offers for distribution, or else there will be labor-checks outstanding which it has no means of satisfying. Somebody might bring forward some such objection as this:

"I understood you to say that the prices will be rigidly fixed. But what if Demand and Supply should play you tricks? Suppose a fabric goes out of fashion, so that your citizens will not buy it at all, or at all events refuse to pay the price that is put upon it. Is your Commonwealth going to force it down the throats of consumers? You Socialists do not propose to abolish a law of Nature, do you?"

This is our answer: We admit that Demand and Supply is a natural law; that is, that if consumption and production does not fit together throughout the entire extent of both, mischief will be the consequence at all times, and Socialists are not such fools as to suppose, that they can decree away any natural law or force. We do, however, suppose, that we may in time become as much master of the force implied in Demand and Supply, as we already are of other natural forces. We have not decreed away the laws of steam, and yet we make now the steam propel our ships across the ocean and carry our burdens across the continent. We can change or remove entirely the conditions under which those natural forces act, and, thus, without abolishing any law whatever, compel them to act in a more beneficent manner; or to become latent, that is, to suspend their effects altogether.

Indeed, we see almost every day how powerful private individuals under our present system *do* control *Supply* for their own sinister purposes. The combinations of railroad companies between each other or among themselves and oil-companies of which we spoke in *Chapter II* are such interferences with a natural force which, if it only were permitted to act spontaneously, would act most beneficently, and as to *Demand,* it may be worth while to note that the freaks of fashion originate usually in the private cupidity of manufacturers and even in that of insignificant tailors and milliners.

The Commonwealth will use its vast power over the conditions of

Demand and Supply to establish and preserve economic equilibrium. It undoubtedly can by proper foresight and abundant statistics accurately adjust the supply of all products to the demand for them; make Supply and Demand balance each other. This function of *Statistician* will be one of the most important within its sphere, and the principal way in which it will control the workers in their industrial pursuits. We think the Commonwealth will thereby be quite successful in keeping prices steady, and in making the chance for Demand and Supply to play any "tricks" extremely small. We think so, because we see with what accuracy the manager of a large hotel hits upon the proper quantities of the innumerable articles of food, required by his guests.

But Demand and Supply will, as a matter of course, whenever it gets the chance, make the prices vibrate above and below the real value. Thus, should the supply anywhere be excessive, either from miscalculation or from the whim of fashion — which by the way, we may rest assured will be pretty effectually curbed by Public Opinion in a society like the Cooperative Commonwealth — then the goods may have to be sacrificed, and the prices correspondingly lowered. The Commonwealth may have to stand the loss, as the universal insurer, which it will be abundantly able to do. Should, on the other hand, the supply be deficient, as must always be the case with a limited number of products (particular kinds of wine, for instance,) in such case the Commonwealth will raise the price to correspond to the demand and be to that extent a gainer. Very likely this gain and loss will generally balance each other.

Of course all export and import will be under collective control. A part of its receipts, so much as it judges will not be needed for home-consumption, the Commonwealth will exchange for such foreign products as there will be a home-demand for, and which it cannot itself produce so profitably or successfully, whether it be on account of climate or other causes. The lines of our commerce will therefore very likely come to run from North to South rather than from East to West.

That is an arrangement that everybody will be satisfied with, a consummation which will change the discord which now obtains in regard to a tariff into complete harmony. It will satisfy those who now sincerely advocate a policy of protection. We cannot agree with Henry George when he cannot see anything but "fallacies" and "absurdities" in the protection-theory. This theory is so much in harmony with the present tendency of the State in the direction of Socialism, that we cannot but sympathize with it. But the trouble is that our "protective" tariffs *do not protect those who need protection,* but protect simply the profit-rate of employers; the trouble is, that our tariffs are adopted and maintained in hypocrisy, again *hypocrisy* and nothing but HYPOCRISY.

There is, on the other hand, this sound element in the free-trade theory that it is foolish for this country to produce here what we can get much more profitably and better from foreign countries. But those who agitate so violently for it, evidently, do it because a free-trade policy would put money into their pockets. As long as one set of individuals see profit in one policy and another set in another, the tariff can but be a shuttlecock, tossed back and forth by conflicting interests. To frame a tariff law that will pacify all interests is about as ingenious an idea as to pray to God for a mild winter without prejudice to the coal-dealers.

Now we come to one of the most important differences between the condition of the workers under the New Order and their condition under a system of private enterprise. Now the wages of the workers — and also wages of letter carriers — are determined, as we have seen, in the last place by what it costs to live and raise a family; in the Commonwealth, as our definition shows, the workers will be rewarded according to results, whether mechanics or chiefs of industry or transporters or salesmen. The productive workers will each receive for every day's common labor a check, entitling him to one day's common labor in return — less his share of the impost, (his premium, it may be called, which he pays to the National Insurance Company, and his part of the public charges.) Those engaged in unproductive vocations will receive similar salaries out of the rent or impost-fund. They all will thus receive the full value of their labors, and whenever they buy anything, they will simply pay wages and salaries, and no profits.

"Yes, it is easy to say, that every one, whether he be teacher or physician or chief of industry or artisan or hodcarrier will receive a day's labor for a day's labor, by which I understand you to mean a day of common labor for a day of common labor. But how is such a comparison of common labor (of a day of the hodcarrier's labor for instance) to be made with skilled labor or professional labor with perfect justice to all? And who are the persons who are to be intrusted with such a delicate and dictatorial function? You Socialists seem to treat this important matter with too great flippancy. Such a gradation of labor is, in fact, entirely visionary, and that is enough to relegate your Cooperative Commonwealth into the realm of Utopia."

Hold on, sir! The New Order will, *by no means,* hinge upon this matter. It will be realized, because Nature ordains it, because at a certain point in time, Society *will have to realize it,* or decay.

And when we shall have arrived at that crisis, we hope that the leaders of the Revolution will not be such visionaries as to commence by trying to do *perfect* justice to anybody. They will know better, than to assume to themselves the attributes of gods. They will, we hope, be practical men who simply try to be as just as they can be, consistently with the best interests of the whole. And we think, that they can not better show their practical common sense, than by adopting the gradation already made, that is, by retaining for an unlimited period the *ratio* of wages which, at the time of the change, will obtain in the various branches of *manual* work and for the different qualities of workmen. This ratio will furnish them a sufficiently accurate "gradation of labor." *

To go a little into details: Suppose they go to work and establish, first of all, a normal day, say, of eight hours, and pay the workers twice the wages which each one has been receiving, on an average, for the ten years immediately preceding. We have no doubt, that the wages can be raised and the working day shortened *that* much with perfect safety, considering the enormous advantages of Cooperative Industry, which we dwelt upon in the preceding chapter. Anyway, a few months' experience will teach them, whether they have raised the wages too much, or not high enough.

And please bear in mind that the members of each branch of industry and every calling will settle that matter of remuneration

---

* [Gronlund inserted the following note in his revised edition: "Here I wish to call attention to the second *decidedly unsocialistic* idea which Bellamy introduces in 'Looking Backward,' — *equal wages; i.e.,* that every person, whatever his work, his industry, or his needs, is to start on every New Year's day with the same income. Socialism must not be saddled with this proposition, which is both impracticable and unjust." — Editor's Note.]

for themselves. They will be entitled as a body to the proceeds of all the labor they have embodied in the product they create, and *that* they distribute among themselves just as they please — subject to appeal to the Commonwealth as Arbitrator. Dr. Green, the President of the Western Union, is reported to have remarked in his evidence before a Senate-Committee: "I shall never agree that the operators should have, or believe they had, the power of fixing their own salaries." They nevertheless *will have* that power sometime, doctor, as sure as the world moves!

But in regard to the work of the chiefs of industry and professionals they, undoubtedly, will institute a new "gradation of labor." There will be no more $50,000 or $25,000 or even $10,000 salaries paid. These fancy salaries are now possible, and now considered proper, only, because large fortunes can at present be made in what is known as "business." When "business" is done away with; then their services will be compared with manual work, as they ought to be, and be paid for accordingly.

That constitutes one of the points, in which our postal system is not yet socialistic. In the Cooperative Commonwealth, the Postmaster General will not receive $10,000 while letter carriers must be satisfied with $800.

Of course, in instituting the new "gradation" in the labors of the teacher, the doctor, they will make allowance for the many years of study these men have needed to properly qualify themselves. But just in the same way the watchmaker's labor will be, and is, rated above that of the hodcarrier, because his years of apprenticeship must be compensated for. It means simply, that both professional and skilled labor is multiplied common labor.

Do not here object, that if the rewards of captains of industries and of the professions are thus reduced to a level with manual labor, men of genius and of natural gifts will then part with the management of affairs and with the professions.

They will not, unless you also can show, that they, also, will leave the world on that account.

They will find their ulterior reward in the zest of intellectual activity, the joys of creative genius, the honor of directing affairs and the social distinction they will enjoy.

Do not object, either, that such a compensation runs counter to the Socialist principle, that everyone is entitled to the full proceeds of his own labor; that, therefore, a manager who by his skill causes a factory to earn $100,000 may claim that amount as his reward.

A man is entitled to the full proceeds of his labor — against any other individual, *but not against Society*. Society is not bound to reward a man either in proportion to his services, nor yet of his wants, but according to expediency; according to the behests of her own welfare. Man's work *is* not a *quid pro quo* but a *trust*. The other construction would lead to the absurdity, that no existing fortunes could give any idea of the monstrous accumulation of riches of the heirs of a Kepler or a Newton, or still more of a Robert Fulton, a Watts or a Morse, if these men could have claimed all the results of their inventions.

It will thus be seen, that the labors of those invested with the "delicate" function of apportioning the rewards — who these persons are likely to be we shall consider in the eighth chapter — will not be so very herculean, for the first generation, at least; nor need these persons be at all "dictatorial." We do not call our Congress "dictatorial," when it fixes the salaries of the President or of Judges.

This will be the glorious achievement of the Cooperative Commonwealth: that the whole proceeds of Labor will be distributed, exclusively, among those who do the labor. But what needs to be impressed upon Socialist workmen especially, is: that common prudence should make them turn the cold shoulder to the idea of *ideally* just wages, and on the other hand, make them satisfied with the present *ratio* of wages — at all events till a more perfect, and at the same time expedient gradation of labor has been perfected.

When the Cooperative Commonwealth has worked for a couple of generations; when the student and the watchmaker are supported by the State during their years of study and apprenticeship and furnished all appliances requisite to their training, *then* another rule may obtain. Then, perhaps, as some Socialists now contend, one hour of the teacher's work and one hour of the hodcarrier's work will be paid for alike — though it must be observed, that, for instance, in difficulty the teacher's work does not at all resemble the work of the hodcarrier — but to speculate upon that in our generation can properly be termed "Utopian."

It is worth while for workingmen to study the case of the tailor association, founded by Louis Blanc at Clichy in 1848, which had to give up equal pay.

We now, lastly, come to the greatest economic achievement of the Coming Commonwealth. Our definition said, that its citizens would be, consciously and avowedly, public functionaries. That, alone, is an object worth striving for, worth dying for.

When reformers call our workingmen "white slaves" and speak of their condition as "slavery," many well-meaning persons deem these terms extravagant and attribute them to demagogism. Now, in all soberness, are they extravagant?

We shall entirely omit any reference to extreme cases of oppression on the part of employers towards their employees, and confine ourselves to what all wage-workers must submit to — whether they be mechanics, clerks or telegraph-operators. And let us remark that here, as wherever we have spoken of "wage-workers," we have excluded and do exclude domestic servants of every sort. We have already seen that these workers are obliged to go into the general market with their labor, which is their ware, and there sell it for a price, vibrating now a little above, now a little below, what is necessary to their subsistence.

Now, what does this "selling their labor" amount to?

We know a man who, though he is far from being a Robert Owen, may very well in regard to sincerity, kindness and hatred of all shams be compared to that philanthropist. He was a prominent Abolitionist, but is not particularly averse to the present industrial system, which, indeed, has enabled him to gather in quite a respectable fortune by the simple process of buying and selling. We think he is a good sample of the best kind of employers. To his clerks he is fond of remarking: "Your time is mine, you know" and he puts this theory into practice to its fullest extent. If any one should suggest to him that he, the model of an employer, was a — slaveholder, (!) he would be very much surprised.

Yet what does this phrase imply? "Your time is mine" means "your body is mine, your actions are mine for so many hours out of the twenty-four. You must do nothing, say nothing, go nowhere as *you* please but as *I* please. *I* want you to do this thing now, or," of course it is understood, "I discharge you." His clerks are subject to his individual, *irresponsible* will; their preferences are not so much as thought of.

What in the name of reason is that but slavery? Was not "your

time is mine" the very essence, the definition of negro-slavery?
True, a master could sell his slave; but there certainly were many
masters who did not dream of ever selling their negroes; were these
therefore less *slaves?* True, a master could whip his slave; but our
employer can discharge his clerks whenever it takes his fancy,
which probably would have worse consequences for the clerks than
a whipping would. The fact is, these were mere accessories. *Slavery
is not yet abolished.* The very principle, *subjection,* which ruled
under ancient slavery, under serfage, and negro slavery, rules yet
under the wage-system. That makes the system essentially immoral;
it demoralizes the employer as well as the employee.

And this relation becomes absolutely unbearable, if, as very often
is the case, the employee has more knowledge, more brains, a fuller
head, in short, than his employer — for it has rightly been said that
all that is necessary to success in business is "great concentration,
continuous application and *an absurdly exaggerated idea of one's
own importance"* — it *is* unbearable, when the employee feels that
in a social system where position depended upon merit *he* would be
the one in authority.

There is no halting place between Subjection and Inter-dependence. Independence cannot be had for all. The employer we referred to boasts of being independent. The trouble is he is too
independent: one man cannot be independent, without making
others dependent on him. The wage-system is only Subjection in a
milder form, perhaps; another instance of the chronic hypocrisy of
our age. That is shown very well by the constant talk about the
relation of the wage-workers being one of *contract.* Well! if it is, it
is a very one-sided contract, one where the employee has but to say
"Amen." By selling his labor *the wage-worker virtually sells himself.*

The Cooperative Commonwealth will abolish slavery by the roots
by raising all private employments to the dignity of public functions. This change, while it will not essentially alter the existing
mode of exercising them, will yet alone transform their general
spirit, for it will forever, *first,* do away with Dependence of one
individual upon another; *next,* take away from those in authority
the irresponsible power of Discharge, and, *lastly,* relieve the worker
from the necessity of going into the market and selling himself as a
ware.

Do not, however, suppose, that there will be no subordination under the new order of things. Subordination is an absolute essential of Cooperation; indeed, Cooperation is Discipline.

Do not suppose, either, that Demand and Supply will cease altogether to have an influence on Labor. As a natural force, it will exert itself whenever it gets a chance, but the coming Commonwealth will see to it that, whenever it does act, it acts beneficently. We shall see here in what manner.

It is as we have stated, for the Commonwealth to determine, in its character of Statistician, how much of a given product shall be produced the coming year or season. That is preeminently its sphere, however much the workers of the different branches will otherwise be left to manage their own affairs. Suppose in a given industry production will have to be narrowed down to one half the usual *quantum*. It follows, that in such case the workmen can only work half the usual time and that there will only be one half the usual proceeds to be distributed among them.

What must be the result? Evidently the men's remuneration will have to be reduced one half, or a corresponding number of workers will have to pass over to some other employment — for the consequences of such a disorder, which may be permanent and is not the result of either miscalculation or misfortune, will, certainly, not be borne by Society at large; and the Commonwealth, while it guarantees *suitable* employment, can certainly not guarantee a *particular* employment, to everybody.

A change of occupation, however, will in that Commonwealth be tolerably easy for the worker, on account of the high grade of general education, and because all will have passed through a thorough apprenticeship in general mechanics. Certain critics of Socialism object that no person under it will have any effective choice in regard to employment. The above shows how little foundation there is for such a criticism. But we should like to know how much "effective choice" the vast majority of men now have in regard to employment or wages, or place of abode or anything else.

Another critic once remarked to the writer in regard to the Commonwealth absorbing all social activities: "What a tyranny, to forbid a Meissonier to paint a little bit of canvas and sell it for $100,-000, if anyone would buy it?" Why, it would be tyranny to forbid it. And we have no reason to think it will be forbidden. We therefore also said that there might be citizens who would acquire labor-checks by parting with something valuable to other citizens. But, really, we do not suppose there will be any citizen in The Cooperative Commonwealth, when some time has elapsed, who has got $100,000 to squander on a bit of canvas, and none should deplore it, for if that fact would deprive the Commonwealth of *Meissoniers,* it surely will not rob it of *Raphaels or Michael Angelos.* It is just one of the curses of this age that it has out of artists made lackeys of the rich. Phidias, Raphael, Michael Angelo, ministered to the People.

We now shall consider how it is possible to have due subordination in a State where all dependence of one individual upon another is destroyed. The political expression of Interdependence is — *Democracy.*

CHAPTER VII

DEMOCRACY *versus* PARTY GOVERNMENT

" 'Behold! Now I, too, have my twenty-thousandth part of a Talker in our National Palaver.' — What a notion of Liberty!" — *Carlyle*.

"I believe that party, instead of being a machinery necessary to the existence of free government, is its most dangerous foe, and that in order to get anything which really deserves the name of republican government, we must destroy party altogether." — *A True Republic* by *Albert Stickney*.

"Nay, must we not rather confess, that that unlovely creature, the habitual office-seeker, is as natural a product of our political and social conditions as the scrub-oak is of the soil, when it has been laid waste by the removal of the primeval forest?" — *Richard Grant White, North American Review, July 1882*.

At this stage, certainly — and probably as soon as the idea of Collective Control of all the affairs of the Nation was broached — many an inquirer exclaims with supreme disgust:

"So you actually propose to increase the spoils of office a hundred, yea a thousandfold! What a bedlam you would make of these United States at election times!!! And then nothing short of a revolution would ever suffice to dislodge the party in possession of the government, however much it may have mismanaged public affairs. Why, this is enough to prove the Utopian nature of your scheme!"

Wait a moment, friends. We have so far only shown you the front-view of our Commonwealth, its economic side. Your objections would be unanswerable and your disgust in order, if the Socialist *Regime* implied the retention of our present political machinery.

We insist on a *political* change hand in hand with the economic change. We insist on new machinery for the new motive power; on new bottles for the new wine. Our political program is just as vital a part of our prospective Commonwealth as our economic program is. The political machinery of our country would be most clumsy and unsuitable to the workings of the New Order. It would of necessity have to be discarded for something more suitable, just as the young man has to discard the clothes of his boyhood which he has outgrown.

This frank avowal will, undoubtedly, hurt more prejudices, than even our economic ideas did.

"What! do you, Socialists, dare to think of laying your impious hands on this glorious Constitution of ours? What a sacrilege!"

Softly! Listen to the following:

"The idea that some men now hold, that this Constitution is the one perfect piece of political machinery that the world has ever seen, is a weak growth of later years. The men of 1787 knew better. No one of them thought it the best form of government that could be devised. It was the only form on which they could then agree. They began an experiment — we have its results. Is it possible, that from those results we can learn nothing? And are we forever to use the machinery of a past age, throwing away all the teachings of later years?"

He who wrote those sentences is no Socialist. He is an American to the manor born, and a matter-of-fact lawyer. His name is Albert Stickney, author of "A True Republic," published by the Harpers. His 4th and 6th Chapters ought to be read by every inquirer as an introduction to the political ideas of Socialists. The fact of Stickney being a lawyer makes him exceedingly keen in exposing the defects in our political machinery, while his practical commonsense, in which he shows himself a typical American, renders him one of the best advocates we could have. As Ricardo prepared the way for our analysis of our present economic relations, and Spencer for constructive Socialism, so Stickney performs that service for us with our countrymen in regard to the political changes which we contemplate.

In the two chapters we have called attention to he discusses first, with a wealth of illustration, the evils and abuses of party-rule as we have it here. If that were all, he would not have done anything extraordinary. Most people admit these evils. But most men, also, think them mere accidents of the time and that they are far outweighed by the good results which party brings. Stickney's merit consists in showing, that parties — by which term must always be understood *permanent* parties — have no good results at all, and that it is *our frame of government which is responsible for those evils.*

He says very pointedly:

"When we said (as we did in effect in our Constitution,) all public servants shall depend for keeping their offices, not on whether they do their work well or ill, but on carrying the next election, then, instead of giving them each a separate interest to do his own work well, we gave them all one common interest to carry the next election. We made it certain, that they would combine and form parties, for the purpose of carrying elections.

"But there was another point. The knowledge which all men had, that at the end of a fixed time there would be a large number of vacancies, made it certain, that other men who were not in office would combine for the purpose of getting out the men who were in office, and getting in themselves. The term-system was certain, then, to create two great parties for the purpose of carrying elections. The men who were in formed a party to keep office. The men who were out formed a party to get office.

"Whether they wished it or not, our public servants were driven by this point in our system of government to make this work of carrying elections their regular profession. In that profession they gained great skill. In that work they were sure to have more skill than the ordinary citizens who gave their time and thought to other things. The professional must always beat the amateur. . . . The natural and certain result was that party leaders, for party purposes, controlled the elections of public servants, and the action of public servants after they were elected."

But enough of quotation. Stickney comes to the conclusion that the *term*-system will have to be abolished; but the term system is the very corner-stone of our "Constitution."

That is certainly a very vigorous way of questioning that instrument — especially for an American lawyer.

We shall have to be broader in our criticism than Stickney (though we can hardly be said to be more radical,) for the objective points at which he and we aim are rather different. He wants a machinery which shall insure good work in the affairs with which government is now charged. We want a machinery fit to transact *all* the affairs of the Nation.

The New Order cannot use a machinery which allows the reigning party to be master of the situation.

Now the successful *party* appoints the people's rulers, and all public affairs are conducted with a view to *party* interests.

For as Stickney remarks:

"The people on the day of election have at most the choice between two men or sets of men; and with the point who these two sets of men are to be the people at large have little or nothing to do. It may be said, that the people can have something to do with the selection of the candidates. However that may be, it is the fact, that they do not, and we are here considering *the way our system really works.*"

No one will deny that all our elective officers, from head to foot, are elected, not by the people, but by the caucus of the party which happens to be successful. And the caucus or convention is simply an irresponsible gathering of men whom selfish interests draw and bind together. Listen to the "N. Y. Tribune," now a good party-organ:

"The Republican vote in this city (New York) two years ago was 81,730. It is the simple truth to say that not more than fifty men had anything to do with the actual choice of the delegates who went to Saratoga (1882) with a pretence of representing the great body of voters."

Next, official action has ever since Thomas Jefferson founded the first opposition party, been directed to the service of party interests instead of the people's interests. Our officials are and must be pliant men; if not, they are driven from public life; these are matters of notoriety. Even such an honest man as Lincoln had to make scandalous appointments. His Secretary of the Interior declared, that, if he dared, he could run his department with half his force of clerks and for half its cost. Such another would-be-honest president as Hayes had to pay for electoral votes with the people's offices.

Our institutions, instead of subserving public interests, are political *fortresses.* "Think what is at stake this fall — *a total of two hundred and thirty places in the county of Oneida!*" exclaimed a Utica paper during a late election. And yet people who superciliously call Socialism a Utopia imagine that an act of Congress can give us civil service reform! Do they really believe that figs will grow on thistles?

No, attend for once to the essentials: destroy these parties which at present are the people's masters; which, as Stickney so abundantly proves, in a normal State are unmitigated evils and these trifles are certain to right themselves. But please distinguish between combinations of men for the purpose of carrying measures — which always will exist — and our permanent parties, standing parties as they may be called. In our party contests men do not battle for *measures,* they fight for *candidates.* "Our parties do not elect men to put into action certain principles; they use principles as battle-cries to elect certain men." Take a glance, for instance, through the socalled "political records" of *Harper's Magazine.* We find from first to last, nothing, *absolutely nothing,* but the names of men and the offices for which they, respectively, have been nominated or elected. "Politics," then, from being the Science of Government has become — Cooperative *Office-seeking!*

It was wise to form a party as a necessary organ of resistance to negro-slavery. But when that object was gained, then the need of party was gone; from that moment the Republican party became nothing but a faction, stuffed full with dollars.

The New Order cannot use a machinery which renders our legislators the people's masters and allows them to conduct public affairs with a view to private and class interests.

Our history furnishes some signal instances in point. The people have quite frequently demanded the resignation of their representatives; State legislatures have demanded it of their senators — instances therefore where there could be no doubt of the identity of the constituency — and what has been the answer?

"You have no business at all to demand my resignation. It is absolute presumption in you to do so."

A perfectly correct answer according to our constitution. They might with perfect propriety, constitutionally speaking, have added; "You call yourselves Sovereigns, and verily think yourselves such. Deluded Nobodies that you are! You were Sovereigns the moment you elected me, but in doing so, you abdicated in favor of me. Please wait till my term is out. *Till then I am the Sovereign.*

Then you can once more call yourselves "Sovereigns" for a moment in order to elect some other Master over you."

Is not that literally true? — And yet our Government is called a *Democracy!*

We, with Stickney, propose to put an end to this *term*-system, but we go further and say that the whole system of *representation* is unfit for a higher civilization.

Is not Carlyle perfectly right when he sneers at that kind of "liberty" which consists in having, as a voter has in our country, a forty-thousandth part of a *Talker* in our "National Palaver?" And even that Talker, though he is called *my* representative, may not, to that infinitesimal fraction represent *me*. That is a nice sort of "representative," *against* whose election I voted and perhaps worked. No matter! by voting at all I express my willingness to submit to a possible or probable majority against me. But I should have had to submit, if I had not voted at all; so whether I vote *against* him or *not at all*, that man is still *my* "representative!"

Very many schemes for doing away with this monstrous feature have been propounded, preeminently that of the Englishman Hare, which is almost perfect in its way, but which is absolutely impracticable, as long as we have standing parties.

All these schemes, moreover, are in themselves failures, because they aim at giving theoretical improvement to that which is fallacious in itself, for that is what representation is.

How can I say that what my representative will *tomorrow* that I also will?

"Nice sovereigns!" Rousseau said, "whose only function in government is to obey."

The simple and plain fact is that our boast of "self-government" is *mere cant;* the "representative" or "parliamentary" government was not *intended* to represent the People, but is a rude device for securing power to our *leading classes;* that is why we find so many lawyers — the retainers of our Plutocracy — in the legislative seats. Hence it is an essentially temporary expedient.

The New Order will have no use for Presidents and Governors who, for their term of office, are masters of the situation.

Our President is, even when he rebels against his party, exceedingly powerful for mischief, at all events. But when loyal to his party he is a veritable *king*, a dress-coat-king, 'tis true, but more powerful than any crowned king.

He cannot declare war, but he can create one. He cannot make treaties, but he can force them on the nation. He can nullify the laws by his pardon. His will and temper is the only rule for his veto power. He acts, Congress talks. He has a thousand means at his command to show favors to Congressmen. He is every year for many months the uncontrolled monarch of the country. In war he is almost absolute. And yet our country is called a *Republic!* — But then, it must be admitted that it was only an accident that made us a republic.

The New Order will know nothing of such an office.

It will know nothing of it because, as Goldwin Smith said in an excellent article in the *Atlantic Monthly* for January 1879, entitled: "Is Universal Suffrage a Failure?"

"It (the Presidency) is at once the grand prize and the most powerful stimulant of faction."

The Presidency is truly under our system "the grand prize" that fosters an ambition which no citizen in a republic *ought* to entertain and which has ruined the usefulness of so many of our best men.

The Presidency is the chief "spoil" and source of other spoils. We all remember the frankness of Flanagan in a late National Convention: "What are we here for if not the spoils?" When the Cooperative Commonwealth abolishes this chief spoil with all other spoils, and thus stops their pay, our standing parties will dissolve for want of cohesion, as standing armies do, when their pay stops.

But what does this discarding of these prominent features of our government mean? It means that the only political machinery fit for the Cooperative Commonwealth is Democracy.

For however hazy the meaning of that word is, nobody can fairly object if we, temporarily, define "Democracy" as that form of administration where *no one* of the public officers *is at any time* the *master of the situation;* where, consequently, *none of the public affairs can at any time be conducted with a view to private or class interests.*

The New Order will, further, discard the system of appointments *from above*, which is simply the principal means by which our ruling classes exercise their power.

It will throw overboard the doctrine of the three "coordinate" powers; that is, the doctrine that the functions of government should be distributed among three departments: the legislative, executive and judicial, wholly independent of, and yet checking each other.

This doctrine amounts to this, that laws should be enacted in one spirit, interpreted in another, and executed in a third spirit, which is preposterous. The theory of checks and balances is one born of passions, engendered by struggle against arbitrary power; *not* one born of philosophical observations. This fact was entirely misconceived by Montesquieu — that embodied Empiricism — and strangely enough, also overlooked by our practical forefathers, as noticed by Prof. Goldwin Smith in the article above mentioned.

The New Order will have no use whatever for a Senate.

It is useless. As John Stuart Mill remarks: "In times of violent excitement, the only times, when it might produce more good than harm, it is destined to become inoperative." Those who object, that the one chamber system has always been the forerunner of the usurper, seem never to have thought of the circumstance, that *the usurper has always introduced the two-chamber system.* With the National Senate will go the doctrine of state-sovereignty, which, though decrepit, is not yet dead. The doctrine is a relic of our infancy, when we were small, undeveloped scattered communities such as all civilized nations have started with. It is worthy of observation, that dual sovereignty has been the historical development of Great Britain, Germany, Sweden, Italy, Spain and France, as well as our country.

The Cooperative Commonwealth will only know of a Nation, with a big, *very big N.* Our present state-lines only work mischief. Parts of New Jersey and Delaware belong as much to Philadelphia as any part of Pennsylvania does, and New Jersey, Rhode Island and Connecticut are far more intimately connected with New York city than is Western New York.

"And when you, thus, have succeeded in doing away with the Term System, the Representative System, the Presidency, the three Coordinate Powers, the Senate, State Sovereignty and Appointments from above — in short with our whole Constitution, be good enough to tell us what other constitution it will please your Cooperative Commonwealth to give us."

An inquirer will very naturally, at this stage, ask some such question. It would remind us, that we have not yet made our fundamental position in regard to political changes clear.

Constitutions are not at all things to be given or taken away at pleasure.

What is a Constitution?

When we speak of the Constitution of the solar system, we mean by that term the attraction of the sun which so regulates the movements of the planets that this movement cannot be otherwise than what it is. When we in the same sense — the proper sense — speak of the Constitution of a country, we do not mean that piece of paper which is called a "Constitution," but *the organic power that makes necessary the institutions which we find.* It is therefore a fundamental mistake to think, that our country with her *written* "constitution" occupies a peculiar position.

Every country has and always had a constitution. A king with an army at his back is a large part of a constitution. The motto of Louis XIV: *"L'etat c'est moi"* ("I am the State") was as fully the constitution of France as any constitution she, or any country, ever had. The peculiarity of modern times consists simply in a piece of paper, simply in the giving written expression to the organic power. But if such a written "constitution" does not correctly respond to this organic power — as the "constitutions" of France during the Revolution did not, and as the "constitution" of the present German Empire does not — it is not worth the paper it is written on. If it, on the other hand, does so respond, it is like a swiftly flying buzz-saw — dangerous to go too near to.

The short history of our own country, even, bears us out in this view. Our present "constitution" is a very different one from what it was in 1850. The point of change was the period when people prated about "upholding the constitution." Whenever a "Constitution" needs being "upheld," it is going, or gone. During that period was promulgated the "Dred Scott" decision, which, undoubtedly, was a correct "constitutional" decision. Yet it was but an idle breath, or, if it had any effect, it was to make our people, (so approvingly styled "a law abiding people,") subvert the very "constitution," that was the sanction of the decision.

What was the matter?

The organic power in the Nation was simply changing. Mark! it was *the Abolition of Slavery which amended our "constitution,"* emphatically *not* the amendments to the "constitution" which abolished Slavery.

Is this Socialist view of the organic law of a country not far more philosophic than the vulgar one, held by our "statesmen" or even by such an eminent authority as Judge Story, who reduces the whole science of government to — a eulogy of the "Constitution?"

It remains true, reader! No army of lawyers, nor of soldiers, can uphold a "constitution," when the centre of gravity of Society has changed its position.

Socialists, then, have no thought whatever of "laying impious hands" on this glorious paper "constitution" of ours, or of "giving" to, or imposing upon, our country a new frame of government of our own; just as little as we fancy, that we can change its economic conditions.

It is the Logic of Events that will accomplish both these changes.

But mark the radical difference between the economic and the political revolution.

The economic relations of the Cooperative Commonwealth will evolve out of our present industrial conditions, as we attempted to show in the preceding chapters. But the form of administration of that Commonwealth will not be an outgrowth of our present form of government.

It is true, that the political system we now are living under is an outgrowth of our colonial system, but the representative, parliamentary system (the only one with which our country in her short history has been familiar, and which at present prevails in a more or less developed form in all civilized countries except Russia) is not an outgrowth of the feudal system, prevailing during the Middle Ages, nor was the latter an outgrowth of the ancient forms of government.

For forms of government are nothing but *forms*. They are not the substance of society. They are only coats, that may, or may not, fit the backs. But they are not the backs; economic conditions are the backs. Or, to use the other appropriate figure: forms of governments are nothing but machinery, but economic conditions are the steam, without which the machinery is useless.

It will be seen from this, that those are egregiously mistaken who charge Socialists with having a "faith in the sovereign power of political machinery." We believe, on the contrary, that forms of governments, in themselves, amount to nothing; that civil liberty, by itself, is hardly worth the trouble of agitation, that political freedom won, nothing may yet be won — but emptiness.

We believe, that economic and industrial relations are everything, wherefore also we devoted the first six chapters to them. Just as the steam-loom took the place of the hand-loom, and the steam-thrasher of the flail, when steam became the motive power instead of human muscles, or as the man must discard his boy's jacket, so we say the Cooperative Commonwealth will have as it grows into existence to relegate the whole machinery with which we are now familiar: President and Representatives and coordinate powers and statelines to the lumber-room of the past.

That is what this capitalist *regime* did as soon as *it* had grown up to manhood. It dispensed as fast as it could with every feature of the feudal system and substituted for it the system which allowed it to work to the best advantage, to-wit, the representative system.

If, therefore, we want to form any conception of the political or judicial administration of the Cooperative Commonwealth, we must imagine this present "constitution" of ours wiped out, first of all. Our inquirer and those opponents of Socialism who call attention to the incompatibility between it and our present frame of government, are therefore perfectly right: The United States would, in truth, become a bedlam at election times.

We hail it as a good sign, that an American lawyer like Stickney, and with him the whole new generation, is getting into the habit of questioning even "the wisdom of our forefathers."

Well, they *were* wise in their generation. They conformed to the organic power of their day. Let us and those who will come immediately after us be as wise in our and their generations! At any rate we cannot help ourselves. *Democracy* is what we are inevitably tending to, which will crush the Republican and "Democratic" parties as easily as if they were egg-shells.

And do not have any fear, that we shall then or ever be without a constitution. No, not for one moment. The new constitution will form itself as naturally as the ice forms upon the water, when the freezing point is reached.

But we must now know, not alone what "Democracy" is not, but what it *is,* and not so much, what the *word* means, but what the thing *really is* which we have in mind when we pronounce the word.

The word comes from the Greek word "demos," which means "the people." That gives us, however, just as poor an idea of what "Democracy," is, as the information that "Evolution" is derived from a word that means "to roll out" enables us to know what evolution is. That it is which has given us the definition found in dictionaries, that "Democracy" is "government by majorities," government by "counting of heads," as Carlyle has it. But government of majorities may be just as "undemocratic" as the rule of any other class.

No, let us turn to the "back" which the "coat" is to fit.

We saw that the Cooperative Commonwealth will incorporate the *whole population* into Society. It will destroy *classes* entirely. And with classes will go all "rule."

The "*whole* people" does not want, or need, any "government" at all. It simply wants *administration — good* administration.

That will be had by putting every one in the position for which he is best fitted, and making everyone aware of the fact.

That is what Democracy means; it means

Administration by the Competent.

CHAPTER VIII

ADMINISTRATION OF AFFAIRS

IN THE COOPERATIVE COMMONWEALTH

"Our self-government is amateur-administration, government by amateurs." — *Greg*.

"The feeling of Equality is growing fast. It makes men chafe more and more under the personal power of individuals, on a political level with themselves. But they will submit willingly to power that comes from above and is impersonal." — *Dr. Woolsey, Communism and Socialism.*

"In your trades-societies you have acquired the instinct of trusting your leaders, of acting with decision, concentration and responsibility. . . . The mass supplying breadth and energy of principle; your agents giving it concentration and unity. Let your watchword be: 'Confidence in tried leaders! Loyal cooperation each with all!'" — *Frederic Harrison, Order and Progress.*

We have now two definitions of *Democracy*,* one negative, the other affirmative, which together complete our conception of a *Socialist* Administration: that of *competent* and *qualified* functionaries, *whose interest is entirely coincident with their duty.*

But right here we shall be challenged. It may be said that this may be a good conception of a good administration, but that it is not "Democracy." Some will quote Frederic Harrison to the effect that "Democracy exists when each man holds himself as wise a ruler as his fellow; where Government is a scramble open to every glib talker." Others think with Carlyle that in a Democracy the people solve every problem by saying "let us take a vote" and

---

* It is annoying, that when we in our country use the word "Democracy," we have to apologize for its debasement from being appropriated by that party of negations calling itself "the Democratic Party," whose only affirmative principle is the decrepit doctrine of "State-Rights."

counting the heads. Others, again, will point to the article by Jesse Jones on "the Labor Question" which we in a former chapter mentioned with approval, and remind us that Jones there takes for granted, that our future economic system will conform to our primitive political system; that is, assumes that all affairs will be conducted on the "town-meeting"-plan. "What is that," they will ask, "but the Abomination of Frederic Harrison and Carlyle?"

This is a perfectly fair objection, to which we shall give an answer that cannot possibly be misunderstood. If the "town-meeting-plan," if that which Frederic Harrison, Carlyle and Jesse Jones agree in calling "Democracy" is properly named by them, then *we must find another name for the Administration of Public Affairs under the New Social Order.* The object of *Chapter VII* was not so much to show that our present form of government, our written "constitution," is *un-democratic,* as to point out that it is utterly unfit to furnish a good administration of the people's affairs. The object of this Chapter, in the first place, is to suggest the machinery that we have reason to assume will be adopted to carry on all the affairs of the Coming Commonwealth. This is the important matter for consideration, which we shall not allow to degenerate into a dispute about words. Yet, we shall also claim, that the Administration of the Future has an eminent, perhaps an exclusive, right to the name of "Democracy;" but that is a subordinate matter.

The "town-meeting" plan, the plan of "counting heads," will evidently be wholly unsuitable in the Cooperative Commonwealth. If our public affairs *now* have altogether outgrown that primitive plan, how much more when "public affairs" will mean *all* affairs, with industrial affairs in the foreground? No argument should really be needed to convince anybody, that a Nation that conducted all its affairs as Jones will have them conducted would very soon become bankrupt.

But this, that such an Administration as we have indicated in our definition will be the very one *needed* is not all: it will be the very one which the future Constitution — *real* constitution — of Society will necessitate.

We have already emphasized as much as we could, that the great achievement of the Coming Commonwealth will be to incorporate the *whole* population into Society, to shift the Centre of Gravity of Society, *to make the Working-Classes the organic power of*

Society. The great body of our people are manifestly dictated to as much as any other people. Though legally, that is, *theoretically,* the people here are governors, *practically* they have no more power over legislation than they have over Crises, over Production or Commerce. And the reason is, simply, that the Working-Classes have not yet got the real social power, for whatever is the strongest power in Society is the governing authority.

Well, all the evidence we now possess tends to prove that the Working-Classes, when *they* once become the organic force in the State, will favor such an Administration as we have defined.

Study the Trades-Unions here and those of England and learn from them, how workingmen go about their own affairs. Have the members of these Unions ever shown any anarchic spirit? Amongst the many things that have been said of and against them, have they ever been charged with evincing any instinctive thirst for each man having his own way? — which is the spirit of Anarchy. Is it not, contrariwise, true, that they always have been willing to acknowledge that some were wiser than themselves, and that, when they thought they had hit upon the right leaders, they have been willing to thrust their whole collective power into their hands? In short, is it not true, what Frederic Harrison says of them, that "they trust their leaders and act with decision, concentration and responsibility."

Now, these Working-Classes, who represent so to speak, the whole social body, of which the other classes only are special organs, will decide what the Administration of the Future is to be.

We avoid, purposely, saying that they will have the *political* power, for "political" power, "Politics," "Politicians" will be unknown terms under the New Order.

Political power is, fundamentally, nothing but the organized power of classes, or men, or sets of men, to "govern" others; that is, to dictate to them what they shall do and what they must not do. In our Commonwealth, where there will be no "classes" at all, there will be no set of men who can by "sovereign authority" dictate to the rest of the Nation, but every citizen will *actually* perform his appropriate share of the administration.

Again, the terms "State" and "Society" are now apart in *speech,* because they are in *fact* apart. But under the New social System they will, as we have seen, come to cover each other, become synonymous. Between the economic and Social organization, and the "political" organization of the Future State there will not be a particle of distinction.

Before we proceed to outline the Administration of the Future we wish to repeat the warning that we gave, when the economic features of the New Order were under discussion: *Socialists lay no claim to be "architects,"* hence do not insist upon details from us! Speculations here in detail would be liable to be far more Utopian than those in economic matters, since, as we have seen, the administrative features of a given society are but the ulterior results of its economic relations. We can, however, pretty safely predict that the following features will take the place of those we have discarded.

Appointments will be made from below. This is the second respect in which our Post Office Department is not a socialist institution — the other respect, as will be remembered, was the discrepancy in salaries. At present the Postmaster-General or President appoints the postmasters, and they again their subordinates and the letter-carriers. Under Socialism it will certainly be the reverse. There the letter-carriers will elect their immediate superiors; these, we will say, the postmasters and these in their turn the Postmaster General. Why should it not be so?

Are not the letter-carriers just as competent to elect their superintendents as the Chief in Washington is to appoint the postmaster of Boston? The qualifications of an elector are evidently these: a knowledge of the capacity of the candidate for a given office and a knowledge of what the duties of that office are (quite a different thing from a knowledge of *how* to *perform* those duties.) Who possesses these qualifications in a greater degree than those who are to be his immediate subordinates, and who, perhaps, have worked with the candidate throughout a series of years?

Understand! by appointment from below, we do not mean, that, for instance, the whole people of a city shall elect their postmaster. Such a principle is altogether too much in vogue now. We maintain exactly the reverse of it: that a man is not qualified to vote for a candidate whose qualifications he is ignorant of, for an office the duties of which he is not acquainted with. It will be admitted that it is quite a different proposition, that the workers in a factory should elect their Foreman, teachers their Superintendent &c. This is the only method by which harmonious loyal cooperation of subordinates with superiors can be secured. No one ought to be a superior who has not the good will of those he has to direct.

Understand, also, that *Appointment* from below does not necessarily imply *Removal* from below.

Think but a moment over it, and notice the important and beneficent results that will flow from such a system.

We said that every citizen would be *actually* a part of the Administration. This that he will have a voice in the election of his immediate superior, will be one way, and perhaps the most important way, of being such part. *That kind of Suffrage will be worth something.* We have now cut what we call "political power" into such little bits, that a single man's share of it is hardly thought worth having at all. But his vote will count for something in a shop when a foreman is to be elected; will indeed, confer such a dignity on him, that he will be a different man from the servile "hand" of our present irresponsible autocrats.

Again, this system will furnish one of the securities for good administration. It is not likely that under it there will any longer be any "government by amateurs." Then the greatest ability will in every sphere of activity in all likelihood gravitate towards all positions of influence, (just as we find it to be the case in the English Trades-societies according to the most competent authority) and *the subordinates will be aware of the fact.*

Instead of any term of office, long or short, *we shall have a tenure during Good Behavior.*

The directors of affairs will hold their offices as long as the people's interests are best served by having them hold them, *but not one moment beyond.* They all, from Foreman up to the Chiefs, will have to do good work, and will not stay in their office one week, nay, not one day, if they fail in their duties, ay, *if they fail to give satisfaction.* Every such officer will be held responsible, not for good intentions, but for *accomplished results.* Of all causes for removal the best of all will be one, unrecognized now, the misdemeanor of Failure. "Good Behavior" will mean first of all: *Efficiency.* And as a very important part of the work of every officer will consist in overseeing others, he will be held responsible, if the work done by those under him is not done well. He will be driven to enforce the utmost efficiency from every one of his subordinates. His holding his place will depend on what they do, as much as on what he himself does.

This personal responsibility and instant dismissal for failure will permeate the whole service from top to bottom. This is what the Cooperative Commonwealth will need, for as Stickney well remarks: "If his future advancement (and we add: the tenure of a functionary) depends on a king he will serve the king; if on party he will serve party; if only on doing his work well, he will do his work well. It is no miracle. It is nothing but a law of human nature." Which remark we commend to our Utopian Civil-Service-Reformers who wish, and no doubt sincerely, to reform the service in the same direction as Socialists do, but want to retain Party-government.

But, on the other hand, when a good man has got into the proper place and performs his work well, he will go on and do it as long as he has a mind to stay. We have tried that plan to some extent and we have had some good results from it. Everybody will admit, that our judicial tenure of office has had a great deal to do with the fact, that our judiciary has been so pure and uncorrupted as has been the case — while the greatest blot on its fair fame (the Electoral Commission business of 1877) can be just as directly traced to the evil influences of *party*. The principal objection we have to our Judicial Tenure is that "Good Behavior" means nothing but "remaining *respectable*." In a Socialist Administration a judge would not remain one day in office when he was notoriously unfit to perform his duties, as was for years the case with members of our National Supreme Court. Again, whatever opinion is entertained of the expediency of West Point and our army, Socialists will cheerfully admit the high moral tone of the Army Service — until lately, at any rate — compared with our Civil Service, which is directly traceable to the secure tenure of office of the former.

The Directors of Affairs, furthermore, will be trusted with all the power necessary to perform their work well. They will not be hampered by any petty technicalities. The people will abstain from meddling with details, as long as the results are satisfactory. That is the sensible practical method which workingmen always adopt whenever they associate to accomplish anything, as also is exemplified in the English Trades-Unions. Workingmen know, that the direction of affairs ought to be a function of the competent, as much as the planning of a suspension bridge is, and not a play for numbers. They always, as Frederic Harrison puts it, "put confidence in tried leaders."

Some one may here object that when in that way under Socialism all the high talent of the country is concentrated in the Administration, it will be exactly the "Bureaucracy" we find in Prussia, Russia and China.

It would indeed be a bureaucracy, if it were proposed that our civil officers under our present system should have a life-tenure of their places. But it will be quite a different thing, when, as in the Cooperative Commonwealth *every* citizen has a life-tenure *somewhere*, and when "good behavior" means something else than not to commit an infamous crime. Is a physician a bureaucrat? When a patient has found a good physician he keeps him and follows his directions, and yet we should say, that that patient's power over this physician is not nugatory, though he does not direct what medicines shall be administered.

Such a tenure during "Good Behavior," as we have defined it, will be another security for good administration. Whenever the directors of affairs have such power as is their due, when they are secure in their positions and permitted to do the best they know how, we can be sure to find merit in the commanding positions, for it will ever remain true that the direction of affairs has wonderful charms for all men who have any gifts, fitting them for it.

Instead of representation *we shall have,* what is technically called, the *referendum.*

By the "referendum" is meant the submitting all bills of a general nature to the people they are intended to affect, before they have the validity of laws, as already exemplified for some years past by Switzerland to some extent, both in national and cantonal affairs.

We claim, that this feature represents exactly the function which the people are fitted to perform and which it is every way expedient they should perform.

They are peculiarly fitted to perform this function of ratifying, or rather, of *vetoing* measures (with which our President and governors are at present and — as we contended in the previous chapter

— improperly entrusted) while they are peculiarly unfitted for the function with which they are now constitutionally invested: that of selecting men of whose qualifications they can know nothing for offices of the duties of which they are ignorant.

The people should leave the framing of laws to the wisest and most competent. But because I should not attempt to make my own shoes, since I am no shoemaker, that is no reason why I should not decline to buy a certain pair of shoes which the shoemaker has made. I need not be a shoemaker to know, whether the shoes pinch me or not. Exactly so with laws and institutions. The people are amply qualified to say that they *do not want* certain laws.

John S. Mill says in regard to representative bodies, that their proper office is "not to make law but to see them made by the right persons, and to give or withhold its ratification of them." "Good sense" and "good intentions," the only requisites for that function, we must assume in the body of citizens or we must, indeed, despair of the Nation.

By the way, it was Robespierre — for whom, however, neither the writer of this nor Socialists generally have any great admiration — who first proposed the *referendum,* by advising the king to say: "My people, here are the laws I have made for you; will you accept them?"

The *referendum* is expedient, because the stability and goodness of all laws and institutions depend on their suitableness. We have compared political institutions to coats that may or may not fit the backs. The *referendum* will insure, that "the coat will fit the back," in other words, that the measures adopted are commensurate with the development of the people. If the coat does not fit, if a given measure does not suit them, they will simply reject it.

It is expedient, because it and it alone will arouse and keep alive in the people the interest in public affairs.

It is a notorious fact that the voters in our country and in all countries are absolutely indifferent to — we may say truthfully, that they look with a sort of contempt on — the electoral franchise; and the humbug of representation that we adverted to in the preceding chapter is a sufficiently good reason. Voters will naturally remain indifferent, as long as a political campaign means but a strife for *candidates.* Whenever they do vote, they will continue to do so from the same reasons which solely influence them now, to-wit:

habit, or the desire to advance a friend or a "hero," or the chance of getting a drink.

But when the voters have measures before them, — not merely general, and therefore vague, constitutional provisions, but *direct, special measures* — to discuss and then to ratify or reject, it may fairly be expected, that they will take a considerable and increasing interest in public affairs. Then, also, they will very likely come more and more to appreciate the fact, that Suffrage is not a right at all — if it were, votes would, indeed, be things to be sold or given away, at pleasure — but a *public trust*.

The *referendum* is expedient, because bills will then be intelligently discussed before they become laws. We shall then no more witness the indecency, that important laws the provisions of which even often are unknown to the legislators are enacted in the hurry of the last night of a session, under the spur of the party whip. Then we shall no longer see huge volumes of trash issuing yearly from legislative halls, but shall have few, and none but necessary, laws.

"But this is all nonsense to propose to get along without representatives. The people of a large country, like that of ours, cannot possibly pass upon all laws."

Yes, we know, that once upon a time somebody made a remark of that kind, and that it has been echoed and re-echoed ever since. Humanity does really resemble a flock of sheep which are known to be so conscientious, that if you hold a stick before the wether so that he is forced to vault in his passage, the whole flock will do the like when the stick is withdrawn.

Why cannot the people, even of so populous and extensive a country as ours, vote upon all laws? Do not, as a matter of fact, our people vote to reject or accept the constitutions of their several states? Do they not practically vote for the President? What reason in the world is there, why they cannot just as well vote upon a law as upon a constitution or upon men?

And what reason is there for the people to have "representatives" at all? True, they needs must have men to direct affairs and to do certain work for them. These men are their *agents* for certain purposes, but in no sense their *representatives*. It is their fictitious "representative" character which permits Pennsylvania legislators to drag along the scandalous extra session and prevents their being kicked out of their seats as they ought to be. It is this "representative" character that is the father of all parliamentary nonsense, blundering work and the "practical politics" in which Garfield was such an adept, and of which he fell such a signal victim.

Under the Socialist *Regime* the Administrators will form a *working* Body, not a *talking* Body. The people in their organic capacity will watch, stimulate and control them but not meddle with details. Their agents will have been put into the positions they occupy, because they know better than anybody else how to contrive the means and execute the measures demanded. They will *administer* the Nation's affairs as a pilot directs and handles a ship, but the direction of the Ship of State will be indicated by Public Opinion.

But the pertinacious curiosity of critics will, undoubtedly, not be satisfied, before they have a sketch of such a Socialist administration before them for examination.

Well, anybody can construct such an administration in his imagination as well as we can, if he only will keep steadily before him these three requirements: *first,* that all appointments be made from below;* *next,* that the directors stay in office as long as they give satisfaction and not one moment beyond; and, *lastly,* that all laws and regulations of a general nature must first be ratified by those immediately interested. We have no better means of guessing how those who come after us will construct their administrative machinery in detail than anybody else; and modern Socialists are not fond of laying down rules for the guidance of coming generations.

In order, however, to show that an administration without President, without national or local "debating societies" of any kind is really possible, we shall draw such a one in outline; but please bear in mind that Socialism must not be made responsible for this fancy-sketch of ours. We do this the more willingly, because, as our thoughtful readers must have observed, there is one highly important provision that we for good reasons have left entirely unnoticed.

Suppose, then, every distinct branch of industry, of agriculture, and, also teachers, physicians etc. to form, each trade and profes-

---

* [In his revised edition Gronlund inserted a note at this point dissenting from Bellamy's provision for the election of officials by retired functionaries, which Gronlund felt to be a reversion to the primitive practice of government by elders. — Editor's Note.]

sion by itself, a distinct body, a Trades-Union (we simply use the term, because it is convenient) a guild, a corporation managing its internal affairs itself, but subject to collective control.

Suppose, further, that, for instance, the 'heelers' among the operatives in a shoe-factory in Lynn come together and elect their Foreman and that the 'tappers,' the 'solers,' the 'finishers,' and whatever else the various operators may be called, do likewise. Suppose that these Foremen assemble and elect a Superintendent of the factory, and that the Superintendents of all the shoe-factories in Lynn, in their turn, elect a — let us call him — District-Superintendent. Again, we shall suppose these District-Superintendents of the whole boot and shoe industry to assemble themselves somewhere from all parts of the country and elect a Bureau-Chief, and he with other Bureau-Chiefs of related industries, say, the tanning industry, to elect a Chief of Department.

In the same manner we shall suppose, that we have got a Chief for every group of related mechanical and agricultural and mining pursuits, a Chief for the teachers, another for the physicians, another for the judges — see next chapter — further, one or more Chiefs for transportation, one or more for commerce — in fact, suppose, that there is not a social function whatever that does not converge in some way in such Chief of Department.

However, we do not want too many of those Chiefs, for we mean to make a working Body, not a talking Body, out of them. We mean that these Chiefs of Department shall form *The National Board of Administrators*, whose function it shall be to supervise the whole social activity of the country. Each Chief will supervise the internal affairs of his own department, and the whole Board control all those matters in which the General Public is interested.

But just as all inferior officers this National Board will be nothing but a body of administrators; they will be merely trusted *agents* to do a particular work; they will be in no sense "governors" or "rulers;" or if anybody should choose to call their supervision and control "government," it will, at all events, rather be a government over *things* than over *men*. For they will decree no laws.

If a general law is thought expedient, one that will affect the people at large or those of any one department, then we suppose this National Board simply to agree on the general features of the measure, and thereupon entrust the drafting of the proper bill either to the Chief whose department it principally concerns, or, what might be the usual course, to the Chief of the Judges. When this draft has been discussed and adopted, the Board will submit it to the people either of the whole country or of the department, as may be, for their ratification. The National Board is thus no law-maker, therefore no "government" but an executive body *strictly*.

But how shall we exact that responsibility on which we laid so much stress; which we considered the very keystone of Democracy? That important question we have hitherto not touched upon at all, for the simple reason that there is absolutely nothing in the tendency of things that can guide us to any solution. The constantly reiterated demands of the working-classes and their mode of procedure in their own affairs teach us what course they will pursue as to Appointments, Tenure of Office and the Passage of Laws but nothing definite about *Removals.* And yet this point is second to none in importance: How shall we prevent these Foremen, Superintendents and especially the Chiefs of Departments from being at any time *the masters of the situation?*

Well, the writer of this can say how it *may* be accomplished, but does not at all pretend to say, how it *will* be done.

Experience has shown, that responsibility to many is, in ordinary cases, no responsibility at all. We therefore hold, that if these directing functionaries are to be made responsible for their work, *they must be made responsible to some one person.* But who is the proper *one* person?

We noticed, that every directing officer should be responsible not alone for the work he himself does, but also for the work of *his subordinates.* He must see to it, that they do their work well. Is not this a sufficiently good reason why every directing official should be given the right instantly to dismiss any one of his subordinates for cause assigned; inefficiency being, as already stated, the very best of causes. When then a foreman was inefficient, he would be removed instantly, without trial, by his superintendent; he again might be removed by his bureau-chief — *perhaps for abuse of power in removing the foreman;* — this bureau-chief again by his department-chief.

But the latter official, to whom shall he be responsible? Some would say, to the whole Body of Administrators. And yet the very obvious objection might be raised to such an arrangement, that it would really be no responsibility, for are not these administrators all equals, and interested in upholding each other in power?

Suppose we make every Department Chief liable to removal by the whole body of his subordinates.

That is to say, suppose, that, whenever the workers of a given department, inclusive of Foremen, Superintendents and other officials, become dissatisfied with their Chief, they all meet in their different localities and vote on the dismissal of that Chief, and that he be considered removed from office the moment the collective judgment of the whole department is known, if that judgment be adverse to him. Then the Bureau-Chiefs immediately proceed to elect another Chief of Department who can be removed in like manner, if he should not suit the workers.

That feature, then, of the plan we have sketched which must be charged to the personal bias of the writer of this is, that, while the subordinates elect, *the superiors dismiss*. This feature we hold will divide power between skill and numbers in the proper proportion. We deem it a pretty good application of the famous proposition of Harrington in his *"Oceana"* who wanted power divided on the principle which governs two children in fairly dividing a cake: that the one halves the cake, while the other chooses its portion. This feature will create perfect harmony between responsibility on one hand and subordination on the other. The Foremen elect their Superintendent, but the moment he is elected, he is independent of them; how else could he be responsible for himself and *for them* to his superior? But by making the Chief of all in each department responsible to all his subordinates, we have vindicated the ultimate rule of that impersonal Power: Public Opinion.

One point yet remains unnoticed. Can the foreman also dismiss any of his workers for inefficiency or other cause? It will easily be seen, that this is a quite different matter from the dismissal of a directing official. When the latter is removed, he is simply put back among the rank and file, until elevated by a new election. He has no right to his office. But whereto could a worker be removed? He must be employed somewhere. Of course, there must be some kind of remedy by which Society could protect itself against any rebellious or negligent worker. For such cases a trial by his comrades might be provided, the issue of which might be removal to a lower *grade* or some sort of compulsion.

Now, is this not Democracy?

It is certainly Administration *by the People.* Every citizen will actually help in administering affairs by having something considerable to say about who is to be his immediate superior. This feature is really the greatest of all, by far; it provides a kind of a primary election which is not child's play. And that it will work well in practice the Catholic church may teach us: cardinals elect the pope; priests nominate their bishops and monks their abbots. That church, by-the-way, — the most ingenious of human contrivances — can teach us many a lesson and we are fools if we do not profit by them.

Such a system as that we have sketched insures *Equality.* It will not make all equally wise in all matters, but it will destroy all *irresponsible* power, abolish every trace of dependence on *individuals.* All authority will be a public trust; whenever there is Subordination on the one hand, there is on the other Responsibility. Instead of a slavish subjection to anybody's autocratic will, there will be loyal submission by all to the common impersonal superior. That is a difference which the penitent operators of the Western Union who lately signed certain so-called contracts(!) ought to be able to appreciate. It by no means implies negation of all impulse, all initiative from those who are the wiser, for *equality* is not *likeness;* it rather is synonymous with *variety,* just as the same soil in freedom produces all kinds of trees.

Such a system, finally, establishes the best security for the *best administration;* it will furnish us those "real rulers" for whom Carlyle yearned. Here again we can appeal to the experience of the Catholic church, which knows how so to possess herself of her priests, that they are as wise, acute and pushing for her as the most consummate man of the world is for his own interests.

But Public Opinion — the *organic* opinion of the people, not what they separately think, — the Public Conscience, will rule these "real rulers."

In three ways this impersonal Power will assert itself: by the *referendum,* by giving or refusing those highest in authority a vote of confidence, and last, though not least, by and through the *public journals.*

Our journals have really a far more representative character than Congress or our legislatures, and, further, they are "representatives" in constant session. True, they do not represent the people, for they represent in no sense the working-classes — these are as yet to all intents and purposes perfectly dumb — but they represent very well our comfortable classes, our ruling classes, the "Messrs. six per cent." This will all be changed in the Cooperative Commonwealth.

Some will here remark: "If newspapers are, also, to be collective property, as we suppose they are, and published only by public authority, we do not see much chance for any opinion, aside from 'official' opinion, to assert itself."

Let us observe that our present journals have three functions:

First, they are *news*papers. To gather and give the news is their principal object. And that is the main reason why they represent the well-to-do classes, exclusively, for it takes lots of money to get the news.

Next, they are *public criers*. They devote, in fact, most of their columns to pushing and puffing all sorts of private enterprises.

Lastly, there is a little space left for "editorials," in which garrulous writers, in the pay of the "Messrs. six per cent," do the thinking for their employers; since they represent mediocrity, it goes without saying, that it is very ordinary thoughts they furnish, none very exciting — narcotic, rather.

In the Coming Commonwealth the first two functions will be separated from the one last mentioned.

There will probably in every community be published an official journal which will contain all announcements of a public nature and all the news, gathered in the most efficient manner by the aid of the national telegraph service, but no comments.

But we are assured that besides these there will also be published many private journals, true champions of principles and measures. True, the printing press will be a collective institution — but it will be open to every one.

Anyone — whatever unpopular opinions he may entertain, however hostile to the administrators he may be, — will be entitled to have anything decent printed, provided he is ready to pay for the work done, or to guarantee by himself or friends that the cost will be defrayed. Of course, a line must be drawn somewhere, as has at all times and in all countries been done. Public Opinion has always insisted upon, that there is something it will not tolerate — and so it probably will always be and so it ought to be.

Some one has happily characterized Carlyle as the man who "brought us out of the Egypt of shams into the desert and — left us there." Carlyle did a splendid work in bringing us out of the shams of representative parliamentarism, but he was sadly mistaken when he wanted us to go back to the forms of the Middle Ages. The "Eternal Silences" have decreed Democracy, which in the fullness of time will transform the party-ridden American people into a self-assertive people, transform the goose into an eagle.

CHAPTER IX

ADMINISTRATION OF JUSTICE

IN THE COOPERATIVE COMMONWEALTH

"Our judicial system: a technical one, invented for the creation of costs." — *Romilly.*

"Distinguished pleaders defeat justice while establishing points of law." — *Frazer's Mag. Nov. 79.*

"There never was such an infernal cauldron as that Chancery on the face of the earth! Nothing but a mine below it on a busy day in term time, with all its records, rules, and precedents collected in it, and every functionary belonging to it also, high and low, upward and downward, from its son the Accountant-General to its father the Devil, and the whole blown to atoms with ten thousand hundred weight of gunpowder would reform it in the least!" — *Charles Dickens.*

It is evident that in the Cooperative Commonwealth there will be far less litigation than now. Everyone familiar with the business of our Courts knows, that cases arising from contract contribute by far the largest part of that business. If these were extirpated; if our Courts had to deal, only, with cases of torts and criminal cases, the great majority of our high-prized lawyers, now crowded with "business," would have to seek pastures new. Now, such cases will in the new Commonwealth necessarily be, if not entirely done away with, immensely reduced, at all events, on account of its taking all enterprises of any social account into its own hands. As to criminal cases we may be pretty sure that they will diminish materially.

Probably nearly all the cases brought before the national courts for determination will be those arising between the Trades-Unions, Guilds, Corporations, or whatever they will be called, and their members, or between the Guilds themselves, or, finally, between them and the Departments.

Further, when discussing the *referendum* we remarked, that its introduction would naturally tend to reduce considerably the bulk of our statute-law and to prevent frequent changes in the same. The immense reduction in the *subject matter* of legislation, mentioned in the preceding paragraph, and, more than all, the wiping out of all State-lines and State-jurisdictions, will contribute materially to the same end. We are now in matters of legislation pretty much in the condition France was in before her Great Revolution. Her laws, it was said, were changed as often as were her post-horses; we may be said to change laws as often as we do railroad-cars.

Under the future Social Order we may hope to have a handy, compact and yet accurate and comprehensive code of *lasting* statutes, so that the requirements of law will not needs be a mystery to anybody for ever after.

And yet, though such a change in itself will be of far-reaching importance, it will constitute but a small fraction of that revolution which the two principles of Collective Control and Democracy will bring about in our judicial system. For that which gives value to all laws is the method of administering them; *and that method will itself be revolutionized.*

In the first place, our present method of administering justice is that of *Warfare.* Our method makes of the profession of law the art of gaining a victory; of a Court of Justice a battleground; it uses witnesses as soldiers and rules, precedents and technicalities as weapons and engines of war. Without perceiving this you cannot possibly reconcile the professional code of the lawyer with personal morality.

Listen to this code:

If a lawyer wins a case by superior vigilance, he has done just what his duty requires of him, *even if he knows he is on the wrong side.*

It is a proper move for a lawyer, adroitly to lead his adversary away from unassailable legal positions, or manoeuvre him out of superiority of evidence.

A lawyer must steer around, must *dodge* the law against him.

A lawyer should see to it, if he may not surprise his adversary, *or even the judge,* into some action which will render a new trial probable should the verdict be against him; for instance, make the judge overrule an objection *by stating a flimsy ground,* while he conceals the true one. Indeed, our shining lights of the bar do daily act on the comprehensive rule, that they may do anything to gain the victory, except suborning witnesses and forging precedents.

This code of the profession becomes perfectly comprehensible in the light of the theory, that a law-suit is a campaign of war. In fact, it cannot be defended on any other ground than the one which allows perfidy and deceit in war. A general *must* vanquish the enemy by all means, and in the same way it is made the duty of the most conscientious counsel after he is retained, to have this thought steadily in his mind: "How shall I bring the judge and the jury to decide for my client? How can I cripple and obstruct my opponent? How can I make my case *appear* to have the law on its side?" without for a moment inquiring into the justice of his case. To this miserable theory, that the profession of law is the art of warfare, of strategy and manœuvring, is due, exclusively, the spoliation, the evasion, the failure of justice, almost synonymous with law.

Thus it explains why the profession so persistently sticks to the cumbrous jury-system and to the unanimity of twelve jurors.

By the way, do you know why there always must be exactly twelve? Lord Coke, the apostle of the Anglo-Saxon lawyer, enlightens you: because there were twelve apostles, and twelve tribes of Israel!!!

Whenever you find a lawyer with a poor case, you can be sure that nothing will make him waive his grand constitutional right to a jury. He has been taught that the lawyer must use as allies even the erroneous prejudices, even the *ignorance* of mankind. Then there is the delicious uncertainty about the verdict of a petit jury, which exactly chimes in with the warfare idea. There is a chance for a verdict in his favor, for a disagreement, and, lastly, for a new trial. Hence such rhetorical laudations as this: "No better tribunal has yet been devised than a jury of twelve intelligent, honest and fair-minded men." Any suggestion that three such men, with a majority to decide, would do as well, is frowned down by the profession. For — that would *very much diminish the chances.**

* An article: "Is the Jury System a Failure?" in the *Century* of 1882 by Albert Stickney, whom our readers know from a former chapter, is worth perusal.

Again, to this theory that it is the duty of the profession to fight battles and win victories is due the fact that the decision of a case very seldom hinges on a statute law and general maxims of equity, but almost always on some precedent, that is, some similar case, preserved in one or other of the thousand American or English "Reports."

The citizen who supposes, that the "law" he is governed by is the *statute-law* of his state is very much in error. The statute-law is the most insignificant fraction of our laws. The "law" is something no lawyer can learn in a lifetime, both on account of the bulk of the Reports (to which in America alone a hundred volumes are added yearly) and because he never can be absolutely certain what is good, and what bad law.

But even if a judge should be told all the decisions on a given point that are valid, *he has no guide in them at all.* There stand the decisions in two rows: On one hand those in which a question has been decided one way; on the other those where the decision has been the contrary way — length of rows as nearly equal as the heart could wish. He takes his choice and either way he bows to the name of some "learned" judge, some "authority!"

The fatal conclusion thus is, that our administration of justice depends upon caprice. The profession *divines*, rather than ascertains the law. And all our legislation, in spite of all codes and all "reforms," is by the address of lawyers made to rest on precedents.

Why?

Because the theory of warfare requires snares rather than guides; it requires as much *uncertainty*, connected with as much *precision* as possible. To say that lawyers have no interests in the uncertainty of the law is to say that glaziers have no interest in the breaking of windows. Because precedents are their engines of warfare, our lawyers tenaciously cling to them and have a horror for broad principles. They unwittingly consider that a virtue which furthers the peculiar, sinister interests of their class.

The same theory, also, requires the innumerable technicalities, rules and forms, that have as little to do with justice as English wigs and gowns have. Our constitutions really perpetrate a witticism, when they guarantee "complete justice, conformably to the laws," for these laws silently *assume* these slippery rules and subtilties. To guarantee complete justice *conformably to rules that thwart justice* is like guaranteeing liberty inside locks and keys and shackles.

From this warfare-theory follows another great evil — an outrage upon every idea of justice. A war demands money, much money. No man, therefore, can commence or defend a lawsuit without a replete pocketbook. It is one of the most expensive speculations he can venture into, and the longest purse is pretty sure to win.

Our paper-constitutions pompously guarantee "justice freely and without purchase, completely and without denial, promptly and without delay." Instead of that this warfare theory gives us the triple-headed monster of Expense, Vexation and Delay.

And, lastly, this warfare theory has a demoralizing effect on the lawyer. It gives far more credit to him who wins a bad case than to him who wins a good one. It compels our legal men to be partisans, to be what Jeremy Bentham sneeringly called them — "Messrs. Eitherside." There is no radical difference between that "representative of the bar" who for a fancy fee is the partisan of one party today, against him perhaps tomorrow, an advocate of one theory one moment, its opponent the next moment, and the common pettifogger. The latter is simply an irregular guerilla. What do we say of the soldier who is today in one camp, in another tomorrow? The rules which this theory makes obligatory on the lawyer, the arts he must practise, if practised in any other position, would be deemed dishonorable.

And the study and practice of the law under this method cripples the lawyer intellectually. Take him who has raised himself to the summit of learning by wooing that "jealous mistress," the law with "twenty years' lucubrations," the condition fixed by authorities. In what has he become "learned?" In the conceit of centuries and the debris of society. Buckle is right: "Learning" serves Ignorance as much as it does Progress.

Take, next, the successful practitioner. What does he gain by "establishing points of law?" — some of which are as unprofitable as the medieval puzzle: how many souls can dance on the point of a needle? He becomes alert, smart, undoubtedly. But the practice of law has the same effect as the action of the grindstone; it *narrows* the mind as well as *sharpens* it. Especially is that the case with practitioners who devote themselves to special branches of the law. They get to have a positive aversion to enlarged views and care no more for the interests of mankind beyond the narrow limit of their pursuit than the man who spends his life in putting on the heads of pins.

And yet the indifference of legal men to the public welfare — as long as there are cases to try — by no means keeps them away from public affairs. On the contrary, a lawyer takes as naturally to politics as a duck to water, simply because politicians and lawyers are equally intriguers. The consequence is that their vicious maxims, antiquated systems and contracted views are carried over into the broad field of governmental affairs, taking the place of enlarged views, suitable to the situation and height of the times. Lawyers as a rule make our laws, although a superstition prevails, that this is the work of the people; but it is an absurdity beyond measure, that no executive officer, in purely administrative matters, can take a step without consulting a cramped, in such affairs essentially ignorant, law officer, placed at his elbow.

In the second place, it is a part of our method that the judges make law for the people.

What are those precedents we mentioned, which make up by far the greater part of the law we are governed by, and which, in our country alone, are manufactured at the rate of a hundred volumes yearly? They are nothing but "judge-made law," "counterfeit law" in the words of Bentham. Of such "law" here one example, only:

Our national constitution provides, that no state shall pass any law, impairing the obligation of contracts. Chief Justice Marshall, by our lawyers surnamed "the Great," took upon himself to say — in the celebrated Dartmouth College case — that this provision should be so construed *as to prohibit the people from altering charters and withdrawing privileges, granted by themselves to corporations.* And such is the law since that "great" decision was promulgated.

No, one more instance, for it is too interesting to omit. Do you know, why Christianity is a part of the Common Law of our country? Because an English judge, Lord Mansfield, mistranslating two words of a dictum of somebody in the 15th century, called *ancien scripture* (Norman French, meaning: ancient *writing*) — "holy scripture!!!"

And this extraordinary power of our judges means, that they can provide a law for cases *after* they arise. As Bentham said: "They proceed with men as men proceed with dogs. When your dog does something you want to break him of, you wait till he does it and then you thrash him for it. That is what judges do to suitors whom they make reluctant heroes of a leading case." They, thus, exercise a power which is expressly forbidden to the legislators.

But that is not all.

The people's "representatives" pass a certain law. The people obey it and act under it. Afterwards a judge delivers himself of this piece of wisdom to some poor wretch whom he has got within his jurisdiction: "I declare that law to be *no law at all*. You were presumed to know that all the time. When you acted under this so-called law, you did so at your peril." Is not that to make the minister of the law superior to the law itself? Certainly it is. Hear Horatio Seymour in an article in the *North American Review*: "The great distinguishing feature of our government, where we stand alone among the peoples of the earth, is placing the judiciary *above* the executive and the lawmaking power."

Yes, and above the people in their organic capacity. The fate of the *constitution* which the people of California lately adopted may lead us to doubt, if it is possible for the people in their primary capacity to frame an *organic law*, that will not be so *mis*construed by judges as to defeat the very purposes they sought to accomplish.

Against lawyers and judges, then, the people are a cipher. Let the people signify their will in a way they think cannot be misconstrued — the judges come with their dignified countenances, saying: "You, people, do not at all know what you will, for you will quite the contrary of what you have said." Some people talk of priestcraft and ascribe all sorts of horrors to it! The priesthood that is dangerous may not be the one that preaches on Sundays, but the "learned" ones to whom on week-days law and reason, justice and the public welfare are merely subjects of play or caprice.

Now we can say for certain that under the Cooperative Commonwealth this method will be radically changed, — our two Socialist principles will not permit its continuance. We may be certain,

First, that judges will not be allowed to make counterfeit laws.

That will be a necessary consequence from the democratic principle, that what the people have *not* sanctioned is *not* law. Every case will be decided on its merits — according to the law as the people have sanctioned it, *without regard to any precedents whatsoever.*

Precedents, then, the dry worthless historical knowledge on which our legal men have constructed their sham-science, called "jurisprudence," will thus be swept away under their feet, as was done in France by the Revolution and the Code Napoleon. That this code has been covered up with new precedents, twenty times as voluminous as itself by the lawyers having commenced their refinements over again, thus clogging the wheels of justice as much as before, is due to the suppression of the principle of democracy.

Second, it will follow, even more necessarily, that *judges will no longer be permitted to nullify laws,* since in the Cooperative Commonwealth what the people *have* sanctioned *is* law.

This monstrous guardianship of the judiciary over the people, dictating to them and their representatives, as last resort, what is law and what lawbreaking, which also Jefferson denounced as undemocratic, and of which the British Constitution, that we otherwise have tried so faithfully to copy, knows nothing, will cease to "distinguish us among the peoples of the earth."

We may be assured,

Third, that *the whole tribe of lawyers will be abolished* and with them the whole warfare-theory and all its quibbles will be swept away.

The New Order, with its practical economic organization of all public affairs, will have no use whatever for our "Messrs. Eitherside." Abolish the warfare, and the profession of the lawyer is next to useless.

Lawyers are now necessary evils — necessary on account of our method of administering justice, just as the old Roman lawyers were necessary, because in Rome a suit was a religious rite, requiring ceremonies that only could be performed by the initiated. So because, and *only* because, a lawsuit is now a warfare and because technicalities and precedents are mysteries to the uninitiated; finally because of the innumerable conflicting personal interests, we undoubtedly could not at present very well dispense with lawyers.

But when this multiplicity of interests is done away with and the present method of administering justice torn up by the roots, then their occupation will be gone. And the Coming Commonwealth is not likely to squander the public treasures on useless functionaries.

Fourth. To sue for justice will be absolutely costless.

That is easily done, as soon as lawyers are abolished.

"But if justice be free, all will avail themselves of it and there will be no end to litigation."

Is then an appeal to law worse than a trespass? The New Order will not so consider it; it will consider the least injury to any of its citizens an injury to itself. Give me a license to do any person at pleasure the minutest wrong conceivable; allow me to pour a drop of water upon his head *against his will; that person is my slave.* Our Commonwealth will know what a *groundless* suit means: it will know of no such thing as a *frivolous* one. Besides, it is the modern sparing justice that feeds iniquity. Be assured, that swift and unbending justice, with the fining of malicious or litigious complainants, will check litigation.

But it is natural, that inquirers should not yet be satisfied. They will ask: "What kind of procedure, then, will the Cooperative Commonwealth introduce? So far you have only been tearing down the present system, except that you have promised us *one* positive achievement, to-wit, a handy, intelligible volume of laws. *What* system, now, will take the place of the incubus you have relieved us of?"

We remark here as we did, when the economic administration under Socialism was discussed, that Socialists have no ready-made plan to lay down for the guidance of those who will be called upon to organize the Coming Commonwealth, least of all a detailed plan. They must be guided by their own judgment, the then condition of affairs and the temper of the people. But we grant, that we ought to show, if but in the merest outlines, how the New Social Order may get along without lawyers tolerably well. Only bear in mind, that Socialism is not responsible for the system we shall suggest.

It will be observed, that of our present machinery almost everything has been thrown overboard except statutes and *judges.*

We assume, that the New Commonwealth cannot dispense with judges; we do not mean our present *lawyer*-judges (their "services" will certainly be dispensed with,) but men especially trained to judicial functions, as others are trained to theirs. The notion, which many within the Socialist ranks entertain that justice can, and ought to be, dispensed by the "people," is one they would be radically cured of, if they could have some years' experience in the trial of cases. Justice by the "people" would be mob-justice. It would be what "lynch" justice is now. It would in its best form be an article not superior to the scandalous judgments for which country Justices-of-the-Peace out West are so famous.

We can give good reasons for such belief. True, in our Commonwealth there will be, as we have seen, no difficulty in *ascertaining* the law; further, there will be little or no difficulty in *interpreting* the law. But it requires, and will likewise in that Commonwealth require, some judgment to *apply* the law, and what is the most important consideration of all, it requires a good deal of education and training to *ascertain the truth* where the facts are in dispute, as they are nearly in every case. It is impossible to ascertain the truth, without knowing how to estimate the force of evidence, and that knowledge cannot be acquired, without having a *Science* of Evidence and having studied it as much as any other science needs to be studied and having learned the art how properly to apply it.

Men trained in that science, and trained to be exact logicians, will undoubtedly be needed, and they will occupy very distinguished positions.

We apprehend, that in the future Commonwealth our sham "science" of jurisprudence, which in its essence is nothing but a "science" of precedents, will be supplanted with a true science of Evidence, something else than that confused collection of arbitrary rules, called "rules of evidence" which Jeremy Bentham many years ago so sharply and caustically criticised.

Assuming, then, that we in our Commonwealth will have a body of trained judges we shall also assume that they will form themselves into a Department like other functionaries, with their Chief among the Board of Administrators, whose peculiar function it possibly may be to draft all proposed laws.

But we pass over to the particular task we have set ourselves: the procedure in case of a lawsuit.

Just as little Switzerland will furnish us a model of really popular democratic administration in the "referendum," so it is possible, that little Denmark will furnish us a model of popular administration of justice in her socalled "Courts of Conciliation," which have been in existence in that country since 1828 and during that period have given immense satisfaction, so much so, indeed, that similar Courts have to a certain extent been adopted by other countries in Europe. The distinguishing feature of those Courts is *that no lawyers are allowed there*. All suits whatsoever, without regard to the amounts involved, must, in the first place, be brought before these Courts. The judge takes down the oral complaint of the plaintiff and the oral defense of the defendant and renders judgment accordingly. If, however, either of the parties are dissatisfied with the judgment, the judge refers the case to the regular Courts, in which Courts, however, no other evidence is allowed to be introduced but that which was laid before the judge sitting in the Court of Conciliation.

A vast amount of litigation is settled yearly by these Courts, because it is the duty of the judge to explain the laws governing the particular case to the parties, and also, undoubtedly, because lawyers are excluded.

Our Commonwealth would do very well in following this Danish model, and only improve on it in making the judgment of such a Court *conclusive* on the parties. This would fulfill the most important requirement, namely, render lawyers superfluous, and taking down the verbal statements of the parties would dispense with the useless lying "pleadings" of our present system.

But the Coming Commonwealth might in another way utilize that model, by ingrafting some of its features on another mode of determining suits at law which is undoubtedly becoming more and more popular. We refer to Arbitration, which at present would be far more used than is the case, if the tendency to resort to it were not constantly obstructed by our lawyers, who naturally enough consider it an inferior commodity — something like neckbeef.

Suppose the plaintiff in a given suit were required to select one of the Commonwealth's judges, who would take down his own statements and those of his witnesses and then notify the defendant of the commencement of such a suit. He on his part would select another of the judges, who would proceed in a like manner. These two judges would then confer together, giving each other the benefit of their views of the law on the basis of the statements taken down, which would be legal evidence, subject to cross-examination, however, in case of discrepancy. If the two could not agree on a decision, they would then select a third judge, and the decision of the majority would be the judgment. The same proceedings might very well obtain in criminal cases, the judge representing the

State being selected by the judges of the district from among themselves.

If it be objected, that trials then would lose their publicity, we answer, first, that arbitrations now are mostly private, and, next, that publicity is often more subversive of justice than otherwise. Wrongs to women are by publicity often aggravated rather than remedied. And administration of justice is by it not infrequently turned into a mighty abettor of the blackmailer.

We said, that our Commonwealth might improve upon the Danish model by making the judgment of the trial-judge conclusive on the parties. We mean that.

There can be no doubt, that the expense and interminable delay of our lawsuits are mainly due to the many appeals. This expense and delay are, also, the reason why in most of the States we find so many appellate Courts constantly being established at the *instance of lawyers,* of course, and never once an appellate Court abrogated, for do not lawyers want expense and delay?

Why not dispense entirely with appeals under the system of arbitration suggested?

What is the philosophy of appeals?

By no means, that the appellate judge is better fitted to render a righteous judgment, for, not being face to face with the parties and their witnesses, he evidently is *not.*

No, the first reason of appeals is that the trial judge may have somebody *to stand in awe of,* so to speak. But the judges of the future Commonwealth, being freely selected by the parties, certainly need no one to stand in awe of.

A second reason of appeals to higher Courts is that the interpretation of the laws may be uniform.

That, however, might be accomplished just as effectually, and much more conveniently, by a provision, that the judges shall inform their Chief of all cases and their particulars, where a disagreement has taken place; next, of the cases where they have deviated from the strict law in favor of equity and of all points arising, not yet provided for by law.

We say "deviated from the strict law," for the judges should have discretion. No law should be inflexible. It would be well to re-adopt the old maxim of the Roman law "*Summum jus, summa injuria*" ("the strict law is often the height of injustice").

The Chief would then approve or disapprove of the judgment rendered, or of the deviation from the law resorted to — a sort of reprimand or otherwise — and introduce amendments to the existing laws, if thought proper. *But the judgment below would stand as rendered,* and neither the judgments nor disapprovals should ever become precedents, or we should soon again be in the meshes of the lawyers. *Nothing would be law that has not been submitted to the people and obtained their sanction.*

Under such a procedure there would not be the least excuse for our infamous bail system. Infamous, because there is hardly a crime so great, but that under that system a friend of Vanderbilt or Astor can get out on bail and have the inestimable privilege of being at liberty to collect evidence in his favor and otherwise prepare for his defence; and because there is, on the other hand, hardly a misdemeanor so trivial but that a poor man cannot get out without bail. Infamous, because poor innocent witnesses are under that system doomed to spend weeks and months in jail. There will be no excuse for it under our procedure, for all cases can under it be decided quickly.

Just as we are the worst party-ridden of all countries, so we certainly are the most lawyer-ridden one. And the lawyer-class is the most mischievous of all classes, the one that most clogs the wheels of progress. When the Supreme Powers issue their decree, that the Established Order is at an end, then with the *Messrs. six per cent* must go their retainers, the *Messrs. Eitherside* and lawyer-judges. It is even more important to insist upon their taking back seats here, where they claim to be the people's guardians, than in England, where they have never ventured to deny the nation the right to change its institutions at its pleasure.

On the other hand, the very principle of Democracy demands *competent* and *qualified judges,* the more so as the very highest of the social activities is to see justice done. We may also rest assured, that the Guilds and Departments of the New Commonwealth will insist on trained functionaries to whom to submit their differences for arbitration. When legal training is freed from legal cobwebs, then we shall have . . . . . . *natural* procedure instead of *technical* procedure.

CHAPTER X

WOMAN IN THE COOPERATIVE

COMMONWEALTH

"The only school of genuine moral sentiment is society between Equals." — *John S. Mill.*

"Why is she constituted a woman at all? — Merely that she may become a sort of second-rate man?" — *"Biology and Woman's Rights"* Quarterly *Journal of Science, Nov. 1878.*

"Work is withheld from woman in theory, only to be more harshly and clumsily inflicted in practice." — *Value of Life.*

The Position of Woman — of that half of humanity out of whose wombs the coming generations issue — has generally been taken as the measure of a people's advancement.

Yet, woman has hitherto always been a stepchild, is even so now, and in our country, in spite of our boasted "chivalry." If the man of toil is to be pitied, much more, indeed, is the toiling woman; if a husband suffers from an unhappy marriage, much more a wife; and the distance between the greatest man and the lowest slave has always been far less than between the high-placed lady and the woman of the street. If the Cooperative Commonwealth would not be likely to affect a vast improvement in the lot of woman, it would not be worth hoping for.

We have good grounds for expecting that she will under the coming order of things be raised as far above her present position as the woman of the Middle Ages was elevated above her sister of Ancient Greece or Rome.

Yet, bear in mind that Socialism, in its essence, has to do with *economic* relations. There is no Socialist Marriage or Family Life;

we may add, there is no Socialist Education or Morals, but neither is there any Socialist Politics or Justice. Nevertheless, Socialism will, as we saw, revolutionize the Administration of Affairs and of Justice. This will be done by a *direct* effort: by discarding the present machinery and contrive other instruments, suitable to collective control of all national affairs. But Socialism will, also, have many *indirect* effects of vast consequence. Production and distribution of wealth being the roots of Society, *they determine the soundness of its trunk and the quality of its flowers and fruit.* Hence it comes that Socialism, by refashioning economic relations, will regenerate Society throughout all its activities, and, more particularly, will have, most marked effect on Woman, on Education and on Morals.

While, however, the influence of Social Cooperation in the other two respects will be a manifold one, as we shall afterwards see, Woman will be affected in a peculiarly simple, though not the less effective, manner. The Coming Commonwealth will place her on *an equal footing* with man, *economically,* that is all.

But here it is even more important than elsewhere to settle what we are to understand by "economic Equality." We cannot do this better than by comparing the Socialist view with the demands of that persistent class of persons, known as "women's rights" champions, of whom John S. Mill was a representative.

These latter demand that the avenues to *all* employments be opened as freely to women as they are to men — in other words, they agitate for *free competition* between the sexes.

Well, we should say that the door to most *industrial* employments *has* for a long time been open to women of the working classes. According to the U. S. Census of 1880 there were 632,000 women engaged in manufacturing, mechanical and mining industries, one-sixth of the whole working force. In some industries the proportion is far greater, notably in the cotton mills, where there are considerably more women than men employed.

Have these women's-rights agitators ever . contemplated the result? Which, under our present industrial system, simply is, that competition is rendered yet more savage; that wages sink to a lower and lower level; that a whole family, on an average, comes to earn no more than the head of the family used to earn by himself.

Of these 632,000 females many thousand were married women and mothers of children. What kind of family life do *they* lead? What kind of training do *those* children get? Ought we to hanker after more competition?

Again, of the force that used to be employed in the Census Bureau in Washington to work out the results of the last census the great majority were women. It is a fact, notorious to those in a position to know, that these women performed their work in a very slovenly manner, evincing next to no interest in what they were set to do. Would, on the other hand, not that kind of work have afforded an excellent training school for aspiring young men, in every way far better fitted to perform it?

Now, *we* say that the worst that can befall both sexes is for woman to *compete with man in man's work*. We contend, *with* Mill, for *equality*, but, *against* Mill, that woman should not become a *second-rate man*. That is to say, we again urge the vital distinction, which is constantly overlooked, between being *equal* and being *alike*.

Woman is different from man in intellect, different from him in temperament, different from him in muscles. There is a peculiarity of construction in the bones of the pelvis and chest which forbids her to be as much on her feet as man. We may, further, suggest certain notorious, physiological facts that demand, in contrast to man, that woman shall have a *periodic rest* of, say, three days every four weeks.

In other words, instead of free competition between the sexes, we contend for *special vocations* for the sexes.

That, of course, is not to be thought of under the present system. The proportion of women to men in shops, mines and factories will undoubtedly continue to increase. In disregard of physiological facts manufacturers will go on requiring their female employees to be on their feet from morning till night, and retail-dealers will stick to the rule against sitting down. As a matter of sentiment they may think Plato's proposition to mix the sexes in all things preposterous, but *the system demands it*. It is just the same thing in regard to wages. Sentimental people deplore the fact that women are paid less than men for the same work. There is not help for it under our system: *the law of wages demands it.*

Quite otherwise in the Cooperative Commonwealth. *There*

woman will become a functionary, she will have suitable employment given her, and be rewarded according to results, just the same as man.

Suitable employment, mark you! Woman will there not take the place of man. The sexes will there *keep pace with each other,* but — in accordance with the teaching of physiology — *walk* in *different pathways.* That will simply mean that the principle which is the basis of our civilization, to wit: *Division of Labor* will be extended so as to embrace *both* sexes. If that principle is good for man, why not for man *and* woman? Indeed, we shall find that this extension of Division of Labor will furnish the desideratum of the Coming Commonwealth: *competent* workers in every field of labor. Woman will surely not be dragging behind, for we must remember that whatever of greatness woman hitherto has accomplished she has achieved in violation of the conventional code, but Nature with *equal* laws always tends to *diversity.*

"Will there be work enough for all women who choose to engage in public activities?" you may ask.

Why! even now, in this crude civilization of ours, there is an abundance of work which woman only ought to do. Why should not our women insist on having female physicians (we do not mean surgeons) to attend them? Is that calling more un-womanly than nursing? The Woman's Hospitals in Philadelphia and other places whose medical staffs and students are women are most excellent institutions, and mark the coming change.

And imagine once the innumerable humane institutions of the Cooperative Commonwealth! They will afford woman a thousand opportunities for the exercise of her peculiar natural gifts — we need only instance the Kindergartens, spread over the whole country, of which we shall have more to say in the next chapter.

How will this affect woman? Just as it will man.

As his becoming a public functionary will destroy the accursed dependence on the irresponsible will of some individual for a living which now obtains; as it will make him a *freeman,* so it will make her a *free-woman.* Woman now is dependent on some man for a living: on father or brother or husband or employer — that is why men arrogate to themselves to say *what* is woman's sphere. Destroy that dependence — we do not say make her *in*dependent, for "independence" is not a Socialist word at all; all will be dependent *on* *the Commonwealth* and *inter*-dependent — give her the *power of earning* her own living *at pleasure,* and *the economic equality of woman is achieved.*

But, undoubtedly, the idea that all women, even "ladies," might come to earn their own living will shock many a "chivalrous" gentleman in these hypocritic times. What would life be to them without "delicate and spiritual" women to whom to pay homage!

Well, the consideration that the equality which we advocate will hardly give us any female sailor or blacksmith ought to console them somewhat. But we admit that they have some reason to be horrified.

For these same persons generally fancy, that it is *their* appreciation that gives value to woman — a view, not so very different from the Mohammedan view. In the Coming Commonwealth woman will certainly not, as now, form her character with the express aim of pleasing the man-fool. But she will have fuller opportunities than she ever yet has had of developing her specific gifts of womanhood. Then esteem will be substituted for vapid compliments.

However, this power of earning her living does not mean, that in the New Social Order all women, or even a majority of them, will be in the service of the public. Nothing will prevent the daughters from remaining at home, assisting their mothers or caring for their fathers, and nothing will compel married women to neglect their domestic affairs. It simply means that every woman will be enabled to earn her own living, honorably, and pleasantly *whenever she chooses so to do.* And this power is essential to the dignity of woman, whether married or single.

After what we have said on Suffrage in other chapters we need not dwell on that other, the principal, demand of our "women's rights" champions, that women now should vote as much as men.

We, of course, suppose that in the Coming Commonwealth woman will be intrusted with the Suffrage to exactly the same extent as man — we say, advisedly, "intrust" for, all these champions to the contrary, Suffrage is *not* a "right," nor is it a *privilege,* but a *trust.*

But what would the mere power to cast a ballot help woman now, supposing it were given to her? Suffrage is one of those things which are so very valuable, when you have not got it, and so very worthless when you have. The ballot has proven anything but a magic wand to the toiling workingmen, and it would be still more impotent in the hands of toiling women.

The ballot would not bring strength to the lightless eye or the thin hand of the needle-woman of this age of competition; it would not remove the causes which now make woman prefer almost any marriage to working for a living. It might enable her to say a word about laws of divorce, but would not enable her to support herself when divorced. The ballot in her hand might suppress lewd houses, but would not prevent men from leading victims to the altar of their passions like sheep to the slaughter-bench.

Neither are we blind to the consideration that if woman could exercise the suffrage to-morrow with the State as at present constituted, the result would in all likelihood be detrimental to progress, for it is undeniable, that they, taken as a whole, are far more conservative, even reactionary — no fault of theirs, though — than men. In the words of Admiral Maxse: "Those who think unorthodox, that is, unusual thoughts, they (*i.e.* women of the present time) believe to be wicked. They turn instinctively from all initiative movements. Even superior women rarely have sympathy with the struggles which determine the life of a nation. They are only interested in public affairs within the limits of the parish." But in the Coming Commonwealth all these objections will disappear, for they can all be shown to be due to their one-sided education.

Let us, however give credit to these persistent "women-rights" agitators for one thing. We are told, that in some settlements on the African coast free negroes are taunted by the slaves with having no white man to look after them. That so many of our women have got beyond the standpoint of those slaves is in the main due to those agitators.

But for woman to expect, that her emancipation will be worked out before that of man is altogether illusive. And this is a sufficient reason, why all agitators for women's rights ought with enthusiasm to embrace Socialism, which will enable woman to right, herself, all her other wrongs.

Take marriage.

The New Order will necessarily, by the mere working of its economic principles considerably modify that relation. And is that relation such an ideal one now, that it would be a sacrilege to touch it?

Is marriage not now, at bottom, an establishment for the support of the woman? Is not maintenance the price which the husband pays for the appendage to himself? And because the supply generally exceeds the demand — that is, the *effective* demand — has woman not often to accept the offer of the first man who seems able to perform this pecuniary obligation of his?

This is rather a commercial view to take of this "holy" relation, but is not, as a matter of fact, marriage regarded by altogether too many as a commercial institution? Do not, in fact, the total of young women form a matrimonial market, regulated by Demand and Supply? Nothing is more natural than that it should be so now. It is most human, that in our present Social Order parents as well as young women should look upon marriage, without prospects of subsistence, with horror.

Now, the Cooperative Commonwealth will dissipate that horror. It will enable every healthy adult man and woman to marry whenever they feel so inclined, without any present or prospective misgivings in regard to their support or the proper education of children. Socialists are charged, ignorantly or insidiously, with attempting to destroy the family. Why! *we want to enable every man and woman to form a happy family.*

Somebody may here interject, that it is very inexpedient for people to marry young, since they must necessarily be wanting in judgment. To that we reply, that by "young people" we mean developed, *adult* young people — children will in a proper social system remain in the care of their teachers till they have grown to maturity; further, that nothing contributes so much to the chastity of a Nation as the marriage of its young men as soon as possible after reaching the adult state; and, lastly, that experience does not teach us, that judgment in love affairs increases with growth in years. The fear of overpopulation consequent on early and universal marriages we have already shown to be baseless.

Next, the Coming Commonwealth will destroy the matrimonial market.

When Wealth ceases to be a means of living by the labor of other people, and especially when an honorable and easy living is within her reach, we may suppose, that a woman will rarely consent to marry for anything but love, will no longer consent to be bought to be a piece of furniture of any western Turk. Here, again, it is the *power* of earning that will confer true dignity on womanhood.

Again, this economical equality of woman will greatly affect for the better her position as wife.

Our marriage laws are the code of the stronger, made by lords for dependents. True, in many states of our Union some modifications in regard to property have been effected in favor of the wife. But even in that regard the enormity everywhere prevails, that the wife as survivor of her husband has only a life-interest in the third part of their common estate, though she may have — and if she has been a farmer's wife certainly has — contributed fully as much to its acquisition as he. The husband, if he be the survivor, on the other hand, takes all her property. So that other injustice is everywhere law, that the wife, if the husband obtains a divorce from her, is driven homeless and penniless into the cold world, while, if the husband be the sinner, she never will get more than a third of the common estate.

But the essence of the wrong is, that in law the wife is nothing but the husband's property. Witness our scandalous actions for se-duction, in which the husband sues for "damages" for enticing away that which is his. Now the husband can say to his wife: "Your will is mine and my will is my own." Now the wife must content herself with what her husband pleases to give her. In fact, our system gives support to that fallacy that a husband "gives" his wife money as much as to that other fallacy, that the employer "gives" work to his employees.

"That is the reason" as John S. Mill says, "why the family which should be a school of sympathy, tenderness and loving forgetfulness of self, is still oftener, as respects its chief, a school of wilfulness and overbearingness and unbounded self-indulgence; the care for the wife and children being only care for them as part of the man's own interests and belongings." And all that because he is the "chief!"

The New Order will make husband and wife — *equals,* and it will do it simply by giving the wife *power* of earning her living by fitting employment.

Not that Socialists, as we before remarked, expect a majority, or even a goodly number of married women to earn their own living, in fact. It is just because a great many of them are now compelled thus to work, that we can justly charge this capitalistic era with destroying family life. We emphatically hold, that it is the husband's province to provide for the necessities of his family, (much more so in the coming Commonwealth where it will be so much more easy to do it) and that the wife has done her full share of the common labor, when she manages her household properly.

We simply want to see the wife invested with the *potentiality* of economic independence of her husband, to be realized any time she sees fit.

"But when the wills and wishes of these 'equals' clash, who is to decide between them?"

It is only a delusion to suppose constant collisions between husband and wife when they are made the equals of each other. It is far more likely, that equality will create mutual deference for each other's wishes, and mutual concessions. That is the way equality works among men. Even now honorable men — gentlemen — fear trespassing against each other not the being trespassed against. "The only school of genuine moral sentiment is society between equals" as Mill says. Indeed, whenever man and wife are now really happy together, it is by ignoring and despising, not by asserting, the subordination of woman to man which they hold in theory.

Need we fear any lack of mutual concessions among two equal persons of opposite sexes who love each other? Is it not exactly the function of love to make of two such persons one: the true social unit? To create that most remarkable oneness where each merges his and her personality in the other; where each gratifies himself or herself, the more they sacrifice themselves for each other? And if, unfortunately, love does not make them one, isn't it absolute presumption for any outside power to declare that they *shall* be one, and that one — *the husband?*

And that leads us to consider, that the Coming Commonwealth will enable the *divorced* wife, also, to support herself by fitting employment.

As the effect of this, undoubtedly, will be to induce wives to seek divorce, whenever they are unhappily mated, we shall here have to confront the question:

"Does Socialism favor divorce? and are Socialists free-lovers, as they are charged with being?"

We answer, Socialism, as an economic system, must only be charged with the consequences which may logically be drawn from its economic principles. Because Socialism will facilitate divorces, it follows not at all that it favors them.

Again, Socialists are *not* free-lovers in the popular acceptation of that term.

The doctrine, that husband and wife should be at liberty to leave each other, and form other connections as caprice or inclination may dictate, we hold to be a dangerous doctrine, and one especially dreadful to women, so long as mostly every man has got a sultan in his body. Marriage is a most needed *test* of man's love for woman, and when she stakes all her plans of life on his promise, he has contracted a series of weighty obligations that the Commonwealth should hold him to perform.

Quite another thing is it, that Socialists generally hold, that there are many cases where a divorce is far preferable to the further cohabiting together of the parties. But we need not be Socialists to hold that view.

Thus *John S. Mill* said: "Things never come" (with a married couple) "to an issue of downright power on one side and obedience on the other, except where the connection altogether is a mistake, *and it would be a blessing to both to be relieved from it.*" And Mill was no free-lover and not a Socialist.

Jeremy Bentham said: "The interpretation which the law now enforces of the contract of marriage is: We shall not be at liberty to separate though hereafter we come to hate each other as now we love each other! This is shocking." He, on the other hand, considered it very sensible for the woman, in entering into the contract, to say to the man: "If I give myself up to you, you shall not be at liberty to leave me without my consent," and right for the State to enforce such a contract. Bentham, therefore, would grant a divorce, whenever the wife should be a willing party — and Bentham was no free-lover nor a Socialist.

Fichte, the great German philosopher, held, that *man* always entered into the marriage relation, avowedly prompted by sexual passion. The chaste *woman*, in submitting to her husband's embraces, was really prompted by the like passion, but without acknowledging it, even to herself; without in fact being aware of it. Her apparent motive in giving herself over to him is her love for him, her confidence in him. Fichte considered this veiling of woman's real by her apparent motive to be the essence and rationale of *chastity*, explaining why mankind requires that virtue — imperatively — in a good woman, but not absolutely in a good man. He, therefore, would have divorces granted in all cases, where the wife for any cause desired it, and to the husband in case of adultery by her: for in either case it was evident, that the wife's love for her husband had fled, and without love on her part she would degrade herself by connection with him and render the relation *eo ipso* immoral.

It must be remarked, that Fichte by no means claimed, that love in man is a fiction, but he maintained, that his love is a growth during marriage, sown and nourished in him by his wife's love for and trust in him.

Now, Fichte has not generally been considered a free-lover, and though he may be looked upon as the forerunner of German Socialism, he cannot well be called a Socialist.

We are thus in pretty good company, when we say, that where there is dislike between husband and wife, their union is an unmitigated evil to both, and not least to their children, if they have any; that the welfare of children demands the highest order of wedlock; and that marriage without mutual love breeds pestilence to all, however persistently our present Social Order styles it "sacred."

But so it is. This hypocritic age combines in regard to all sexual relations the sternest total prohibition in theory with the vilest laxity in practice and stops aghast at the whispers of any mediary or modifying suggestions.

The other day we noticed a dainty lady, the wife of a wealthy person whom she hardly could have married for love, sweeping by a fallen sister, as if fearing that the hem of her garment might be touched and defiled.

The former had, under our supposition — and it is notoriously true in very many instances — sold her person for money *under cover of* marriage. The latter does the same thing *outside* of marriage. Now, no hypocrisy, please! In all candor: what is the difference between the two?

And it is not fair to look upon the latter as she is. Look on her as she *commenced to be* what she is.

Perhaps she was seduced and then left to shift for herself. Society now persecutes these victims of man's lust, as if it intended to force them to kill themselves or their children.

In very many cases she is pushed toward the pit by poverty, by the small pay she receives for her toil under this wage-system. Poor girls are every whit as virtuous as boarding-school ladies. Yet, think of it, how much harder, how very much harder it is for the former to be pure than for the latter! Is it remarkable, is it anything but human for them to give way to temptation, to accept the bribes of the beast in man?

Let us admit that many fall because they like fineries and adornments too well. This, however, is no bad quality in itself; it is merely an uncultured manifestation of a truly feminine characteristic: pride of appearance.

But that of which this fallen woman stands the representative is a horrible evil. It is called "*the* Social Evil," and called so very properly by people who skim along the surface of things. It is a most loathsome ulcer on the social body, but *the* evil which causes this ulcer to break out is in the *constitution* of society. *It is our economic system that also here is at fault.* And the fact that this system serves as a hothouse for such plants is the most damning fact.

The "evil" is said to be incurable. Indeed, so it is in our Established Order, since it is the cause of it. The only "remedy" this Order has for it is policemen, prisons and asylums with prison rules. But that it is *not* in itself incurable has been proven by the Mormons. It is unknown among them, because they have no unmarried element for lust to prey upon. We admit, of course, that their mode of bringing this about is as bad as the disease.

The Coming Commonwealth will cure it in the only proper way.

It will protect and hold sacred every pregnant woman, whatever she may be, for she will enrich it with one member, at all events innocent.

It will see to it that there are no giddy young girls running round on the streets by themselves at night.

But the economic changes we already have considered will be the most efficient cure by far. For

It will, as we saw, enable all young people to marry who want to. The great majority of women, undoubtedly, will choose marriage; and we believe experience teaches that married women exercise a far greater influence everywhere, also in public affairs, than the unmarried.

But there will always be some women whose special vocation will be the Public Service; these will be cheerfully enrolled among the public functionaries, for there will be use and even need for every one of them.

Woman will then have full opportunity of developing all the possibilities of her womanhood, as man those of his manhood — and that is Equality.

We may add that the Coming Commonwealth will relieve woman of all drudgery in housekeeping. Our progress in that respect has evidently not at all kept pace with our progress in other respects. Some feeble attempts have been made in that direction by individual enterprise, but they have nearly all been limited to the well-to-do classes. Hardly anything of that kind has been, or will be done under the present Order for the immense mass of toiling women who most need it.

The New Order will, we may be assured, do away with much worry in private houses in the way of washing and cookery, without sacrificing one jot of privacy or real home life.

Thus we shall have for all, women as well as men, that true luxury of which now the great multitude, rich as well as poor, know nothing, *leisure:* the prerequisite for all development, all *education.*

CHAPTER XI

EDUCATION IN THE COOPERATIVE

COMMONWEALTH

"All these were years ago little red-colored pulpy infants, capable of being kneaded, baked, into any social form you chose." — *Carlyle.*

"The education of children is a *trust,* whose principal effects are to be felt after the death of the parents and teachers." — *The Value of Life.*

"The power of education is almost boundless; there is not one natural inclination which it is not strong enough to coerce and, if needful, destroy by disuse." — *John S. Mill.*

An Episcopal clergyman, of great influence in his denomination, once expressed himself to the writer hereof almost exactly as follows:

"The dispensation of Divine Providence determines the social grade of children on their reaching adult age, just as their pecuniary condition is settled. If a father is a vagabond, why! his children must suffer from the iniquity of the father: that is God's law. It is absurd to claim, that a child has a 'right' to a liberal education, or to such an education as is, at present, given in our public schools. To take the property of a citizen in order to give the children of his poor neighbors such an education is as unjust as to compel him to furnish food and clothing to those same children. In short to demand a liberal education for all children is not less monstrous than to demand roast beef and plum-pudding for them. I can assure you, that this doctrine is held by a very great number of the most thoughtful Christian people, Protestants, not less than Catholics, and I am convinced, that, however unpopular this doctrine seems now, the country will in fifty years adopt it in sheer self-defence."

"I am well aware," he continued, "of that well-worn argument, that ignorance in a people is too great a danger in a State, and especially in a Republic, but there is evidently no more danger in ignorance than in physical destitution. And then," he added, "we are very willing, that the children of poor people should be given, as a Christian charity, a *minimum* education; that they should be taught to read and write, so that they can read their bibles and their ballots. But this is something very different from the education, now furnished by our public and high-schools. Again, you must not understand me to say, that *the State* should furnish that 'minimum' education. I think this is not the State's business at all, for it is not a charitable institution."

I could not help smiling at this idea of a minimum education; it reminded me of the mistress who was quite willing her maid should learn to *write,* but not to write *like a "lady."*

Well, this is a pretty frank declaration of a representative of our luxurious "society." He is confirmed by the following sentiments, taken from a Presbyterian periodical: "It is God's decree, that children shall inherit the culture and position of their parents and that which they provide for their children. Knowledge, culture and virtue are not to be extended beyond the fortunate youths for whom their parents secure them. The sad law holds good, that ignorance and its consequences must needs be hereditary."

There is here a remarkable sympathy between the thoughtful Presbyterian and the thoughtful Episcopalian.

Now, these gentlemen who uttered these sentiments are certainly frank. They are not bad men; quite the reverse. They are intelligent, above the average. What if they are right? We mean, what if their sentiments are sound, *from the standpoint of the Established Order,* of course?

Is it not true, that the destitution of the masses is just as dangerous to a republic as ignorance is?

Would it really be more "monstrous" to demand roast beef and plum-pudding than to ask for a liberal education?

And is it anything but robbery under the euphonious name of taxation when the State, which recognizes the fleecings of its enterprising citizens as "sacred" property, puts its hands into their pockets and devotes what it extracts to purposes that are objectionable or indifferent to those citizens?

And pray! If the present Social Order is to continue for ever,

what business have these working masses — these necessary evils!
— anyway with a *liberal* education? Their virtues consist in being
humble, frugal, temperate, industrious and contented with the sta-
tion "to which it has pleased God to call them." It is notorious, that
education contrariwise makes them self-assertive, gives them expensive habits, makes them hanker after comforts and luxuries, causes
them to fret under toil: in short, makes of them rebels against their
superiors, and the more "liberal" the education, the more unman-
ageable rebels. By all means, then, if they must be educated at all,
let it be so much "minimum," that it will not endanger their
"virtues!"

Our *"liberal"* friends have only one line of defence left: that it is
cheaper to build schools than jails, that education diminishes crime.
But neither of these propositions is true. Our schools cost more than
our jails; and the fact is, we build jails in the same proportion that
we build schoolhouses.

Neither reason nor facts sustain the assumption, that ignorance
has any particular relation to crime. Mere intellectual training does
not make good citizens, but will undoubtedly make out of clumsy
lawbreakers refined rascals.

The most reprehensible crimes are by no means committed by
ignorant persons. Bank-burglars are often as intelligent as bank-
presidents; forgers as a rule as educated as railroad-directors. In
France, where a generation ago two-thirds of the inhabitants could
neither read nor write, there occurred in a given period fourteen
times less crimes than in Prussia where compulsory education prevailed. Already De Toqueville remarked that in our country crimes
increased with instruction, and the census of 1880 has informed us,
that the Northern States with their costly school-houses and still
more palatial jails are more criminal than the uneducated South.
Suppose we take all the States east of the Mississippi, and compare
those north of the Ohio with those south of the same river, we find
that the criminals detained in penal institutions of every kind on the
1st of June 1880 amounted in the former to 1 in 827 of the population, but in the latter only to 1 in 932.

Thus the spokesman of our "thoughtful Christians" — the cream
of our employers, capitalists, comfortable classes — seems to have
all logic on his side. Will then really in, say, fifty years our public
schools, high schools and state universities be closed?

Ah! there is one thing to which he is blind.

He sees very clearly that we are fast approaching the economic condition of older countries, that the gulf is daily widening between Dives, the few, and Lazarus, the teeming multitude. He is also keen enough to see that for the Class-State to maintain free education for the poor would be to commit suicide. If all are to be well educated who will do the menial, servile work of the ruling class? How can there be masters if none will consent to be subjects? It is clearly to the interest of the governing class that education be limited to the elect few and that the masses be kept in ignorance.

But he leaves entirely out of account — as who does not? — the present tendency of the social organism in the direction of Socialism, of Interdependence. Oh, if we could with propriety emphasize that central fact on every page of this book! For we have *not* written these pages, in order to show that the Socialist system is a *good* system. They have been written in vain, if it will not have been brought home to our readers that the fact that Society is moving irresistibly toward Socialism is the one important fact; that we are going to have the Socialist State whether it is good or bad, and that every active individual in our country is, consciously or unconsciously working to that end in some way. This, therefore, is the central fact of Society and the red thread running through these pages as well. We, nevertheless, also insist upon this, but only in the second line, that the goal itself, the Socialist State, will prove an immense good even to those who now deem it an abomination.

Now, this very fact that all progressive countries are committed to the common school system is, as already noticed in a former chapter, both an indication whither the stream flows and one of the chief impelling forces. Our Liberals are perfectly right when they feel that they must uphold and extend universal education and that to give it up would be to turn back to barbarism, but they have none but fallacious reasons to give for the faith that in them is.

The fundamental and all-sufficient reason for giving all as good an education as possible is that *the Socialist State is upon us.* It is not a matter to be fought out between "Liberals" on one hand and "thoughtful Christians" on the other; it is simply one phase of the contest between the Established Order and the New Order. The ancients told a story how their old god, Saturn, was wont to devour his children as soon as they were born, but that one of them, Jupiter, managed to evade his father, until he grew strong enough to overpower and dethrone him. This fable will get a new significance in the approaching undoubted victory of the social system which is soon vigorously to assert itself over the present system which would strangle its offspring, if it could.

This throws quite a new light — a kind of electric light — on this blurred subject of education.

Society hitherto has been burdened with a vast number of unassimilated members and in consequence has clung to a large part of its crudeness. But the Interdependent Commonwealth cannot get along in that way at all. Just as it assimilates the masses, it must elevate them; it is the unavoidable condition for its own welfare — its very existence. Why, many of our readers already will have observed that such a Commonwealth as we sketched in our *5th* and *8th* chapters *presupposes* universal education.

And that the *finished* Socialist Commonwealth in fact does; wherefore also we called education the true starting point of the New Order. But many will go on and say that the first thing, then, to which we should have called attention ought to have been this matter of education and not the economic condition of the people. No, not so, as we shall presently make clear.

A book, called "Dynamic Sociology" by Lester F. Ward was published a short time ago by the Appletons. It would be a most instructive book if it were not so voluminous, and so terribly learned — and yet we cannot agree to its two principal propositions. These are: Happiness is the end of human life — which seems at least doubtful to us — and Education is the initial means to that end. Let the State only give a scientifically perfect education to all and the whole problem is solved, according to Ward. Education is, so to speak, a crank which, when properly applied, will, with comparatively little effort, turn the otherwise so unwieldy social machine.

So it will. Education indeed, can accomplish wonders; no thick volumes and pretence of much learning are necessary to prove that.

But how get the State to take the initiative? Who shall decide what is the scientifically perfect education? How get the parents to cooperate with the State? And what is the use, anyway, to try to educate children who are poorly fed, poorly clad and poorly housed?

All these first steps are taken when we get the Cooperative Commonwealth.

We have seen that Social Cooperation demands first, and last, and at all time *Competence*. In order to get the greatest ability in every branch of affairs and in every post of duty: in order to sift out the most competent for the direction of affairs, and in order to make the citizens pass with ease from one employment to another, when required, all citizens will have to be trained all-sidedly and to the highest point. Monotonous toil now crushes out millions of potential luminaries of Society; if the true merits of mankind are to be brought out, it must be done by equalizing the opportunities for all.

And "minimum" education will not do at all. Simply to teach children to read and write is the same as to teach them the use of knife and fork without giving them a particle of meat; or as to furnish them the key to a larder, containing poisons as well as victuals, without telling them which is food, and which poisons. In fact, children are more likely to choose the poisons than the food: witness their voracious consumption of trashy novels and other vicious literature. The highest grade of education will be the best possible investment for the future Commonwealth.

Again, the Interdependent Commonwealth will take care that all children *do* get roast beef and plum pudding and that they, besides, have warm clothes to their backs, clean linen to their bodies, and comfortable shoes to their feet, and warmth and light at home, and these goodies will be provided before their education is thought of.

Again, the Interdependent Commonwealth will relieve children from the task of being bread-winners. The 182,000 children who according to the Census of 1880 were employed in manufactures in our country were not thus robbed of the bright days of childhood solely because employers could coin money out of them. The horrible fact is that their parents cannot make both ends meet without the labor of their children, and that in Massachusetts where a few weeks schooling yearly is required by law of children between 10 and 15, many parents feel themselves tempted to evade that law by false swearing in regard to the age of their children. It is an infamous system that bears such fruits. And yet there are political economists whose hearts are so seared and whose understanding is so obscured by being trained in that system that they glory in the fact that children can be utilized in augmenting the wealth of the country! These hundred thousands of children, as well as the urchins who gain their own precarious existence and partly that of their parents as newsboys, bootblacks, cash-boys, will have the most important period of their lives — that in which *character* is formed — saved to them, as soon as their parents are secured a decent living.

But that is by no means all. This that not only the children but that the parents also will have roast beef and plum pudding is of vast importance to the cause of education. For it will relieve the fathers and mothers of the body- and soul-devouring *care* which is the special curse of our age; it will give these fathers and mothers, to whom now even reflection is forbidden, LEISURE, and thus make them effective allies of the Commonwealth, because leisure is the incentive to all progress.

The bread-and-butter-question is therefore the fundamental question. We see here again how Socialism, by revolutionizing the economic relation of Society, will revolutionize all other relations.

Education, then, will be the second important branch of the activity of the New Commonwealth. Let us now consider what organ is likely to be intrusted with the function of education.

In the discourse above referred to our Episcopal Mentor also laid it down:

"God has instituted three coordinate authorities: the Family, the Church and the State. The Family is *imperium in imperio* — a dominion within the dominion; — the parent is exclusive master within that dominion."

Well, we can pretty safely assert to the contrary that the Coming Commonwealth will not acknowledge the Church as a coordinate "authority."

There was a time when the two were coordinate authorities. At that time it was still doubtful which of them was destined to be the embodiment of the social organism. Out of that struggle the State has already virtually issued as the victor: the "Church" is in all

civilized countries already virtually nothing but a voluntary association. "God" thus has already decided against the pretensions of the
Church; and this, as we already noticed in the fifth chapter, is the
most important step, perhaps, in the movement of the State toward
Socialism.

And we can also be assured that the Church will not be made the
organ of the State for education purposes.

There is one all-sufficient reason: *the Church is not competent.*

Circumstances for centuries gave education into the hands of the
Church, and she then perhaps performed that function as well as
could be done. Let us grant that much. But we are not living in the
Middle Ages. So far from being in our age an institution of enlightenment, the Church is now looked upon by all well-informed people as an institution to darken men's minds. We simply state facts.
The men of science assume the falsity of all theological dogmas.
The Church is incompetent, because she knows nothing worth
knowing — we are again simply stating facts. The Church has still
some influence, partly on account of our hypocrisy, and hypocrisy is
prevailing as it is, just because this is a transition age; but the
Coming Democracy will want to *know* and will wage an unrelent-
ing war against all shams.

We, furthermore, maintain that neither will the *Family* be acknowledged a coordinate authority.

This, however, is a much more important assertion than the
former, and is not quite as evident, though on reflection it will be
found just as true. But we cannot fail in passing to remark that it is
amusing to see the solicitude the Church has for the authority of
the Family now, when her own importance is on the wane. When
she had supreme power, she certainly did not consider the Family
coordinate with herself.

The first evidence we shall adduce to show that the Coming
Commonwealth will assert supremacy as against the Family is that
which we everywhere throughout this book place at the head: the
logic of events. *Just in the same proportion the State has aggran-
dized itself, the Family has dwindled in importance.* The State
commenced to repudiate the "dominion" of the Family the moment
it forbade parents to destroy their children; it absolutely rejected
that "dominion" the moment it, the State, fixed the age of majority,
when the child is entirely emancipated from parental control.

Why! the system where authority is vested in the Family, as distinguished from the State, is that patriarchal, barbaric, system from which we are more and more retreating. Proudhon is decidedly right when he says: "It is on the model of the Family that all feudal and antique societies have organized themselves, *and it is precisely against this old patriarchal constitution that modern democracy revolts and protests.*" It is yet sometime said that "blood is thicker than water," but that is not often the case now; and this fact that the Individual has become almost independent of the Family is merely the preparatory step to the supremacy of the State.

Next, in the very nature of things, Family-Supremacy will be absolutely incompatible with an *Interdependent,* a solidaric, Commonwealth, for in such a State the first object of education must be to establish in the minds of the children an indissoluble association between their individual happiness and the good of all. To that end family exclusiveness must be broken down, first of all. A public spirit, *i.e.* the spirit of all being members of one social organism, must be substituted for family-spirit. Now please do not misunderstand the Socialist position in this respect! We do not make war on the *family;* on the contrary, our aim is to enable every healthy man and woman to form a family. But we *do* make war on family-*exclusiveness* — perhaps a better word than "selfishness" — on family-*prejudices* and family-*narrowness* and we are glad to be able to say that our common schools are doing very much to break down that spirit.

To hear some fathers talk of what is commonly called "compulsory" education, one should suppose that a man's children were literally a part of himself. When they are not allowed to be masters over their offspring, to choose what is wrong for their children — and we know that as to education the greater the need the greater is the dislike — they call that an infringement of their "liberty;" the fact is, they do not value *liberty*, but irresponsible *power*.

Children do not belong to their parents; they belong to Society. The observation of Franklin, that, if we go back but a few generations, we necessarily come to common ancestors expresses the truth, that we are more the children of Society than of our several families. Again, the education of children is of far more importance to the State than to parents, since the effects of it will be felt by Society, and principally *after* these parents are dead and gone. It is because through it Society accomplishes the end of its being, that all education is a public *trust*.

Just as little as parents will the many denominational and private schools and colleges which we now have do. Even granted that the education in, say, the Quaker college of Swarthmore is fully up to the standard of any public college, the New Order cannot get along with such one-sided, awry, cramped men and women as necessarily must issue from such a one-sided school.

Lastly, the same objection applies to the Family as to the Church: *it is incompetent to teach.* That is the main objection against Herbert Spencer's justly popular book on "Education." He assumes throughout his treatise (which might better have been called "Home Training") that parents are competent to teach their children. Why! the fact is, that even now most children of the age of twelve are more fit to teach their parents in all more important branches than the reverse. If any man might be supposed qualified to teach his son, it was James Mill, and yet we know from the pen of John Mill that he would have been of greater service to the world, if he had been trained in a public school. Now it is true, that in the New Commonwealth mothers will be far better qualified to assist in the development of their infants than now, yet their general incompetency will still remain, on account of the higher grade of education which will obtain. At all events, a sufficient objection is and will remain that seeming paradox, that parents know none so poorly as their own children; they prate of qualities which no impartial person can discover.

The Coming Commonwealth must radically do away with all and any form of quackery and amateurship, in educational matters especially. Education is essentially scientific labor. A competent and qualified body of educators must therefore be raised up to whom the whole function of education can be intrusted.

Teaching is now a "business" and a temporary one at that. To teach in order to get pocket-money, or wait for a chance to get into some other "business," or for a chance to marry, if the teacher is a woman as generally is the case, does not qualify for the grand art. The time teachers in our country practice their profession is simply their own training period. We cannot have that genuine education which the new Commonwealth will demand, before we have teachers who have themselves been genuinely educated, next, thoroughly trained as teachers and who then will devote themselves with their whole soul to their profession.

Here again, and more clearly than at any other point, we see how all-important, how indispensable the economic side of the New Order is to all other progress. For these teachers will not be raised up, before we have given them a dignified position economically. Teaching is now a temporary "business," because it is one of the most unprofitable positions, and because the teacher occupies a very low round in the social ladder. In the New Social Order he will be rewarded proportionately to his important function and need take no thought for his advancing age. Furthermore, he will be a member of a corporation of the highest dignity in the State; a corporation embracing the teachers in the most elementary schools, as well as the professors in the various universities — genuine universities for untrammelled scientific investigation in all departments — and whose directors, superiors and representatives in the National Board of Administration we shall suppose elected and dismissed exactly as they will be in the other departments.

This corps of educators will have in their exclusive charge the whole education from top to bottom and all scientific investigations. They will be perfectly untrammelled, for such a system will enable them to say to all charlatans in their department as the bakers, artisans and agriculturists can say in theirs: "mind your own business, sir! You are not competent to say aught in this matter."

There is not the smallest reason to fear that this will result in any spiritual tyranny, for the influence of this theoretic body of men is sure to be counteracted by that Public Opinion of the practical majority which we saw will be of extraordinary force in the Coming Commonwealth. We ought rather to hail such a strong and independent organization of a class, devoted to the cultivation of knowledge, as a healthy counterpoise to that Public Opinion. We may also suggest that the present tendency of founding universities in every section and almost every State of our country (though so far it has generally only resulted in founding university *buildings*) may be the sowing of germs of many different centres of science under the New Order, and thus contribute, as it has in Germany, to intellectual freedom and all-sidedness.

Then, and not till then, we can begin to have anything that deserves the name of education. Then, as we have noticed several times, we shall have arrived at the true starting point of the Cooperative Commonwealth. It will thus be seen that, even if all the conditions were ripe tomorrow for the inauguration of the New Order, we could not hope to do anything more in the generation, then living, than lay the foundation, deeply and firmly, for its upbuilding; among other things by training capable persons belonging to the second generation to be the educators of the third — to have charge of this third generation *from its earliest infancy till it reaches the adult age.*

Consider how many, many children are now sent into the world at an age, when those of wealthy parents are still in the nursery; consider that the average time children attend school is in our cities but *five*, and outside our cities but *three* years; consider that such an "enlightened" state as Massachusetts requires only a yearly school-attendance of *twenty-weeks* of her children under fifteen years; consider that in spite of this law 25,000 of her children *never* have seen the inside of a school-room; consider that 10,000 infants *under ten years* are working in the factories of that same *enlightened* State;* consider that all over our country, with *all* our children, schooling stops when the thinking process really first commences, and is it any wonder that our educational results are wretched?

Why! the sixteenth, seventeenth and eighteenth years constitute the most critical period of a boy's life, and left to himself he is, during those years and until he become restrained by experience, really one of the most dangerous members of Society. That these boys turn out to be as noble men as many of them do is a sufficient proof of the inherent goodness of human nature. But when the New Order has arrived, we shall be unanimous in acknowledging that restraint is just needed as a sort of astringent, to give maximum of power. We shall have learned that a young man who is kept under close and continued discipline of proper persons till twenty-one is sure to have a more vigorous and original character than one left to his own devices at an age when mind is yet unformed. And as far as our girls are concerned we shall yet sooner have learned a similar lesson.

You will very likely doubt that such a radical change will take

* For these facts see an article on "Children's Labor" in Atlantic Monthly, December, 1880.

place here where, preeminently, it is the practice to leave the young men and women to shift for themselves. In the same way many doubts might have been raised as to the success of the common school system, judging from the opposition to it from so many quarters at its introduction. Yet nearly all parents now avail themselves of it, driven by an unconscious impulse. And so, when the Great Change occurs, novelties will soon become familiar.

But the greatest novelty will be the new *ideal* of education.

That is the only matter left us to consider. We have nothing to do with what will be taught or how to teach it. That we for our part shall leave to the competent; already too many amateurs have had their say on that subject. But even those now most qualified would be incompetent to frame a curriculum for our future schools, for the ideal of education now will by no means be the ideal of the Coming Commonwealth.

The ideal, the end sought to be attained, now of education is to enable the individual to achieve *success in life, to get the better of their fellowmen* in the struggle for the good things of this world. That is the meaning of Individualism. No matter that in the nature of things but few can achieve that success, and that those who do succeed generally at the end of their career consider their success not worth the trouble, *that* teacher is considered the best who best knows how to qualify his pupils for the battle of life. That is why teachers stimulate the "ambition" of their scholars with prizes, marks, relative places in the school-room &c. That is also why they cram their pupils with facts and common-places of received opinions and persist in teaching them Latin and Greek so that they may afterward quote classical extracts for the sake of effect.

The end to be attained by education in the Coming Commonwealth will be a very different one. It likewise will be to qualify the pupils for the battle of life, but *against nature* and *in accord with their fellows*. That is the meaning of Social Cooperation.

In that Commonwealth prizes will not be used, because they only excite a few while leaving the mass phlegmatic; they will be condemned as *anti-social*. Perhaps in their place the educators will have recourse to Bentham's suggestion of a scholar-jury, scholar-suffrage, leaving it to the scholars themselves to determine by their votes the relative position of each other in the school-room. That will be a proper extension of the suffrage and will bring home to the minds of the pupils, *that all suffrage is a trust.*

Conformably to that new ideal the scholars will be impressed with gratitude for the blessings which all past generations have conferred upon them, and it will be urged upon them that they owe *all* to Society.

They will be taught how to utilize all the sources of happiness which Nature and the Commonwealth supply, for the New Order will want them to have many tastes and needs.

But especially will they be taught to perform well their functions in Society.

It will by that time be fully known, that a man trained for one subject only never becomes a good judge in that one, even, whereas enlightenment and enlargement of his circle gives him increased power and knowledge in a rapidly increased ratio. Therefore a harmonious and balanced cultivation of all the faculties will be the first object. The pupils will be taught all that is known, and though that field seems immense they will easily master it, for they will be led to the bottom of things and learn the fundamental laws and the connection of phenomena. They will be profound and complete human beings, all of them. We are tending more and more in that direction; that is why such *incomplete* men and women, as Puritans and Quakers, have hardly any of their old-time influence left.

Again, a great deal will be done in order to find out the peculiar fitness of every child. Now next to nothing is done to discover the natural aptitude of children, or to substitute choice for chance in the allotment of the various social functions. And so it may be said that *the* mistake which all teachers make is to teach the same lesson in the same way to all.

But Goethe suggests in the second volume of his *Wilhelm Meister*, that every human being is born into the world with a particular talent of some kind or other. In his opinion, it is only requisite to recognize that particular talent in the child, and foster it, in order to develop all its other faculties, and that, if that talent be not found out and developed, it is the fault of the educator. He grounds this suggestion of his on the well-known pedagogic experience, that a teacher can succeed with even the dullest child, as soon as he manages to win its interest for some object, whatever it may be; in other words as soon as he succeeds in discovering *the drift of that inborn talent in the child.* As soon, then, as a scholar is incited to voluntary activity and finds out that he is able to accomplish something in *some one* direction, it would be comparatively easy to awaken his self-confidence, so that he will succeed in other respects. This special talent thus insures the possibility *that every healthy child,* male and female, may have all its human faculties harmoniously developed.

Now we do not say, that it is remarkable that educators have hitherto been entirely deaf to this important hint — for it is not, considering the present ideal of education — but we cannot help here to notice that an obscure teacher in Hoboken, N. J., Dr. *Adolph Douai,* who, were the New Commonwealth now in existence, would undoubtedly be found in the front rank of its leading minds, has been the first and only professional educator who publicly has called attention to this suggestion. We may be sure that the Coming Commonwealth, which can only furnish the necessary favorable conditions for the verification of this thought, will not be slow to utilize it. The institutions that have already shown themselves specially adapted to the discovery and unfolding of these latent talents in children, are the *Kindergartens.* Though as yet but comparatively few of them exist in our country or elsewhere, those who teach in them have been able to discern in many children geometrical talent and aptitude for the study of natural sciences in whom otherwise nobody would probably ever have suspected them. These Kindergartens the Cooperative Commonwealth will in all probability establish in all the nooks and corners of the country, not to say in every family, as the first and most important link in the chain of its educational institutions.

Mr. Bain in his treatise on Education makes an important observation which is pertinent here: "If from the beginning one can interpolate five shades of discrimination of color where another can feel but one transition, the careers of the two can be foreshadowed as widely apart. To observe this native inequality is important in predestining the child to this or that line of special training."

This observation and predestination will be made in the Kindergartens, where also a *taste* for manual work will be imbibed at a very early age. Thereafter we suppose general education and special training will accompany each other, under the eye of the teacher, till the child reaches adult age. We judge so, not merely from considering the natural requirements of the Commonwealth, but from observing the various attempts that now are being made to find a substitute for that slavish and wasteful apprentice-system which happily is a thing of the past, by founding industrial schools, so-called "developing schools," and trying to make them a part of our common-school system.

We do not know whether this hypothesis of Goethe, that all normal men are capable of being educated up to the same level of intelligence and knowledge, is true or not. We know of no fact that militates against it, but think there are many facts that confirm it. At all events, only the Interdependent Commonwealth can furnish the necessary conditions for its verification. Should it be found true, it is easy to see that it will prove of transcendent significance as it will lay the foundation for that perfect, absolute *equality* which is the ideal of Socialism — and yet, mark what an *unlikeness*, what a *variety* there will be!

As the boys will be really educated, so the girls will be. In the New Commonwealth they will no longer be trained to please the man-fool, or acquire only accomplishments which give fullest scope to vanity, luxury and passion. No, they will be equally fitted for *their* appropriate functions as members of society, as wives and mothers, *in institutions adapted for them.* The latter qualification is important, for the motto which is the prominent characteristic of the modern American school-system, that "boys' and girls' schools should be one, and that one the boys" will surely be rejected by the Coming Commonwealth, as one against which physiology protests. But the future woman will, by methods and regimen adapted to her sex, reach the same plane of knowledge and intelligence as man and in that way become his *equal* and true *companion.* We shall then surely have *complete men and complete women.*

But how can the State, when once it has taken charge of education, draw a line where education ends and moral indifference begins?

The great need of the age is to organize, diffuse and assimilate that which is known. Humanity, indeed, does not now so much need more isolated facts, as to understand how all these facts are related to each other, and most of all, it needs to have that deeper, real knowledge made common property. Then first we can enjoy all the fruits of the tree of knowledge. Then, more particularly, we shall again reach a substantial agreement of opinion as to this Universe in which we live, what it means and what therefore is the part we ought to play in it. The anarchy of opinion of this transitory age is an enormous evil. Unity of belief is the normal condition of the human intellect; it is just as natural for healthy men to think and believe alike, as it is for healthy men to see alike.

When one harmonious sentiment thrills through the whole of Society, we may expect a revival of the aesthetic sense of ancient Greece. This Gilded Age with its so-called "promoters of the arts" create prostitutes of art, who exercise it, not for love of it, but to "make" money by it. Imagine if you can, a Raphael painting a Madonna, or Phidias sculpturing an Aphrodite for — profit! Art always is prostituted, when it only serves the vanity of the rich. In the present age poets do not sing for the masses, artists do not fashion their masterpieces for the masses as during the Christian Middle Ages or in classical Greece and Rome.

In Athens the whole people in the amphitheatre witnessed the spectacles, here — how different it is! We have expensive theatres where our comfortable classes can idle away their time, but, as Beecher says, they are not for the poor. The theatre to which the poor have entrance is perhaps the most vitiating of all social institutions. If there is anything that needs the helping, the reforming hand of the Commonwealth we should say it is the stage. It can be made the mightiest educational instrument. In particular, manners and address can be learned to perfection in the theatre, and only there.

Matthew Arnold says, pointedly: "A handful of Athenians of two thousand years ago are more interesting than millions of our contemporary nations — because they present us the spectacle of a cultured *people*. It was the many in the highest development of their humanity; the *many* who relished these arts and were satisfied with nothing less than those monuments."

So in the Cooperative Commonwealth where *care* is forever banished art will once more belong in the midst of the people, because of its eminently educational importance. He who has learned to appreciate the Beautiful will never after have a taste for the Low. Art will re-enter into the open arena of life.

But the greatest effect of this common education and common opinion will be the feeling of a *common duty*.

CHAPTER XII

MORALS IN THE COOPERATIVE

COMMONWEALTH

"Ethics are the finest fruits of humanity but not its roots."
— *Mallock's New Republic.*

"Man has it in his power by his voluntary actions to aid the intentions of Providence, but to learn those intentions he must consider what tends to promote the general good." — *John S. Mill.*

"Mankind, without any common bond, any unity of aim, bent upon happiness, has sought each and all to tread their own paths, little heeding if they trampled upon the bodies of their 'brothers' in name, enemies in fact. This is the state of things we have reached today." — *Mazzini.*

We have said that socialism, considered as simply an economic system, will have a great influence, also, on morals — that is to say, it will greatly affect our relations to what is "right" and "wrong," "good" and "bad," "moral" and "immoral," and, though there is really no such thing as *Socialist morals,* may even affect our conceptions of what is "right" and "wrong."

We have hitherto avoided, and pretty successfully we think, all commonplaces, all words involved in mist. The above ethical terms are, however, such commonplaces. In order to begin, right at the start, to clear away the mist, we cannot do better than quote George Eliot:

"Let a contractor enrich himself by making pasteboard soles pass as leather for the feet of unhappy soldiers; let a speculator retire to private life on ten thousand a year after cheating widows and hard-working fathers of all their savings, you often hear charming women pity such men, when they come to grief, and exclaim: 'He is a thoroughly *moral* man,' meaning thereby, that he is not a drunkard or a debauchee. . . . Is not this misuse of the word "Morals" a reason, why the ablest intellects are supposed to look on morals as a sort of twaddle for bibs and tuckers, as a mere incident of human stupidity?"

Now, to be sure, the economic changes which we have considered will contribute vastly to the establishment of what we call the *decencies.*

Drunkenness, *i.e.* the habit of excessive drinking, which our social "reformers" pronounce the cause of almost all evil, is to the philosophic mind nothing but an effect, especially an effect of *care.* When care is banished, we may be sure that drunkenness will be banished also. It is absurd to suppose that a happy young man will go and get drunk more than once. Bear also in mind, that when the New Commonwealth takes charge of the liquor traffic the dispensers of beer and liquor will no longer have an interest in the quantities sold, and none but pure and wholesome products will be sold.

As to sexual irregularities we can say, that they will hardly be heard of as soon as woman is put in a position to spurn the bribes of man, and as soon as every young pair can marry without any fear of consequences.

But it is far from us to limit "Morals" to this shrunken meaning. To explain what we mean then by the words "right" and "wrong" let us illustrate:

Men for thousands of years used the words "up" and "down" with reference to themselves, and the consequence was confusion: what was "up" to one in one place was "down" to him in another place. It is only a few hundred years back that we commenced to comprehend the real, the *scientific* meaning of these terms: that "down" means towards the centre of the earth, "up" away from that centre, and that to one suspended in space there is absolutely no "up" and no "down."

In the same way theologians presumed to tell mankind that "good" and "bad" actions were to be judged from their effects upon the destiny of the *actor.* "Sins" that were scarlet could therefore under certain circumstance be made white like snow.

Science, and with it Socialism, which bases itself on the verities of things, teaches that there would be no morality at all if man did not need his fellowman; that "right" and "wrong" have reference, primarily, not to the individual actor, but to that greater organism, called *Society*.

Gambling is wrong, is immoral, *not* because it tends to the ruin of the gambler, but because he cannot win unless somebody loses; because gambling, thus, sears the sympathies and, therefore, is essentially *anti-social*.

"Right" is every conduct which tends to the welfare of Society; "wrong" what obstructs that welfare. Bad actions are no longer "sins," but "crimes," and *crimes* can never be white as snow.

Now, human beings have already learned by experience that they must act in a certain way under penalty of being unable to act together at all; that Society could not *exist* at all without *Integrity;* that it could not *progress* without *Sympathy*. We may call integrity the *basis* and sympathy the *crown* of Morals.

It will be seen that there is no such thing as absolute, unchangeable morality. The different stages in the progress of Society evidently require different standards; what was right at one period may be eminently wrong at a later period. Thus if Slavery was, indeed, the first necessary step of our civilization, the first lesson in cooperation, we must pronounce Slavery to have been right then — and the fact that the best men of antiquity: Socrates, Jesus, Aristotle, acquiesced in it tends to prove it so — however wrong it appears in the light of a higher morality. It, also, will be seen, that morals is truly a science, a very subtle science, as it involves a correct philosophy of Society, its tendencies and destiny. Is it any wonder that morals has hitherto been a tissue of rhetorical and emotional commonplaces? Before anybody can say what is "right" conduct, and whether he is a truly "moral" man or not, he must possess all the knowledge and mental development which we have assumed will be the portion of everybody when the New Social Order is in full swing.

But to know what is "right" is only one side of the great subject, rather the reverse than its front side.

The writer of this once listened to a very interesting lecture by Carroll D. Wright, the head of the Labor-bureau of Massachusetts on "our factory system," the leading thought of which was, that our industrial system would be unobjectionable if both parties, employers and employees, would only go down to the foundation and be led by morality and religion.

Therein lurks a fundamental mistake, Col. Wright!

Morals are *not* the foundation, still less religion. They are the top of our system. *Interest — Self-interest — is the foundation, the prime motor, the mainspring of our actions;* so it is, has always been, and will always be.

"Why should *I* do this thing?" "why should *I* not gamble?" has always been the great practical question, and not "is gambling wrong?" It is easy enough to gain intellectual assent to a moral precept, but the trouble is that a man is never tempted by things in the abstract, but when he does something wrong he does it for the sake of some particular, concrete thing.

There is then the greatest possible difference between *end of* and *motive to* morality: and nothing is, not even the most self-sacrificing acts are, done without a motive. That which moves must be primary. Now, Col. Wright! it is not our morality or want of morality which makes our economic relations what they are, but our economic system that makes our morality what it is.

That is the hinge on which this chapter turns.

In former chapters we have analyzed our economic relations. Let us now see how it stands with our *integrity* and note the relation there is between it and our economic system.

First, in order come the so-called crimes against property. Robbery, burglary, larceny, embezzlement, common swindling, murder and arson, when committed in pursuit of wealth (and it is only in that connection we here have to consider them,) are all acknowledged offences against Society. And probably no one doubts that there are more such crimes committed now than in any former age. To take one instance as illustration: For a merchant to become bankrupt was formerly a life-long disgrace; now bankruptcies are so frequent, that they are considered mere incidents of "business" and are facilitated by law. It may be said that there are more opportunities for committing such crimes, but what we here want to make clear is the simple fact, that these crimes *are* more frequent now, in proportion to the population, than, for instance, during the Middle Ages — no matter how it comes.

But now we arrive at the first point that we wish to make. Such practices as those above mentioned are the only ones which we of this age stigmatize as *crimes:* we call by that name only acts that may bring their perpetrators into the penitentiary. Ought not, in view of the philosophic definition of "right" and "wrong" conduct, every grievous offence against Society be so called? To be sure, in that case most of the leaders of our self-styled "society" may come to be reckoned as criminals.

Henry Ward Beecher once told his congregation of merchants, bankers, politicians and speculators: "the laws against larceny have no relations to me. I am on too high a plane to be affected by any temptation to steal." In other words: "Thank God, that I and you, dear brethren and sisters, are not on a plane with that rabble that commit crimes against property!"

Are they on a higher plane?

Herbert Spencer has shown, that Trade in England is essentially corrupt and that there success in business has become incompatible with strict integrity. It is certainly not better here. Are the tricks of trade not offences against Society? Is "commercial cannibalism," as Spencer calls it, not a crime?

Adulteration of provisions has everywhere become a social institution. Is that not a crime?

Are the traps ingeniously devised by speculators for the punishment of ignorance in people of small means, are the corners gotten up in money, stock, wheat and pork not crimes?

Our late income-tax was repealed for the avowed reason, that it could not be collected, because our rich men were far more ready to swear falsely, than to hand over a small percentage of their vast incomes. Were these rich men not criminals?

It is a fact, that directors of gigantic corporations so manipulate things, that the public is taxed heavily to pay dividends on "watered" stocks. Are these men less guilty, because powerful?

It is notorious, that our politicians are corrupt from top to bottom. Even if too "high-toned" to debauch voters, in person, they are ready enough to raise corruption-funds, and never squeamish as to profiting by the bribery. Are these "eminent citizens" on "too high a plane" even according to the ethical code of to-day?

But we shall have to go a good deal farther; *we* cannot afford to compromise. In morals there is no difference between "legitimate" and "illegitimate" offences against Society. *Everyone who pockets gains without rendering an equivalent to Society is a criminal.*

Every millionaire is a criminal.

Every one who amasses a hundred thousand dollars is a criminal.

Every president of a company with nominal duties, if his salary is but a thousand dollars, is a criminal.

Every one who loans his neighbor $100 and exacts $106 in return is a criminal.

Again, it is a fact, that the mere transfer of products is a very low order of labor, requiring only the most ordinary and inferior kind of mental qualities, which, if it received simply an equivalent in return, would be allowed but the very lowest compensation. Yet it is that very mercantile class which absorbs all the wealth by every available form of deception and strategy, while a thoroughly skilled artisan cannot possibly amass a large competence by the diligent prosecution of his trade. This whole mercantile class is a criminal class in regard to by far the largest part of their income; one of our really *dangerous* classes — and the same applies to their cousins, the financial class.

It is damnable hypocrisy in these mere dealers in products and financiers when they pretend to any extraordinary "executive ability;" they know in their hearts, that they have but very little ability, very little skill.

It is hypocrisy, when the poor mechanic who by superior skill produces all the wealth of the world is taught to look up to those who only *handle* his products.

The whole integrity of our rulers can be summed up in one word: cash-payment.

Our mechanics and artisans cannot be filled with too much righteous hate against such shams.

And what about integrity in work? Well, it is bad at the start that the duty of doing one's proper work well is entirely left out of "morals" in popular speech. And yet it is by work that man takes his place among the creative forces of the universe. As has been well said: "Thoroughness of workmanship, care in the execution of every task undertaken, as if it were the acceptance of a trust which it would be a breach of faith not to discharge well, is a form of duty so momentous, that if it were to die out from the feeling and practice of a people national prosperity and happiness would be gone."

The absence of such integrity is a most conspicuous feature in the operations of modern industry, and is the most lamentable fact of all. It was not so during the despised Middle Ages. Then every artisan felt a pride in his skill and in turning out good work. Now shoddy work is abounding. It has come out in the investigations of the Trades-Unions in England, that the men are required by their masters to "scamp" their work, that is, turn out inferior work and that this is just the reason why the masters are so determined to introduce piecework instead of daywork.

Such is our integrity — the *basis* of our morals. This was the first point which it was necessary to establish: that our "best people" are criminals. If they themselves do not know it, it is simply because their understanding is being clouded by their interests and the opportunities of the system.

If this hypocritic age should frankly enunciate its moral code, it would say:

Thou and thine may keep whatever thou canst get.

Carlyle has illustrated this in a drastic manner. He makes one pig ask another:

"What is justice?"

"Your own share of the general swine's-trough; not any portion of my share."

"But what is 'my' share?"

"Ah, there is the rub upon which piggism can settle absolutely nothing. My share? Humph! My share is, on the whole, whatever I can contrive to get, without getting hanged or sent to the hulks."

Now we come to our second point: how is it that we have so far attained to this low level of integrity? Why do people steal, and rob and embezzle?

We claimed in the preceding chapter, that ignorance is not the cause of such crimes. We saw there, that these crimes are abounding in the most educated sections of our own country. Indeed *the most reprehensible of these crimes cannot be committed by ignorant persons.* True, among the lowest criminal class you find much ignorance, but so you find much uncleanliness, many dirty shirts, and frequently no shirts at all. You might, therefore, just as well, perhaps with more propriety, attribute crime to want of a shirt or of soap as to want of education.

More superficial yet is it to attribute the crimes we now are discussing to drunkenness, simply because we find the lowest criminals so often associated with poor beer and whiskey. Drunkenness has very little to do with these crimes, *most of which, in fact, cannot be committed but by sober persons.*

Herbert Spencer finds a sufficient reason for the persistence and growth of crime in the fact, that the code of supernatural ethics which our forefathers had is losing its authority, and the moral injunctions, given by it, therefore more and more losing its sanctions, coupled with that other fact, that while the regulative system of our forefathers is thus decaying, we have not yet got any other regulative system to take its place.

There is no doubt, that as long as people had a vivid dread of purgatory and hell fire, that was a powerful spur to good behavior. Yet, deliberate dishonesty and carelessness, so peculiar to human work alone, is so unnatural, that there must be a weightier reason for this decline of integrity. And then, we verily believe, and have reason to believe, that every man is naturally honest, and that the most inveterate thief would have remained honest if there had not been some *positive* temptation to lead him astray. The decay of religion can never be more than a negative reason.

No, the only rational way is to consider every such crime as an act, preceded by a motive which, if it be but imperious enough, it is not in human nature to withstand; in other words to look upon crime as essentially human.

And when you do that, can you wonder, that our jails are full, when honest men are starving? Is it strange, that men in many of whom vagrancy has become a second nature — often originally from no fault of their own — prefer larceny, or burglary or swindling to toiling ten hours or more daily for a weekly pittance of $5.00? Is it anything but human to use any means to obtain wealth, when Society has made wealth the sovereign power? When one reads in novels and witnesses in plays how the hero and heroine are always rewarded by marrying — wealth? When one everywhere hears a man, in every way no better than himself, as "worth" so many thousands of dollars and sees him the admitted superior of the most worthy of poor men?

The fact is our *integrity* is simply the fruit of our *struggle for life against each other,* and a river can rise no higher than its source.

The economic system under which we are living *creates all* these frauds, dishonesties and this hypocrisy. Men *find it to their advan-*

tage to adulterate goods and to manufacture shoddy articles; indeed, our Established Order compels men to seek their success in overreaching others, makes it a merit in them to be unscrupulous, simply because everybody's interests have been made antagonistic to the interests of every other body. By this capitalistic system of ours Society has been made the hunting ground for the sharpest individuals.

It is evident, that the longer this system lasts, the more will these evils grow, for the struggle for life and success will become more and more intense; wealth will come more and more to mean power, and the chase after wealth, therefore, will become fiercer and more savage. Sermonizing or lectures on Moral Philosophy have never affected and will never affect any state of mind. Prize-essays against embezzlement will not diminish the frequency of this crime.

No, we just see here exemplified what we stated in another place. When our social order is to be changed into another social order, (the case now, and in that other sceptical period before the introduction of Christianity) the change commences from above; disorganization commences at the top: with religion; then it goes down to morals and down to the foundation, until the base has changed its position; then, on the new foundation, on the new economic system, morals and religion will be rebuilt anew. Then the changed economic relations will furnish new *motives* for an enduring morality.

Just as self-interest now is eating away the edges of morals, so self-interest must build up morals, and that the New Commonwealth will make it do. It will make it men's *interest* to be honest; will make them find their advantage in being men of integrity, simply because its very essence is making the interests of everybody identical with the interests of Society and of everybody else.

The following reflections from an interesting work from which we have quoted before: *The Value of Life*, written it is understood by an eminent scientist of New York, are here very pertinent:

"It is no sentimentalism, but the simple expression of fact that the individual occupations of the members of Society cannot be adequately regulated, as long as they are regarded merely as the means for each of these persons to get his or her living. By a crowd of official acts, from the inspection of markets to taking the census, Society, even as it is, expresses its recognition of the fact, that this vast mass of activities, constituting the 'business' of the community, represents the sum of its own vegetative functions, by which all its life, from the lowest to the highest plane of it, is sustained. In the discharge of these functions the money or 'living,' earned by each individual, is really the least important consideration. Thus it is of much less importance, that a butcher grow rich than that the thirty or forty families he supplies with meat receive good meat at fair prices. Whatever value attaches to the individual life of the butcher is multiplied forty times by the sum of those of his customers; it is, therefore, *their* welfare, not his profit which must be the first consideration. In other words: The essential thing is, not that the butcher shall have a living, still less be rich, but that *meat shall be supplied*. The how and where are secondary details, to be regulated not by the convenience of the producer, but by that of the consumer.

"This indisputable line of reasoning overturns the theory, that work is performed for the sake of the producer, (whose advantage, indeed is quite subsidiary) and shows, that it is primarily for the benefit of Society or some group of persons in it. Of course, the worker, by entering into another group where *he* is the consumer, finds his welfare correlatively taken into account. The daily business is thus removed from the ignominy and pettiness of isolated individualism and elevated into an honorable function, while he who performs it becomes invested with the dignity of a public functionary. That the worker receives remuneration is incidental — that the work be thoroughly done is so essential, that it is inseparable from any typical conception of achievement."

That is it. In the New Commonwealth the butcher will be conscious and satisfied that "the *essential* thing is, not that he shall have a living, but that meat shall be supplied." The work of the citizen will be the glad performance of social office, not, as now, the mere tribute to physical necessity. He will be a moral worker, whose best efforts, best ardor and highest aims will be drawn out by the joy which he takes in his work — in all but the lowest work, such routine, manual labor as machinery should remove altogether from human hands. He will soon be habituated to regard his wages, not as a *quid pro quo*, but as a moral claim, as the provision made by Society to enable him to carry on his labor. The question: "why should I do honest work?" will *then* seem just as irrational as it is now to ask "why should I eat?"

Most of the offences to which we have called attention will disappear, simply because the opportunities for committing them will be gone.

And when in the Coming Commonwealth a few hours of daily, agreeable effort will secure to everybody all necessaries, decencies and comforts of life, why then should any rational being want to steal or cheat or rob? And why should anybody want to make a living by crime, when it will be far easier to make it by honest work? And why should anybody care to procure wealth dishonestly, when wealth no longer will mean *Power* over men? When wealth will not be able to coax the meanest of men to be your footman and wear your livery? When wealth simply will mean more to eat, more to drink and more luxuries?

In short, the economic system of the New Commonwealth will have two most important effects on integrity. First, *it will institute a higher moral code* by giving us a truer conception of what is "right" and "wrong" conduct. It will thus make us feel that the man who charges six per cent., or even one per cent. for the use of his money is just as much a criminal, in principle, as the highway-robber; that is, it will once more make us call all interest-charge *usury*.

Secondly, *it will absolutely reverse motives.* Instead of the present Society saying: "help thyself or go to jail!" the future Society will help everybody *by removing all temptation to do what is wrong.*

Here we hear some well-fed, well-clad personage exclaim: "So we are to have only negative virtues in your Commonwealth!"

Only negative virtues? Let us recall what Beecher said of himself: "I am on too high a plane to be affected by any temptation to steal." Of course he is! With a yearly salary of $20,000 there is for him every temptation to *refrain* from stealing. Is his then anything but a "negative" virtue? He should not, like the pharisee of old, speak so superciliously of his "lofty plane," until he was in want of the necessaries and decencies of life, with no honest way open to him to procure them. We have in the foregoing seen what the "lofty plane" of his congregation amounts to; their principal virtue perhaps consists in hating so heartily the offences of other people, not in their set.

The difference between our so called "virtuous" and "vicious" classes is far more a difference of temptation than of virtue. The virtuous person can pride himself on very little else than negative virtues; he is virtuous because everything tempts him to be virtuous. Even so we want everybody, even the meanest of men, to be tempted, *and the Coming Commonwealth will so tempt all.*

Now we pass over to *sympathy*, the crown of Morals.

We have frequently throughout this work had occasion to quote from Herbert Spencer. The reason is, that he is truly the most profound of recent English philosophers, that his influence on all liberal minds in our country has been very great, and that we cannot conceive of any better way of propagating socialist ideas than to show them to be the logical outcome of the best modern thoughts. And Spencer's later philosophy is really socialist. The best socialist lessons can be drawn from his latest work: "Data of Ethics," and especially from the chapter on Sympathy.

Sympathy is *fellow-feeling.* To sympathize is to make the pleasure and pain of our fellows our own; the former we do willingly, the latter unwillingly. We naturally sympathize with pleasant, joyful people; we with difficulty sympathize with sorrowful and miserable persons. Anyone can easily convince himself of the truth of this, by one day attending a funeral and the next day a wedding.

It is therefore but natural that sympathy grows, if those around us habitually manifest pleasure and but rarely pain, while it decreases, if we ordinarily witness little pleasure and much pain. It is also natural that sympathy at present grows but little, since the life usually led under our present conditions is such that suffering is daily inflicted or daily displayed by associates.

And please observe that *sympathy* and *pity* are two greatly different things. Sympathy requires equality; pity regards the object not only as suffering, but as *weak*, hence as inferior; therefore the distresses of those beneath us excite only the same sentiment as that with which we regard the suffering of an over worked cart-horse. It is just because the occasional so-called "charities" of the wealthy have their motive in pity and not in sympathy, that they lack all moral value, though the following remarks of Prof. Adler are also true: "Of what avail would it be if one of the members of the great monopoly which I have recently described were to found an orphan asylum or to build a hospital? Should we really be willing to clap hands as many are supposed to do and cry, Oh, how charitable the man is! Why, he has not begun to give back to society what he has taken from it in the first instance, much less that he should claim credit to himself for his charitableness." In such cases "charity" is nothing but *hush-money*.

And for the very reason that there can be no sympathy without equality, we in a former chapter denounced the subjection of employee to employer as demoralizing. We now wish to speak of a relation than which nothing in the present constitution of Society is more essentially vicious and morally injurious: the relation of domestic servants to their "masters" and "mistresses." We called the wage-workers' condition substantial slavery; that of servants is servitude in substance and form.

American society has wofully retrograded in this respect. In the beginning of this century Americans spoke of their "help;" now it is everywhere "servants!" This is *not* a mere difference of words, but involves a degradation in position. The servant drops her surname, a veritable degradation, for it marks her as a person henceforth of no social account; she is spoken to only to receive orders; she abandons family life, an ordeal not required by out-door workers; she is day and night subject to the bidding of master and mistress, and may be called to account for every hour out of the twenty-four. We think it very much to the credit of American women, that they refuse thus to degrade themselves. They are in pleasing contrast to the so-called "men" who consent to perform menial services for others for — money, or who even with apparent satisfaction act as the liveried flunkeys of our money-bags. Our wage-workers at least keep alive the spirit of discontent, but who ever imagined that our flunkeys could be rebels?

We cannot withstand the temptation once more to bring forward our friend, the uncompromising abolitionist, to point a moral. He, by nature the kindest of men, a champion of the Rights-of-Man theory, once commended the English men-servants compared with American specimens and said: "when I pay a man to be a servant, I want him to be a servant." Suppose a slave-holder once upon a time had said in his hearing: "I bought him for a slave and I want him to be a slave" what would he have thought of such an argument? Thus this system of rich and poor, of master and servant, demoralizes the best of us, for it nourishes our "love of lording it," which is the greatest obstacle to the growth of sympathy.

It is, moreover, evident that the insolent individualism which is the moving power of our present industrial system necessarily stifles all sympathetic sentiments. It incites men to pursue their individual happiness in complete indifference to their fellows. When Herbert Spencer was here, he told us that he had observed, that Americans do not resent small trespasses. Why, if any passer-by would resent having to force his tortuous way on sidewalks, crowded with boxes, or having his face and clothes covered with the sweepings from our stores, he would make himself ridiculous! Spencer got the cart before the horse. Every individual here is a sovereign and says like Vanderbilt: "the dear public be damned!" — and acts accordingly.

Sympathy however has proven itself a far stronger force than individualism. The views we now hold on the subject of Slavery compared with those held by the good and wise of old prove the growth of sympathy during the whole historic period of man. And please mark, that even during this individualistic, sceptical age, in which integrity has so wofully deteriorated, sympathy has constantly been on the increase. The evidences thereof are on every side. Look at all the humane institutions in every nook and corner of our land — asylums and hospitals for every sort of misfortune and malady. Consider how ready men were to inflict bodily tortures a couple of centuries back and how anxious we now are to avoid doing so. Think of the penal code of medieval England and contrast therewith *our* treatment of criminals. Observe finally the relative frequency of the crimes themselves: while crimes against property have notoriously increased, those of brutality and passion have just as evidently grown less as well in number as in atrocity.

Just as we did not have to go very far to look for the reason of the backward state of integrity, so the reasons for the growth of sympathy are easy to find. Pain has been constantly on the decrease and pleasure as constantly on the increase; that is to say, we are much better clad, sheltered and fed than our ancestors were; many plagues which decimated our forefathers during the Middle Ages have been entirely extirpated; many others of their diseases have been considerably alleviated. Thus, again, we find our principal proposition substantiated, that it is material prosperity that is the

basis for all improvement, that economic relations are the foundation of even the highest form of morals.

And in this conquest of sympathy over individualism we have
another evidence, of the most convincing force, that we are irresistibly drifting towards Socialism. Why, even Spencer foresees "an
advanced social state where the manifestations of pleasure predomi-
nate and where sympathy, therefore, will reach a height that we
cannot now imagine."

And what kind of "advanced social state" has Spencer here in his
mind? Hear him!

"The citizens of a large nation, *industrially organized,* have
reached their possible ideal of happiness when the producing, distributing and other activities are such, that each citizen finds in
them a place for all his energies and aptitudes while he obtains the
means of satisfying all his desires.

"And we can imagine the eventual existence of a community
where in addition, the members are characterized by eminent æsthetic faculties, and achieve complete happiness only, when a large
part of life is filled by æsthetic activities."

In these words Spencer, on whom the word "Socialism" probably
has the same effect that a red cloth has on any healthy bull, has
drawn an admirable picture of — a Socialist State, our Cooperative
Commonwealth.

For in the Commonwealth that we have sketched in the preceding pages everybody will certainly find "a place for all his energies
and aptitudes" and obtain "means of satisfying all his desires."

In that Commonwealth ignorance and uncleanliness will disappear. Even so bodily pains, for we may be sure that medical science
and, especially, a developed public hygiene will very soon have
reduced physical suffering to a minimum.

In that Commonwealth will be found that necessary condition of
sympathy which Spencer ignores: *substantial,* perhaps absolute,
equality. The relation then, corresponding to our "domestic
service," will at all events be a moral — a sympathetic relation: that
is, domestics will be incorporated in the family, as members of it.
No one then, surely, will be so slavish as to accept the position on
less honorable terms.

"Is the man crazy?" some will here exclaim, "no one to black our boots, brush our clothes, sweep our rooms, attend us at meals, nurse our children! No one to look after our comfort! No one to answer, when we call 'Pat,' 'John' and 'Bridget!' That will be a nice sort of life, indeed!"

We really think you will have to "look after your comfort" yourself; most of your fellowmen, many of them far more worthy than you, now have to do that. At the public places, of course, you can have all your wants supplied and yourself attended to, but mark! by persons, as much public functionaries as you yourself will be, and conscious of being so, and whom you cannot familiarly call "Ben" or "John," except on an equal footing. But at home you will have to be "served" by members of your family and such people whom your personal qualities will attach to your person.

That Commonwealth, we insist, will be Spencer's "advanced social state" where sympathy will attain such a growth, that we now hardly can conceive of it; for we firmly believe with John S. Mill, that "the present wretched social arrangements are the only hindrances to the attainment by almost all of an existence, made up of a few and transitory pains and many and various pleasures."

We have already considered some of the fruits of that higher morality which thus will be the natural outcome of better economic conditions. We may now add that not only crimes against property, which we discussed under the head of "integrity," but all forms of crime will probably be practically unknown.

Crime, in all its forms, is an evidence of the neglected responsibilities of Society, exactly as the plagues of the Middle Ages were the proofs that the laws of health were disregarded. Now we have a daily birth of so many infants, so imbedded in criminality, that you might lay your hands on each and say, that if not rescued by something akin to a miracle, this child is, inevitably, destined to a criminal career. It is a sad reflection that infanticide would in their cases be absolute mercy! Yet the State stands by with folded arms, cares not a straw for them, permitting them to be trained to crime, furnishing them even temptations, until it catches them with its implacable arms and — strangles them. For mark! children and young persons — and old persons, too, for that matter — are led into a criminal career from precisely the same reasons that keep proper people from such a career: temptation, example and love of approbation.

The New Order will do away with crimes against property — "legitimate," such as the law now takes no notice of, as well as "illegimate" — by tempting all the right way. It will do away with crimes of brutality and passion by its thorough education and exalted sympathy. For this class of crimes does, certainly, depend upon the "plane" up to which one has been educated. As to such crimes Beecher might, with propriety, say of himself, that he is on too high a plane ever to be tempted to commit them, though a given occasion might prove, that he was mistaken even in that. In other words, criminals will be found to be what all socalled "nuisances" at bottom are: useful matter in wrong places.

Of course, for the first few generations the New Order will still have some criminals on its hands. In order to show, that Socialists are not influenced by any peculiar sentimentality in favor of criminals, let us state that we perfectly agree with Herbert Spencer, who would give convicts the barest of boards to rest on and nothing but cold water to support themselves on, until they force themselves — by an internal coercion which they can carry with them out of prison — to work for their necessaries of life and whatever comforts they desire, without subjecting them to any unnecessary pain and degradation as now they are subjected to. But that, also, can only be properly accomplished in the New Commonwealth, where convict labor will become an integral part of the cooperative labor of Society. Convicts will there, certainly, not be utilized by contractors to paste leather and pasteboard together to make a thick sole to impose upon the public, as is said not to be unfrequently the case now.

But the most glorious fruit of this higher morality, the one that ought to be most highly prized, will be this: that a complete accord, a perfect conciliation, will at last be effected between two hitherto irreconcilable sentiments, self-love on the one hand, and regard for our fellow-citizens and the public on the other.

We have several times impressed upon our readers the fact that Socialists take human nature as it is and we have claimed *that* to be one of their greatest merits. It will also have been noticed that our Commonwealth is built on self-love in robust vigor as on its cornerstone. Every man is necessarily his own centre, we hold; he can, as has been said, no more displace himself from self-interest than he can leap off his own shadow.

Now we already have, as Spencer has observed, instances of complete accord between self-love and love for others. We find it in the relation of a mother to her child and of the loving husband to his wife.

Is the mother who is watching day and night over her sick child and thereby imperilling her own health devoid of self-love? Is it not the fact that she is exactly *gratifying herself* in acting as she does?

Go to the bottom and you will find that her sacrifice is made from a direct desire to make it, is made to satisfy an egoistic sentiment or craving, and the strength of that egoistic sentiment is shown in a peculiarly strong light by the adoption of children by the childless.

In the same manner the husband is truly egoistic, when he makes sacrifices for the beloved wife.

Now, in the Cooperative Commonwealth, where perfect harmony will obtain between the interests of each citizen and those of the citizens at large, just as it now obtains between the members of a well-ordered family, there the final development of sympathy will in time merge self-love and regard for our fellow citizens into a concord, kindred to that between husband and wife and parent with children. A *kindred* concord we say, not exactly a *like* concord.

We shall gain pleasure by giving pleasure, but we shall not be thinking of the sympathetic pleasure gained, but only of that given. We even shall in the New Commonwealth willingly and with supreme satisfaction do acts of true *self-sacrifice*. The explanation of that seeming contradiction is, that cases involving self-sacrifice will in that Commonwealth become so rare and therefore so highly prized, that they will be unhesitatingly preferred and not at all felt as self-sacrificing acts; just as we even now sometimes hear it said of somebody: "Let him take the trouble: it pleases him to do so."

It will from all this be seen that we by no means want to "reform" *men*. We do not claim that under Socialism men or women will be any better than they now are or ever have been. We want to reform their *surroundings*, the *constitution of Society*, the *mould* in which their lives, thoughts and feelings are cast.

Socialists want to make it the *interest* of all to be honest, to make it to the *advantage* of all to furnish their best work, to make it *natural* for men to love their neighbors as themselves.

Socialists want all to be able to take a delight in life for its own sake and in everything that ministers to it, and that is the end of morals.

"Yes, it is well enough to enable people to take delight in *this* life. But it is related of Samuel Johnson, that he once exclaimed on being shown over a magnificent estate: 'Aye, sir! these are the things that make death bitter.' It is vain to bid men exclude the thought of immortality from their minds, and think only of making the best of this life and that is what we understand Socialists mean them to do. We understand that Socialists mean to drive religion entirely out of the world."

You misunderstand us, friend! We do not propose to drive religion out of human life. But what is religion?"

It is with "religion" as with "democracy;" to revert to the foreign words from which they are derived helps us very little to get at the essence of what we mean when we use these terms. According to its derivation "religion" means the restoration of a broken bond, it is understood, between earth and heaven. Now, that there is a broken bond to restore, was a fact to our forefathers; at present it is to all but simple-minded people a theologic fiction. If, however, by "religion" you mean this dogmatic theology, Socialists do propose to help drive it out. Socialism *is* the inveterate foe of theology — a fact of which the Pope is well aware, wherefore he is perfectly right in damning it — because Socialism is abreast with the highest intelligence of the time, and the highest intelligence of all progressive countries is at issue with what, only by a stretch of courtesy, may be called the popular religion. This, we hold, is a most mischievous state of affairs, fatal to sincerity, and creating, on the one hand, in the masses of the people a chilling, conceited scepticism in regard to everything that cannot be touched or handled, or giving rise, on the other hand, to sickly spiritual hallucinations. All that in the future will be needed to drive this theology entirely out of human life is to continue that "Titanic laughter — that terrible, side-shaking, throne-and-altar-shaking laughter" — which Rabelais started.

That which is now meant by "religion" is the view we hold of our relation to the great mystery which is all around us, in time as well as in space, and the awe we naturally feel when we think of it. We do not propose to drive religion in that sense out of the world, because it cannot be done, even if we wanted to. Comte tried it and only succeeded in doing what children do who are afraid of the darkness: they pull the bedclothes over their heads and pretend there is no darkness beyond. Nor are Socialists, like the men of the French Revolution, going to commit such puerile follies, as either to decree a deity out of existence or decree him back again.

But there is not the least doubt that just as the new economic system will greatly modify the family-relation, education and morals, so it will mightily affect religion, as we have now defined it. For, please mark this important fact, that as morals and education are the fruits of our economic relations, so religion is the fruit of our morals and education. *The latter are primary:* our gods are but the reflections of our moral and intellectual state. The religion of a nation is the outcome of its highest intelligence in its most solemn moments.

It cannot be denied that the idea of immortality has hitherto been an integral element of everything that deserves the name of religion, that our whole race has and has had a deep and secret longing for life beyond the grave. This longing may be due to the fact that this world was to the masses a veritable "vale of tears;" it has at all events been fostered by Catholicism and other so-called "religions," whose whole strength consisted in offering consolation to people who felt miserable here. It is just possible that when men all live to a good old age and get out of this life all the delights which nature permits, that this longing itself will disappear. But this longing *does* exist in the breast of mankind at present, and is nowhere stronger than in the Anglo-Saxon race.

Now, whether this longing for and belief in immortality is to be a part of the religion of the future is impossible to foresee. We can only say with Prof. Goldwin Smith:

"Suspense of judgment and refusal to accept the unknown as known is the natural frame of mind for any one who has followed the debate with an unprejudiced understanding and who is resolved to be absolutely loyal to truth. To such a one existence is an unfathomable and overwhelming mystery. But let not this suspense of judgment intimate a negative decision. *For a negative decision the hour has certainly not yet arrived,* especially as the world has hardly yet had time to draw breath after the bewildering rush of physical discovery."

We may also add, that Science knows as yet next to nothing about the Mind; there are, however, great promises in that direction in the near future. It is by studying the disturbances of Nature, that Science has succeeded in penetrating some of her inmost mysteries, and even so it is by watching the disturbances of the mind, that Science already has given us glimpses of hitherto unknown powers of the mind. Thus by the study of cataleptic patients it has already been demonstrated, that the Mind has extraordinary capacities, *independent of the orderly agency* of its bodily machinery, and that its perceptions in that condition are as much realities as those of its ordinary condition. It is impossible to say, what light may not be thrown on the question of personal immortality, when once this rich mine has been worked out by Science; then "the hour may have come for a decision," one way or the other. It seems however to us, that the thought of living a thousand years hence *somewhere* with personal *identity* unimpaired, is so rapturous and so inspiring that mankind will not feel inclined to relinquish it until Science lays down its *veto.*

But whatever may be the fate of the immortality-theory, we can be pretty sure that our race will again be practically unanimous on some religion, as they will be on all important matters. They probably will never know whether they have found the objective truth or not, but that is not of first importance, for observe that religion is *subjective, is the human view* of the mystery and our relation to it; if the mystery is ever revealed it will cease to be an object of religion. But *some* theory of life is needed to give harmony, purpose and vigor to active life, and they will certainly agree on such a theory as will explain the mystery to *them* and satisfy their highest intelligence. This is not the place to state the thoughts which the writer of this has on that subject.

Let us only say that this future religion will make *this* world *a real one.* The existing religions fail to satisfy mankind especially because they inculcate that this present existence is vain and that all the affairs of this world are petty and worthless; that some other world is *the* real one.

The religion of the future, besides, will lay special stress on our *interdependence;* it will teach men that the only way in which they can enter into vital relations with the Great Mystery is through *Humanity;* Socialism, in other words, will elevate religion from being a narrow personal concern between the individual and his maker into a *social concern between Humanity and its Destiny.* Humanity will not become a god, as Comte would have it, but *the* mediator between man and the Mystery.

When at some time you are lying sleepless in bed in the solemn hours of the night, do what I often have done: project yourself into space and fancy the insignificant little planet which is our dwelling place rolling swiftly past you, swarming with its ant-colonies of kings and beggars, capitalists and workers, all in the hollow of the hand of that Great Mystery! Is not that a train of thought that should make manifest to us the "solidarity," the interdependence of mankind? What is more natural than that each of us should desire and try to help our species along on the road to its destiny, since the ability has mercifully been granted to us to cooperate with that *Will* of the Universe which our own nature suggests to us!

Who can then deny that Socialists are religious in the highest sense of the word? Our creed can be expressed in these words of the preacher of *Village Politics;*

"The modern Christ would be a politician. His aim would be to raise the whole platform of modern society. He would not try to make the poor contented with a lot in which they cannot be much better than savages or brutes. He would work at the destruction of caste, which is the vice at the root of all our creeds and institutions. He would not content himself with denouncing sin as merely spiritual evil; he would go into its economic causes, and destroy the flower by cutting at the roots — poverty and ignorance. He would accept the truths of science, and he would teach that a man saves his soul best by helping his neighbor."

CHAPTER XIII

THE COMING REVOLUTION

"Be careful, sirs! how you judge God's revolutions as the products of man's invention." — *Oliver Cromwell.*

"The Revolution is a work of the Unknown. Call it good or bad, as you yearn towards the Future or the Past." — *Victor Hugo.*

> " 'Twas but the ruin of the bad,
> The wasting of the wrong and ill,
> What'er of good the old time had
> Was living still."
>
> — *Whittier.*

We commenced this book by quoting these words from a dialogue in "The Nineteenth Century:"

"We see that political systems in all progressive societies tend toward socialistic democracy. We see everywhere that it *must* come to that. We all of us feel this conviction, or all of us, I suppose, who have reflected on the matter. We feel, too, that nothing we can do can avert or possibly long delay the consummation. Then, we *must* believe that the movement is being guided, or is guiding itself, to happy issues."

We now add the response immediately following, from the same dialogue:

"*Hope* that the inevitable may prove the ultimately desirable, but *act* towards it in public affairs as you do in private, *i.e.* — *ignore it altogether!*"

It is, of course, two of "our best people" who thus discourse. The one who warns his friend that the *political* systems of all progressive countries are drifting towards "socialistic" democracy is uncommonly far-seeing and candid. He is undoubtedly right; the simple fact that household-suffrage was introduced in his country under *Tory* auspices proves it. But he is not profound enough. Political phenomena are merely the straws on the surface that show the direction of the current. That all the tendencies are and, especially, that the undercurrent is towards Socialism, towards Social-Co-operation, is the principal proposition of these pages.

Of the surface-tendencies there are, moreover, several of more significance than the political symptoms. Such are: the success of our common-school system and the efforts in other "progressive societies" by the State for the education of the masses; the fact that, though "Individualism" is rampant enough, practically, as a doctrine it is declining in the Protestant countries that gave it birth, and that the sects that were its apostles are now of next to no influence; and, most significant of all, the remarkable growth of fellow-feeling among the masses, due to the concentration of the workers in our cities, for there man meets man and spirit quickens spirit and intercourse breeds *sympathy*, and sympathy combination and enthusiasm, while the agriculturists remain comparatively unsympathetic and weak on account of their isolated situation.

But the undercurrent is the decisive factor. We mean the force that is unfolding the material, the industrial relations of life. Already Goethe remarked of animals that *subordination* and *difference* of parts is the measure of the height of their organization; we have learned that precisely the same applies to the social organization. This undercurrent manifests itself in the concentration of manufactures, of transportation, of commerce, and in the rise of large farms; in short, in the growth of monopolies. These, however, furnish us no halting place. For while these monopolies, on the one hand, have immensely increased the productivity of labor, they have on the other hand, been unable to furnish the requisite effective demand. However paradoxical it seems the result has been, that our large accessions of wealth and comfort have created an extended sense of unhappiness. As a consequence the undercurrent carries us beyond individual monopolies and calls forth the popular cry for collective control of material interests, first of all, of telegraphs and railways.

Now right here this current meets another, a parallel current: that which has been propelling the State unwillingly, in opposition to all received theories, to take charge of one social activity after another; a tendency that perhaps can be made clear in no better manner than by stating that the national expenses of England were in 1841 *forty* times as great as in 1685, while the population had only trebled — of England where the doctrine of "let alone" has had undisputed authority!

How the exercise of national authority has been extended in our country in the last generation we have already noted, and we are convinced that this centralization so-called would have been just as irresistible, though perhaps slower, if the Democratic party had been in power — look at the alacrity with which the Democrats vote for appropriations for rivers and harbors! The proposition of such an astute politician as Blaine to make the National Government the fiscal agent of the States and the deep impression it has made is another sign of the times. But our civil war, of course, was the giant step of our social evolution, and it is very difficult to decide, whether its main issue, the Union, or its side issue, Slavery, will prove of most importance. All other progressive countries, however, have kept pace with us. The struggles for nationality everywhere have mightily advanced the evolution of the social organism. Even the enormous standing armies of the European continent do this, as does everything that drills the masses as a whole and that teaches the people to work in concert. Why, it is through the German standing army that the German peasant has become accessible to Socialist ideas!

Buckle lays it down that "the movements of nations are perfectly natural; like others, they are determined solely by their antecedents." We may, in passing, remark that the fact that this view is now the generally adopted one, the fact that the law of evolution has been discovered and recognized as governing also Societies, is itself *an important step of the social evolution.* In the light of that philosophy it is easy to see that our whole civilization has been a lesson in cooperation, that slavery was the first lesson, that serfdom was the second, that our present wage-system is but a modified form of the latter, and that social-cooperation, *State Cooperation, Socialism,* is to be the system of the future, for this idea is in harmony with all antecedents and all our surroundings, and our whole age cooperates with it.

However, there is something else of importance to be noted. Herbert Spencer, as we have seen, is one with us in holding that Society will in the course of evolution arrive at "an advanced social state." But, besides shutting his eyes completely to the growing influence of the collective authority, he holds that this evolution is a purely blind natural force. Virtually he teaches: "Do not try to do anything at all; it is simply folly. In the first place, you *cannot* do anything; and, next, any effort on your part is unnecessary; if you only let things alone, they will come out all right of themselves sometime *in the far distant future*." It is no wonder that this indolent optimism does not attract the masses. How can Spencer have any sympathy with his fellowmen? What gospel has he or have his disciples for the poor, the suffering and oppressed? The greatest objection, however, to this scientific fatalism is that *it is unsound, fallacious*.

The fact is, that, though Society is truly an organism, the evolution of Society does not take place precisely like the growth of plants or animals. The former is the result of efforts *consciously* put forth; the progress of man requires the cooperation of men. Therefore, while Buckle's view, that the movements of nations depend upon their antecedents is true, it is not the whole truth; it must be supplemented by Carlyle's idea, that "the history of what man has accomplished is at bottom the history of the great men who have worked here." Again it is true that an idea, to be successful, must be in harmony with surrounding conditions, and yet, *that* is not enough: it must also be *incarnated*, so to speak, — made alive — in men and women. There must be a few people, at least, who care a great deal about the idea and who feel a resistless impulse towards its propagation.

Hence we add, that perhaps THE most important part of the evolution is the fact that *there are Socialists in the world at the present time*, that there are resolute men and women, intelligent representatives of all classes, who are determined to lead the world into the new channels! The most precious product of the evolution, therefore, we say, is that practical and energetic band, consisting less of dreamers than any number of men hitherto concerned in any great movement, and yet fired with an ideal that makes people forget their national antipathies — what even Christianity has been powerless to do! The pledge of success precisely are these men and women who act as if the fortunes of the world depended on their personal endeavors, proudly conscious that the fortunes of the world *have depended* on the struggles of just *such men as they!*

One such man — a man with a faith — is a social power, equal to 999 who have only interests.

The distinguishing trait of Socialists is that they boldly aim at a *revolution* and care not a jot about *reforms.*

We know that good people now-a-days shudder at the mere whisper of the word "revolution." It was not always so. There was a time when the eyes of patriots sparkled whenever "The American Revolution" was spoken; there was a time when "The English Revolution" sounded tolerably well in polite ears. Now the term "revolution" seems to suggest nothing but blood and destruction and violence. Yet, it means nothing of the kind. It simply denotes a *complete* change, the *vigorous* adaptation of old social elements to new conditions, *most orderly,* but effecting vast and permanent alterations. That is what all philosophic Socialists mean by a revolution. Their red flag has no relation to blood, or if it has, certainly not to cold clotted blood but the blood that courses warm and throbbing through the veins of every youth and maiden. But "reforms" only attack abuses, and in this are just as unscientific and stupid as bleeding for a fever in olden times was; both being simply crude methods of suppressing *symptoms.* How can any one "reform" away abuses *that are inherent in the system!* Reforms even often do immense mischief: they open the safety-valves and thereby render evils tolerable for the moment, but it is well to bear in mind that evil "evolves" as well as good.

The Coming Revolution is the new social force which will so act on the constitution of Society that the old withered husks are cast off, permitting the social butterfly to emerge from its chrysalis state.

For Spencer is wrong again, when he places his "advanced social state" in the very distant future, and teaches that the progress of Society is altogether accomplished by slow, very slow, gradual stages. Historic experience does not at all bear him out; it tells us, on the other hand, that when a social order has once been attained, there is first a period, quite a long period, of virtual stagnation, then Society begins to move slowly (the stage on which Spencer has wholly fixed his attention,) followed by an advance, constantly increasing in velocity — the nineteenth century is a good illustration of this stage, for are we not moving along in every department with railroad speed? — last of all, the decisive change to a new social system is accomplished almost before the living generation can recover its breath.

Will this New Social Order be "a happy issue?"

That is really a consideration of secondary importance and will perhaps be answered differently according to the standpoint one occupies. To our money-bags, prominent politicians, prominent lawyers, who now lord it over us; to "independent," overbearing, domineering "Philistines," buoyed up at the top, it will probably not seem a very "happy issue," looking at it through spectacles, colored by their class-interests, as they do. For the very gist of the Coming Revolution will consist in unseating them, in abrogating their vested rights, the *divine* right which they have been taught that they have to the fruits of the labor of other people. It will abolish "freedom" as they practise it, that is, the right to do what they please and to make others do as they (the "independent") please. But to the great multitude it will be, we should say, a happy issue, for it will put an end to their *subjection* and put *interdependence* — *genuine* freedom — in its place. And if we consider the welfare of the social organism there can be no doubt about the New System being a happy issue. Instead of the quackery, charlatanism, amateurship which now bears sway in all activities of Society we shall have skill, competence and qualifiedness (if we may coin a word) at the head of affairs, and indeed from top to bottom. Why, the main reasons why the workers will dismiss those who "rule" us now, is the very fact that they have proved themselves incapable of "governing," of administering affairs. The anarchy which now obtains, the discontent of the masses, our crises, our bankruptcies are all so many proofs of their incapacity, imbecility and ignorance. And most important of all, instead of being a *crowd*, not able even to keep our streets clean, we shall have *organization;* instead of gregariousness we shall have association; instead of everybody pursuing his individual petty interests absolutely indifferent, and often hostile, to the interests of Society, everybody will instinctively be conscious of himself as a being who, *of course*, considers the social welfare in his every act.

We can be sure that the Coming Revolution will not destroy an atom of what is really good now. We can be sure that it does not mean destruction as much as upbuilding. We can be sure that should anybody thereafter seriously propose to go back to the present Social Order, he will be laughed at as a fool, fit for the lunatic asylum.

But — *"ignore it altogether!"*

Those who are now at the head of affairs affecting — to ignore! That is a dangerous policy. Those who *will not* see become in time those who *cannot* see. Think of "leaders" who wilfully shut their eyes, and advise "ignore it altogether!" of "statesmen" with the motto: "after us the deluge!"

So, however, it has always been. "Force has been the midwife at the birth of every New Order." But the responsibility be on our incapable "leaders!"

Meanwhile the evolution of society marches forward in spite of all stumbling-blocks; one moment quietly in the brain of the thinker, the next moment unmercifully over corpses! But it does not want blood. On the contrary, it sends warning in advance of every catastrophe. Woe to those who do not heed that warning!

As yet, and first of all, it is a contest of ideas. We aim to put the Socialist idea into the minds of the people, knowing that if it be there actions will follow fast enough. However, as was intimated in the Introduction, the writer of this does not expect that the *majority* will in that way be excited to action.

The majority are always ignorant, always indolent; you cannot expect them to be anything else with their present social surroundings. They never have brought about, consciously and deliberately, any great social change. They *always* have permitted an energetic minority to accomplish that for them, and then — they *always* have sanctioned the accomplished fact.

That our people is no exception was proven by the abolition of slavery. That was accomplished by the emancipation proclamation of Lincoln who was egged on to issue it by an energetic minority; when it was accomplished, the people sanctioned it by amending their constitution; though even now, as a matter of course, "prominent" lawyers can be found who verily believe, that said proclamation was not worth the paper it is written on.

This, then, is our objective point: *a respectable minority;* respectable as to numbers; respectable as representing the most advanced intelligence; respectable as containing sincere and energetic representatives from all classes: the minority to reach which these pages are written. Give Socialists such a minority — give them only 10,000 such men in, say, twenty years from now, in a population of 75 millions, and our country and its future is theirs!

Socialists are the only social philosophers who can be called *purposeful,* the only ones in the whole wide world who can dispense with commonplaces and slippery words and phrases and who present clear cut, definite solutions. It is, of course, to the discontented that they address themselves; they have nothing to say to such as think that the world is good enough as it is. Neither have they any business with that very large class of poor men, clerks especially, who toil on from day to day, in the hope of being some day, by some lucky accident, rich themselves, so that they in their turn can lord it over others. It is that class particularly that fill the ranks of our state-militia and who with alacrity obey the command to shoot down such of their fellows as have been goaded on to rebellion. It is a most contemptible class of men; the motive that leads them is a contemptible one, and yet it is such men who are patted on the back by "our best people" and called "ambitious."

It is, of course, to the discontented wage-workers that Socialists can appeal with the greatest chance of success. To them they can say:

"Look the future confidently in the face. The golden age of which poets have sung has proved a cruel illusion — cruel, for as long as it lasted, it served as the greatest stumbling-block to your improvement. In exchange for that will-o-the-wisp we give you another, a real Golden Age, at whose threshold you stand. If you do not enter into it, your children may." It is to the wage-class that the rankest injustice is being done. To lay bare that injustice is, first of all, the mission of Socialism, and as Carlyle says: "Hunger, nakedness, death even, may be borne sometimes with cheerfulness, but injustice is insupportable to all men."

To the thoughtful among our small middle-men it ought to be easy enough to prove the Socialist State their sole refuge from the cares and troubles that now beset them.

It will not take many years, before the eyes of farmers will be opened to the fact that the vast majority of them must necessarily become tenant-farmers and their farms gobbled up by the rich under a system of unrestricted competition. Then we undoubtedly can convince some, that Socialism is the only system that can secure a civilized life to their descendants.

And even to many in the professions we can with propriety appeal. Indeed, as we already have said, many, if not most of our literary men, lawyers, physicians, journalists, and last, though not least, teachers are among the dis-inherited. Only those at the top — most of whom are in one way or another the retainers of our money-bags — have any motive to side with the Established Order. Of course, all aspiring young professional men start out with great expectations; but what a grievous disappointment does life prove to the great majority of them! Before they reach middle age they will have given up all their grand plans, and they will consider it the summit of success, if they can secure a decent livelihood. Most of them will fail lamentably even in that. To my personal knowledge hundreds of talented persons of that class now live a most precarious existence, and are glad to sleep at night on the lounge in the office of some more successful brother, and do not know for certain whether they will have a meal the next day. Such a man's refinement has become his curse.

To such men the Coming Revolution should be just as welcome as to any mechanic or common laborer. How their talents would unfold themselves and their energies be roused under that inspiring emulation which the New Order will inaugurate! Talent, genius and intellect will in our Commonwealth have their due influence, what they never had before.

Neither ought it to be very difficult to convince such women who take any interest in public affairs and labor for the elevation of their sex that no lasting benefit will be conferred either on Society or their sisters by making women into second-rate men, and very, very little benefit by their obtaining the suffrage in the present state of things; while it is very much to be apprehended that when political "rights" are minced twice as much again as they already are, they will seem and in fact become absolutely worthless. Socialism is evidently far more capable of elevating the female sex both by ennobling the men and by enabling women themselves to assert their dignity.

And everywhere in all conditions of life there are thoughtful, generous youths who cannot keep wondering at the manifestly unjust arrangements of this world. Youths who cannot help asking why so many whose work is only nominal should live in splendor, while those whose daily toil produces all that makes existence enjoyable and even possible have such a hard struggle for life. Youths, who then dream of impossible "remedies" and, like Thomas More in his "Utopia," construct castles in the air. Youths who by and by, when they have been chilled by contact with the cold realities of life under this Established Order, will come to look back on these dreams as mere foolishness!

Ah, youths! "when those phantoms fade, some portions of your better nature will die within you, too!"

Might we not expect that the eyes of such youths, — and even of mature men who have had such dreams *and not forgotten them* — to kindle with enthusiasm, and their hearts to beat quicker upon learning that many of their fellows are bent with all their energies on making glorious realities out of those dreams? As Novalis says: "My belief has gained infinitely to me from the moment any other human being has begun to believe the same." Why then might we not expect many of such men to throw themselves into this movement of ours, *as soon as they find out what it really means?*

It is a slander to say that the American people cannot be excited by an ideal, that they only care for the "Almighty Dollar." Our war of the Revolution was fought for a point of honor. The Rebellion was fought for ideas. But small ends do not rouse anybody's enthusiasm. Civil service "reforms" and other "Utopias" — and small Utopias at that — are not likely to make one's blood throb the quicker. To cut off each head of an ever-growing hydra as it appears is a tiresome process, and will seem an idle, wasteful proceeding to any practical mind. But to help evolve a New Social Order which is "struggling — convulsively, desperately struggling — to be born" is an end, grand enough to fill the noblest soul with the most ardent zeal!

And because it is well known what repelling effects mere words may have on the minds of men, and because "Socialism" once had such an effect on the writer himself, we add: Let not the consideration frighten you, that it is an "ism!" Why, even Christianity was for four hundred years an "ism." Every ideal, that is, every "soul of the future" is an "ism" as long as it is waiting for its body. When

Socialism becomes embodied, it leaves its "ism" behind and is realized as the New Social Order, — *Social Cooperation.*

It is for various reasons just such young men as those of whom we have spoken, of all classes, that we should try to enroll as members of our effective minority and for which I have written this book. Elderly people have already made up their minds — indeed the man who has reached forty and has not made up his mind may pretty safely be put down as a poor specimen of a man. And then there is a weightier reason. Though there is no man living wise enough to say when the Coming Revolution will occur, we can say that there is little probability that it will occur this century. Now, you cannot ask an elderly man to prepare for something which he probably will not live to witness. You, on the other hand, can with the greatest show of success appeal to the ardor and hope and sympathy of youth or young men of, say, 30 years to prepare for an event in which they may be principal actors when they reach ripe manhood. And that is just what that effective minority principally will have to do — *prepare,* prepare themselves and their people for the Great Change. Not, as we already said in the Introduction, to *make* any revolution, but to make themselves, and the Nation as much as possible, ready for the Coming Revolution, to meet it when it comes, peaceably or "clad in iron sandals" and to carry it out. To accomplish this, the first thing needed is organization, next, organization, and, lastly, organization, in order that they may become perfectly acquainted with each other, come to have confidence in each other, and study together the great philosophy and the means of realizing it. That minority ought, indeed, to come to a unanimous agreement as to every principal step that must be taken to make the Cooperative Commonwealth a success from the very start and until it is in full working order.

And they should also, as we said, as much as possible prepare their countrymen. They should continually keep — not themselves, mark you! — but their *cause* before the people. They can do this very effectually in two ways: each one in his own neighborhood, in his immediate circle of personal friends and acquaintances, by direct appeals to their understanding, sympathies and interests, and all, in mutual accord, through the general newspapers of the country. It is folly to waste money and energy in starting special journals for the propagation of new ideas — that is my private opinion. I have always found that there are in every city of any consequence some newspapers of established circulation, ready enough to publish notices and articles, if only they are temperately, and especially *well* written — just such comments and appeals as we may expect from the class of persons we have in mind — force and fire and no froth. But the important thing, always to be heeded, about this latter form of agitation, is that it be carried on *systematically*.

This will be work enough for anybody, however zealous: beside this that minority can do nothing better than — wait with patience.

Wait for what?

For the natural culmination of the present system, (as to which we refer to our third chapter) and for the outburst of Passion.

Passion? — Yes. We are not indebted to Reason for the landmarks of human progress: not for the introduction of Christianity, not for the institution of the monastic orders, not for the Crusades, not for the Reformation, not for the American Revolution, not for the abolition of slavery. Man is only irresistible when he acts from passion. We are first to be philosophers in order to prepare for and carry out the Coming Revolution, but no walls are now-a-days thrown down by blasts of trumpets. The masses of men are never moved except by passions, feelings, interest.

Now it is possible that these passions of our people, or of the British people, will be roused by what may transpire on the continent of Europe. For we have no doubt that the first serious attempt to realize Socialism will be made there. There is Germany, where our ideas have reached their highest development both in depth and in breadth, and whose people seem in the last generation to have modified their former pure reflectiveness. Formerly they paused to reflect so much, that they were slow in action; now they simply make sure beforehand of every detail which might make them hesitate in action.

Then there is France, there is Paris. Not the frivolous debased Paris of the sight-seer, but earnest Paris, for a century the heart of the world; whose victories have been the victories of mankind, her defeats its defeats.

We know what an excitement the French Revolution of a hundred years ago caused in the minds of the people of England, and notably among her working men, then in their swaddling clothes. Certainly, then, in this age the establishment of Socialism either in Germany or France would exercise a tremendous influence both here and in Great Britain.

If we, the American Nation, are anything, we are practical. If we are not apt to originate any new political and social ideas, we have a wonderful aptitude for copying the good points of successfully working models. We, therefore, think, that it might not take very many years — in fact no longer time than would be needful to rub our eyes in order to find out whether we were really awake — before we should set to work to copy that Socialist State.

But the difficulties in the way of success on the continent are so great — the consideration, that even a completely successful revolution in any one of these countries may, on account of their geographical position, not prove sufficient to insure the stability of the New Social Order, — these difficulties form such a threatening shadow on the horizon, that we cannot but tremble for a possible successful counter-revolution.

And then there are really many reasons why either Great Britain or our own country — the *universal colony* — may be considered the place where the New Commonwealth will be first successfully established.

The United States possesses the immense advantage that it can safely make the first experiment, without danger of any foreign interference. We possess the advantage of being an eminently practical as well as a thoroughgoing people, when we are roused. We have within us the reflectiveness of the German as well as the momentum of the Anglo-Saxon, who, if he *wills* to jump across a brook, does not hesitate, but runs and clears it with a bound. We furthermore possess for an indefinite period — to be determined by the fears and blind anger of our masters — the privilege to agitate without restraint by pen and tongue and thus educate and organize the effective minority.

Great Britain has the same advantages, and in addition the glorious precedent: Cromwell's revolution, "the English Commonwealth," the first popular revolt against *divine rights,* "vested" rights. In both countries the culmination of the economic evolution is nearer than elsewhere, that is, division of labor and concentration of wealth are carried further than elsewhere, a fact of tremendous importance, and another fact, only second in importance, in both countries, is the organization of their workers, the splendid Trades-Unions of England and our own *Knights of Labor*.

"Socialism is not suited to the genius of our people" we have heard some say, as if we had patented a new order of life. These Trade-unions, and Trades-assemblies, and Grangers and Knights of Labor precisely prove that Socialism *is* suited to the genius of our and the British people. The central spirit that rules these unions is that of Socialism, to wit, that the interests of all workers are the same, that each must postpone his own advantage to the common good and each yield his individual prejudice and crochet to the collective judgment.

Those of the working-classes who become enrolled in our effective minority can do no better work than strengthen these unions in every possible way. Through them their fellow-workers are sure of getting Socialist *hearts* — the Socialist heads will come in due time. And bear in mind, that it is these organized labor-battalions that are to form the *lever* by means of which the new ideas are to move Society.

Just on account of these organizations, and because they will become invaluable skeletons on the establishment of the New Order (as we have emphasized in another place,) we think that the United States, but particularly Great Britain, are nearer the realization of Socialism than generally supposed.

Most Americans remember the rising of the workingmen in July 1877. That rising was to all Socialists, also to those who held aloof from it, a most promising sign. The first revolt of American white slaves against their task-masters!

That it was accompanied by excesses by the most neglected stratum of Society was unfortunate but unavoidable. This stratum is just the worst heritage which capitalism leaves on our hand.

In a very short time we shall have another series of years of hard time. Remember what we said about "Crises" in the second chapter. We expect another revolt then, more serious than the first. That most likely will also be suppressed with comparative ease.

A few more years elapse. Another "crisis," yet more severe, shows its hideous head. The screws of distress are turned yet more on the wage-workers. Another most serious revolt. Possibly powder and shot will suppress that, too.

But in the fulness of time we shall have a labor revolt that will not be put down. *Then* is the time for the energetic Socialist minority to exert its influence. There is nothing that the people in such a crisis hail more than *leaders*, nothing they hunger and thirst more after than clear-cut, definite solutions.

All the horrors of the French Revolution and the sad fact that Napoleon the First became a necessity were due to the circumstance, that the revolution had no leaders. We do not mean to say, that that revolution was a failure, for it *did* accomplish every one of its objects: the abolition of privileges, the dispossession of the landowners and free competition, but the price paid was exorbitant.

In our civil war, on the other hand, it was the abolitionists that successfully assumed the leadership, and probably exerted all the influence to which they were entitled.

That the Socialist minority must do when *the* crisis comes, and make out of a revolt — another *revolution*.

Be confident that the people will follow. In such times men become awake, shake off nightmares; the experience of years is crowded into hours. Novelties which at first sight inspire dread become in a few days familiar, then endurable, then attractive.

That is one way in which Socialism may be realized.

Here our mind is involuntarily directed to a remarkable book: *The Coming Race*, said to be by Bulwer. It represents a race, living underground in a great number of small communities, as having attained to a perfect social state. It may be considered an ingenious satire on a Socialist Commonwealth, but no matter, it is highly interesting. That which at this point led our thoughts upon it is a wonderful natural force which those people are said to have discovered, which they call *Vril*. It can be stored in a small wand, which rests in the hollow of the palm and, when skillfully wielded, can rend rocks, remove any natural obstacles, scatter the strongest fortress and make the weak a perfect match for any combination of number, skill and discipline. No wonder that these people attribute their equality, their freedom, felicity and advancement to this discovery.

What if this "Vril" is but a poetic anticipation of the civilizing power of that real, energetic substance which we call — *dynamite!*

Again, we all have heard of the "anti-monopoly" movement. That is a war, political and otherwise, of one class of fleecers against another class of fleecers; of industrial and mercantile cannibals against moneyed and corporate cannibals. There is no love lost between the two classes just as little as between two veritable cannibals. No one can tell to what extremities the war between them may not go. But the following correspondence to the *New York Sun* from Titusville Pa., of Nov. 4th 1878, may give us an idea of possible coming events:

"The fact is, the State of Pennsylvania has had a narrow escape from an internal civil war. Had certain men given the word, there would have been an outbreak that contemplated the seizure of the railroads and running them, the capture and control of the United Pipe Lines property, and in all probability the burning of all the property of the Standard Oil Company in the region. The men who would have done this, and may do it yet, *are not laborers or tramps.*"

The Coming Revolution may arise out of a similar struggle between our fleecing classes. Revolutions, however, have no precedents. The wisest of us may err as much as Ulrich Von Hutten did in the days preceding the Reformation. Ulrich was far in advance of Luther when the latter took hold of his mission. Then he wrote in a letter, still extant, to the effect that he heard that a monk had become rebellious. "It delights me" he wrote in substance, "to hear of a rebellion in the bosom of Holy Mother Church. How I wish the two parties may tear each other to pieces!" Yet it was just Luther and not the clear-sighted nobleman whom the logic of events selected as its organ.

Just as impossible it is to say, *when* we may expect the Coming Revolution. But it is worth reflecting on, that a prudent man in 1853 would hardly have taken upon himself to foretell the abolition of slavery in 1863.

But the Great Change is coming.

In the words of Carlyle:

"Will not one French Revolution suffice, or must there be two? There will be two if needed; there will be twenty if needed; *there will be just as many as needed.*"

When the Cooperative Commonwealth is achieved, there will be no room for any more revolutions. For revolutions are caused by the clashings of class-interests, and all class-distinctions are forever abolished the moment the lowest class is fully incorporated into Society.

But there will be plenty of room for progress, for further evolution. Even our Commonwealth, though it may take a long period to develop it, is but a step of the evolution. One Commonwealth after another may decay and disappear, but they will all contribute to the upbuilding of the *Organism* of *Humanity*.

With Organized Humanity will be evolved the Coming Religion, though we already noticed it in the preceding chapter, because people persist in mixing up morals and religion. But morals really relates to the social organism: *it makes the good citizen.* Religion relates to Humanity *and makes the saint.* The Coming Religion will make us feel that we are here for the sake of Humanity, with whose fate it may be found that we are personally far more concerned than is now supposed; it will make holiness consist in identifying ourselves with Humanity — the redeemed form of man — as the lover merges himself in the beloved. Individualism: the deception that we have been born into this world each for the sake of himself, or family, friend or kindred, *Selfness,* will be acknowledged to be the satanic element of our nature.

We therefore more than doubt, we deny Ward's proposition that individual happiness is the end of human life. If it is, the existences that were made miserable in order that mankind might be trained up to Social-Cooperation were failures; they are decidedly not failures, if, as *we* hold, the end of the individual existence is to further the evolution of Humanity, in whose fate it may be found, as we repeat, that we have a greater stake than is supposed. But happiness is a *fact;* as an *incident* of life and not an object of pursuit, it is a blessed fact. It is to man what the odor is to the rose.

That the New Commonwealth will very much diffuse and increase individual happiness there can be no doubt. It will make possible the harmonious exercise and development of all human faculties in everybody — that itself is happiness. It will, by banishing care and giving leisure, enable everyone to become familiar with all that is known about the universe and to explore its perpetual wonders and pore over its numberless riddles for himself — and that is more than happiness, it is *rapture*. Finally, it will be the grandest vehicle for serving Humanity and thereby generate the purest happiness, perfect *blessedness*.

But blessedness it is even *now* our privilege to obtain. We have the choice to live as Individualists and on our deathbed look back in despair on a dreary, hateful life of play-acting, or as Socialists fill our existences with those serious moods that make the grand tone of life, and in the hour of death stand on the mountain-top, as it were, and see with entranced eyes the rays of the Sun that soon will illumine the dark valleys below. I, for my part, deem it worth ten crucifixions to win for my memory a fraction of the adoring love which millions of the noblest men and women have felt for a Jesus.

INDEX

THE JOHN HARVARD LIBRARY

*The intent of
Waldron Phoenix Belknap, Jr.,
as expressed in an early will, was for
Harvard College to use the income from a
permanent trust fund he set up, for "editing and
publishing rare, inaccessible, or hitherto unpublished
source material of interest in connection with the
history, literature, art (including minor and useful
art), commerce, customs, and manners or way of
life of the Colonial and Federal Periods of the United
States . . . In all cases the emphasis shall be on the
presentation of the basic material." A later testament
broadened this statement, but Mr. Belknap's interests remained constant until his death.*

    *In linking the name of the first benefactor of
Harvard College with the purpose of this later,
generous-minded believer in American culture the
John Harvard Library seeks to emphasize the importance of Mr. Belknap's purpose. The John Harvard
Library of the Belknap Press of Harvard University
Press exists to make books and documents
about the American past more readily
available to scholars and the
general reader.*